DEBTMAN walking

DEBT MAN walking

A 10-Step Investment and Gearing Guide for
Generation X

BRUCE BRAMMALL

Wrightbooks

First published in 2009 by Wrightbooks
an imprint of John Wiley & Sons Australia, Ltd
42 McDougall St, Milton Qld 4064

Office also in Melbourne

Typeset in 10.5/15pt Syntax LT

© Bruce Brammall 2009
The moral rights of the author have been asserted

National Library of Australia Cataloguing-in-Publication Data

Author:	Brammall, Bruce
Title:	Debt man walking: a 10-step investment and gearing guide for Generation X / Bruce Brammall.
Publisher:	Richmond, Vic.: John Wiley & Sons Australia, 2009.
ISBN:	9780731408351 (pbk.)
Notes:	Includes index.
Subjects:	Generation X—Finance, Personal.
	Financial security.
	Saving and investment.
Dewey number:	332.02401

Cover design by Popomo

Cover image © shutterstock images/Timothy Large and © shutterstock images/Robyn Mackenzie

Image on p. 17 © Corbis/Deborah Feingold

Image on p. 33 © Newspix/News Ltd

Image on p. 53 © Corbis/Sygma/Collection Spitzer

Image on p. 75 © Universal/Celandine/Monty Python/The Kobal Collection

Image on p. 107 © Corbis/Neal Preston

Image on p. 123 © Touchstone/Warners/The Kobal Collection

Image on p. 153 © Corbis/Bettman

Image on p. 175 © Universal/Gordon/The Kobal Collection

Image on p. 193 © Corbis/Sunset Boulevard

Image on p. 217 © Constantin-Bavaria-WDR/Warner Bros/The Kobal Collection

Printed in Australia by McPherson's Printing Group

10 9 8 7 6 5 4 3 2 1

Disclaimer

The material in this publication is of the nature of general comment only, and neither purports nor intends to be advice. Readers should not act on the basis of any matter in this publication without considering (and if appropriate, taking) professional advice with due regard to their own particular circumstances. The author and publisher expressly disclaim all and any liability to any person, whether a purchaser of this publication or not, in respect of anything and of the consequences of anything done or omitted to be done by any such person in reliance, whether whole or partial, upon the whole or any part of the contents of this publication.

Contents

Dedication

It is possibly the same for other Generation Xers, but every time I hear or read the word 'dedication' I can't stop myself singing Dire Straits' 'Walk of Life'.

As the rest of this book is about reliving memories, I might as well open the book by pinching a couple of lines. Next, from the mouth of Renee Zellweger in *Jerry Maguire*...

To my family—Genevieve, Edward and Amelia—'You complete me'.

Acknowledgements

Unlike children, books can't happen by mere accident. With two of the former and three of the latter (as of 2008), I can speak with some experience there. With a book, you don't get to wake up one morning, wonder a little, pee on a stick and get confirmation that an end product is coming. The kind of book that goes to the printer is not a random one-in-a-billion event.

Books are not the result of the collaboration of a union with just one other person. I'm pretty sure '80s political crusader and morals campaigner Reverend Fred Nile would have had a coronary if the number of people who helped create this book were actually in the same room helping to create a baby. There's a cast as big as Band Aid singing 'Do They Know It's Christmas?'

My darling wife, Genevieve, I've been spelling 'team' with a 'u' in it. This book wouldn't exist right now were it not for your support. That said…your lack of '80s music knowledge is both funny and incomprehensible. Did you *never* listen to songs being back-announced on the radio? How does someone get to know everything about the singers, but nothing about the songs they sang?

To my children. To Edward, who was just 16 months old when the manuscript was finished, 'The Wiggles' isn't the answer to every music question Daddy asks (but more useful than most of your Mum's answers). A helpful answer *might* have been: 'Hey, Dad, the blue and purple Wiggles were part of The Cockroaches and they sang…'. That your fourth ever word was 'book' is very encouraging for an author dad. And Amelia, this entire manuscript was written after we knew someone was coming but before we got to meet you, you gorgeous little girl. Thank you *so much* for not arriving too early.

Years in the thinking, this book probably would have stayed years off being written had it not been for Kristen Hammond, acquisitions editor at Wiley. Kristen chased me with another concept that didn't grab me at all. But her enthusiasm about my Generation X concept was very encouraging. Kristen, thanks for gritting your teeth, not giving me both barrels and getting through the contract negotiations without your head exploding. Your guidance, encouragement and early editing role were important to the book's evolution. That we have such similar memories of the '80s is freaky.

Thanks to everyone else at Wiley and Wrightbooks, but particularly editor Catherine Spedding, Georgie Way, Katherine Drew and Brooke Lyons.

When it comes to unearthing the memories of my youth, I can't decide what is more disturbing: what I had personally forgotten about the '70s and the '80s, or what Gen's friends and my friends could remember. I'm still searching for laws that would allow me to have my parents retrospectively charged with culinary crimes for apricot chicken casseroles. The memories that weren't my own came from a treasured list of people—my Gen X brains trust—who contributed with their own memories of growing up.

Naturally, as back then, there is a boys' team and girls' team. And judging by their responses, they grew up in parallel universes. My boys' team was, largely but not solely, connected to the Tossers Indoor Cricket Club. Thanks to Simon Smith, Andrew Probyn, Steff Pettit, Tony Spark, David Pringle, Rob Clancy, Brent McMillan, Brendan Cahill, Jonathon Evans, Rohan Christie and Steve Kerr. The team led by Gen was made up of Felicity Hamilton (I was searching for an idiot and you provided the father of them all—Frank Spencer), Michelle Coffey, Zoe Kanat, Kimberley Clemens, Sophie Paterson, Liz Wilson, Madeleine Seletto, Edwina Webb, Katie Flockart, Celia Purdey and Odette Kerr.

To the technical readers: my cousin, Danny Brammall, for reading the whole thing and only occasionally reminding me that he knows a better way; Mark Longworth for lending his insurance expertise; and superannuation guru and *Eureka Report* colleague Trish Power for advice with step 10.

Thanks to Max Prisk for his kick-ass contribution to the back cover, Popomo for the cover, Tess McCabe for Debt Man corporate designs, *Herald Sun* photographer Jay Town for the back cover shot, and Kate Jungwirth and David King from EKM Legal for work on my contract.

Thanks also to my brother-in-law Nick Lally for his Yoda-like timely and sage advice ('The answers you seek lie offshore, Debt Man') that led me to find my 'Man in

Acknowledgements

Montevideo', Marcos 'Mark Skayff' Scaianschi, who perfected the calculators for the website <www.debtman.com.au> and, as it turns out, ironed out a crease or two in the book.

To the partners—Spiros Livadaras, Peter Mattmann, Leonie Ladgrove and Kostas Livadaras—and the rest of the crew at Stantins, thanks for your ongoing support.

To the celebrities, songwriters, musicians, actors, directors, designers, fashionistas, cartoonists, casting agents, writers, journalists, sportspeople, politicians, toymakers and chefs of the '70s, '80s and '90s, I thank you on behalf of Generation X for our childhood memories. It was a rockin' time to grow up. First among equals, as far as I'm concerned, is Brian Mannix and The Uncanny X-Men—you typify Generation X in Australia. The songs...the attitude...the 'Party'...the mullets. I'm ashamed to confess, I never bought one of your albums. It still haunts me.

It wouldn't be right to conclude without mentioning two writers out there in the world of Australian personal finance journalism (who must stay anonymous). The first I want to thank for writing a feature that so abundantly offended my innate beliefs that it required a response. The second's writing style I have found objectionable on an almost weekly basis for years (and still do). Needless to say, I read you both regularly and that's what journalism is about. You too may find some of my stuff disagreeable. This book wouldn't have existed at all (arguably) and certainly not in this form (definitely) if you hadn't, unknowingly, annoyed me so much. And so damn often. Thank you both.

About the author

The towering figure of Paul Keating casts a long shadow over my life. The Lizard of Oz wasn't just the Prime Minister of my country, the engineer of my first real economic downturn and the man who took some of the fun out of getting rich by introducing the capital gains tax in 1985. My relationship with PK was far more personal than that. He was my first local MP.

I was born in Bankstown, Sydney, in 1970, the year after Keating was elected to represent Blaxland. Keating didn't use me to practise his baby kissing. Mum assures me I wasn't too ugly (my dad vocally disagrees). Perhaps I just didn't hang around long enough; my parents uprooted me for Canberra when I was six weeks old.

There is, however, video evidence of my time in Bankstown. Grainy footage taken from a shiny new Super 8 camera shows me being carried into the rented family home from hospital, carried by my 22-year-old first-time mum who was wearing a mini-skirt so skimpy it would have made Jean Shrimpton blush ('Mu-u-um, put some clothes on!').

I played every type of organised sport I could—cricket, basketball, hockey, tennis, golf and both of the rugby codes. But that was dwarfed by the amount of time I spent playing disorganised sport—street cricket, kick-to-kick, Frisbee golf, marbles, handball, swimming (including Marco Polo), ice-skating, roller-skating, skateboarding, kite-flying, British bulldog, brandings, bike riding...

This might have been because the Atari 2600 had only just been invented in the US in 1975 and none of my mates had one yet. The Commodore VIC20 was still years away (1980).

I remember furniture that might have been made out of brown velour, the older generation wearing flared pants and winged collars and watching colour television for the first time. I was too young to remember Gough Whitlam getting sacked. But I remember vividly the end of Malcolm Fraser and the start of Bob Hawke, because my dad was the chief political reporter for *The Canberra Times*. As Hawke's Treasurer, Keating would occasionally call my dad and give him a roasting, complete with colourful language, over articles he'd written.

It was in about year 10 that I got my first crack at economics and political thinking. Marist College (Pearce) made George Orwell's *Animal Farm* compulsory reading. Napoleon and Squealer made me aware that the root of all evil is, actually, the removal of personal incentive. Socialism and I never made friends after that.

My parents' rule was that in order to drive the family car (a Mitsubishi Magna) I had to have the insurance excess saved in the event that I had a stack. So while everyone else was whining about 20 per cent mortgage rates, I was getting 17 per cent on my savings.

Watching my dad led me into journalism. I think. I might have been enticed by a career that promised lots of free beer. I started at the University of Canberra in 1989 (the year Keating reintroduced university tuition fees in the form of HECS) and earned a BA (Communications), majoring in journalism.

In the middle of Keating's 'recession we had to have', with double-digit unemployment rates, I entered the job market. News organisations, like most industries in 1991–92, were sacking rather than hiring. The newly merged *Herald Sun* in Melbourne (the butt of Keating's 'arse end of the world') was bucking the trend and I got a cadetship. That year, 1992, was also the year one of Keating's political babies, compulsory superannuation (designed to make sure Gen X and future generations look after themselves in retirement), started.

Journalism was a perfect industry for someone who wasn't keen on growing up. And the *Herald Sun* was certainly a place where I was surrounded by like-minded individuals. There was always a drink to be had and someone was always going to the pub or a club. Reporting eventually led me to business journalism, where I became the deputy editor of the *Business* section. I also wrote about banks, superannuation, insurance, wealth management and tax. At the same time, I got hooked on property (immediately becoming an investor) and the wider potential for debt-funded investment strategies. I have written two property investment books (*The Power of Property* in 2006 and *Investing in Real Estate For Dummies* in 2008).

In 2005 and 2006, I studied for the Advanced Diploma in Financial Services (Financial Planning). I am now an adviser with Stantins Financial Services (licensed with Australian Financial Services) in Hawthorn, Victoria. I still write regularly, as a superannuation and investment columnist for *Eureka Report* and on property topics for News Limited publications. Oops, there he is again—Keating has just bobbed his head up to criticise Kevin Rudd's Government for failing on superannuation. I also appear on radio and television programs as an adviser, and media and financial news commentator.

And I've left my absolute favourite parts of me, the 'grousest' bits, till last. Nothing beats 'em. I am proudly husband to Genevieve and father to Edward and Amelia.

Prologue

Setting the scene…

The film clip for The Uncanny X-Men's 'Everybody Wants to Work' starts out with employee Brian Mannix (The X-Men's lead singer, playing himself) in his office, on the phone. His boss, Mr Thompson (played by the late, great Australian actor and gagster, Maurie Fields), walks into the room. Mannix is on the phone to his lotto agency after he's had some sort of a win.

Mr Thompson: 'Mannix, you mongrel! Get back to work!'

Mannix: 'Yes, Mr Thompson.'

Mannix (on phone): 'Look, sir, how much have I won?'

Mannix grins from ear to ear.

Mannix: 'Mr Thompson…gu-e-e-e-ess what!'

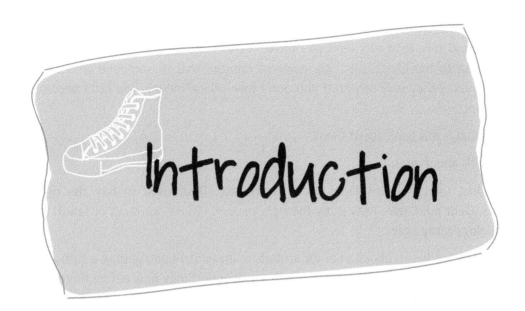

Introduction

Debt is not a financial death sentence.

Not all debt is evil. Debt does not involve selling your soul to the devil. Debt isn't the custom-made pair of concrete boots fitted as you're thrown into the Hudson River. There's no proven link between debt and cancer. Debt played no part in Princess Diana's death. Debt doesn't kill people.

Nor is this book a cheerleader's chant for debt.

Debt Man Walking (despite what some will inevitably read into the title) does not urge readers to collect loans like Barbie dolls or football cards. It does not blindly promote debt. It does not implore readers to covet credit. It does not decree, Gordon Gekko–like, that all 'debt is good' (although some of it is okay).

Don't believe for a second that this book is going to tell you that you'll get rich just by backing up your Holden ute to a bank and borrowing until your nose bleeds. If you believe that, you misunderstand how dangerous debt can be. Too much debt, debt used badly, or debt in the hands of the unsophisticated or untrained investor can be devastating. 'Debt is not the messiah! He can be a very naughty boy!'

Understand this: debt can send you broke. What's the definition of a bankrupt? According to the Oxford, it's 'an insolvent debtor'; that is, someone who can't repay money they owe others. If you don't owe others money, you can't become bankrupt.

So … what is this book about then?

Okay. It's about debt.

But, debt used properly. Debt used strategically. Debt used to buy the right assets. Debt used, dare I say it, by the *right people*. (That's not racist or sexist. It's unapologetically ageist.)

Debt Man Walking is about a holistic attitude to investment *and* getting a particular generation to understand the enormous financial opportunity now before them *and* how that generation, if any, is the best-placed generation to combine their age, appetite for risk and investment debt to achieve their financial goals.

As a result, the debt part of *Debt Man Walking* is not a message aimed at everyone.

It is not aimed at 22-year-olds who've just landed their first job out of university, who are looking to move out of home, to buy their first car, or are considering donning a backpack for the first time. If that's you, put this book down and go out and party! Save some dough, then blow the lot around Europe, or (my favourite) South America. In fact, buy yourself a one-way ticket, land yourself a dead-end job and what doesn't get drunk in an Earl's Court pub should be splurged doing silly things in stupid places. Bum around a little. Bum around *a lot*. That's what your 20s are for. (Plus, the humour in this book probably won't make much sense to you.)

Neither is the central message of *Debt Man Walking* aimed at 60-year-olds. If you are looking to retire, have never used investment gearing before, or have worked your whole life in the hope that you'll finally pay off your home loan with your last pay cheque, then hand this book to the kids and go enjoy your retirement. This book is *too late* for you. You might have already understood investment debt and used it to create your wealth during your working life. Or you didn't. Either way, you're probably beyond gearing up for the first time now. You might end up losing everything you've ever worked for with one major property or sharemarket downturn. (Plus, the humour in this book probably won't make much sense to you, either.)

Debt Man Walking is for Generation X.

'Who?'

Generation X, if you take a fairly wide definition, is those people born in the '60s and '70s. Some will argue that's too broad. It doesn't really matter. This book will be relevant to younger Baby-Boomer 'oldies' and some older Generation Y 'kids'.

Here's a better test.

If you remember The Uncanny X-Men and Molly's Melodramas... If you still had 'youth' when the Berlin Wall fell, *Challenger* exploded and Halley's Comet passed by... If you can remember when Madonna was married to Sean Penn and pretended to be virginal (*long* before the pointy boobs)... If the only Russian words you know are 'perestroika' and 'glasnost', but you can't remember what they mean... If you can remember when *Neighbours* was on Seven and Kylie was singing about train travel... If the words 'Dallas' and 'shot' remind you of JR Ewing (rather than JFK) and a real romantic tragedy was Mulder and Scully never jumping in the sack...

... then you're probably, roughly, roundabout, a Gen Xer.

This book is for you.

Its primary purpose is financial—to get you to think outside the Rubik's Cube. To get you to understand that where you are now is the perfect position to plan to combine your income, your (relative) youth and your ability to take a risk with a dash of 'great' debt to achieve financial dreams. It might bring back some pleasant and/or nasty flashbacks from the '70s, '80s and '90s. But at least the humour is likely to make some sense.

In the never-ending financial battle of good versus evil, *Debt Man Walking* hopes to swing a little lightsabre down on some debt and investment myths. *Debt Man* will show why there's actually three types of debt (the DOG of Debt—we'll explain this DOG in step 6), why there are five universal financial rules (they'll work the same in Rio de Janeiro as they will in Rockhampton) and five peculiarly Australian rules (they probably don't even work in Rotorua, much less Rome). These are the basic rules understood implicitly by people who have already made money.

What's risk? Sure, it's a solo cava-drinking session with the natives in Vanuatu, getting tear gassed in La Paz or turning your back on your bags at Roma Termini.

It can also be buying investments that affect your health. It's great being rich, but pointless if it caused you to die (or lose your hair) before you're 50.

And lastly, what this book is not. This is not a book about the basics of saving.

Debt Man Walking does not focus on telling you how to save $10 to $15 a week by cutting out a morning coffee, $20 a month with an offset account on your mortgage, or how to save money by switching insurance companies. These are great habits to learn, but there are dozens of good (and bad) books out there that cover those topics in great detail (they're as common as a mullet at a Blue Light disco). If this book makes any assumptions about its readers, it's that you understand these basics and you're wondering what the next step is.

In fact, *Debt Man Walking* challenges the assumptions of some of those common money 'rules'. Should Gen Xers really 'save to invest', or should they 'invest to save'? Should you really pay off the mortgage before beginning an investment strategy? In this age of heightened environmental awareness, what is debt recycling and why might you get down and dirty with it? How could 15 minutes of care now, rather than when you turn 55, potentially double your super?

Did Monopoly teach you enough about property to make you a mogul? If you make a lifestyle choice not to buy a home, how do you make that decision work financially? Think you're pretty savvy? Well, do you spend 10 hours doing something badly that you could pay a professional to do properly in an hour?

Sooooo... this is the premise from which *Debt Man Walking* starts. I hope it's different from any other personal finance books you may have read. We certainly grew up in a different era. It was an era when the decades-long Cold War suddenly ended, when Australia was still producing Nissans, when Bon Scott was still the lead singer of AC/DC, when fluorescent clothes were still considered fashionable (seriously, were they really?) and when smoking in cinemas was still legal (as was, unbelievably, cigarette advertising).

Debt Man Walking walks to a different beat. And if the concept grabs you, there are details at the end of the book on how you can take these principles one step further.

Generation X

'Hi, I'm Bruce and I'll be your author and guide for today.

'I'd like to welcome you to the *Debt Man Walking* book tour. We've got what I hope you'll find is an interesting book ahead of us. I hope you brought your tax file numbers—the ones they started handing out in the bicentenary year, 1988—you'll certainly need those. And for those of you who *did* bring your Sony Walkmans, thank you, I'll show you where you can drop them off for recycling a little later. For legal reasons, I'll assume that you've all read the introduction and understand that this is not a book tour for everyone.

'Hey, you sir! You with the cardigan and the bi-focals, I think you've joined the wrong tour. I think you're after the *How to Survive in Retirement on $14 a Week* tour. You'll need to head back to the bookshop, old man. They'll be handing out government-funded Zimmer frames to those who need them on that one, and you might be able to get access to your superannuation while you're there, sir!

'And you, the impatient young woman sending an SMS! Would I be right in assuming that you're after the *Time to Leave Home and Get a Job* tour? Yes? Well, that bus left a few minutes ago. You'll have to wait for the next one. Missy, don't have a hissy fit! It's okay. We know your type. There's another one leaving in about 27 seconds, if you can wait that long.

'Sheesh, some people. Generation X! Is it that hard to understand? The rest of you look about right. Were you all born in the '60s and '70s? If you think you're actually probably the MTV Generation, that's okay, you're in the right place. Hands up all those who remember *Miami Vice*. Goooood. *The Love Boat*? Fantastic. Did all you girls wear legwarmers, à la *Flashdance*? And did you boys own a pair of Dunlop Volleys, adidas Romes or Converse shoes? Hum a few bars to 'The Reflex' by Duran Duran? Brilliant! Remember *Mad Max*? Yep? That's *Absolutely Fabulous!* Looks like the rest of us are right to start.'

Weekends spent writing books are weekends not spent with your wife at the wineries in a bed and breakfast, with your kids at the beach, with your mates playing golf (except that Smithy would never join us anyway, of course) or having a beer at the footy. Not that I'm looking for sympathy.

So, when those friends who I don't catch up with often enough asked what this book was about, my answer was that it was a finance book specifically for Generation X.

The next thing they'd ask is 'Am I Generation X?'

I found this a little unsettling. I was born in December 1970, which makes me smack bang in the middle of what has come to be known as Generation X. Like most people, most of my friends are within a few years of my age, so they are not just part of Gen X, they are its heart and soul.

That they didn't know that they are Gen Xers was a concern. If this book was designed to appeal to Generation X, but Generation X didn't know who it was, then perhaps the whole strategy/idea needed a rethink. After much discussion with a few other book insiders for this project (wife Genevieve and commissioning editor Kristen Hammond), it was decided that no, it didn't. You'll just need to take their minds for a little walk down memory lane. It'll come back to them.

Who is Generation X?

It could be that we don't care to remember that we're Generation X because *they* were right. *They* being the people who popularised the term—an older generation that was writing about a younger generation.

'Generation X' caught on when Canadian fiction writer Douglas Coupland used it to describe disaffected youth in his 1991 book *Generation X: Tales for an Accelerated Culture*. The term Generation X became popular when used in the media as a derogatory phrase to describe a generation of slackers (hence the 1991 movie *Slacker*) who didn't care and who had no commitment to anything in particular. *They* said we lacked optimism, we distrusted institutions and 'traditional' values. *They* thought that we were 'overeducated underachievers'. (Which, of course, makes us vastly superior to Bart Simpson, who is an undereducated underachiever. And proud of it.)

Hmmm. Sounds to me like they were just talking about teenagers and 20-somethings being teenagers and 20-somethings. They insinuated that *they* weren't like that when they were that age (yeah, right!). It's just that they got a very catchy term to describe it. An easy label. They were so impressed with how good and original the term Generation X was that they haven't been able to think of anything else since. If *we* lacked optimism, *they* lacked originality. Generation X is followed by ... Generation Y and Generation Z.

Whatever. (Interesting in itself: in France, Generation X is apparently sometimes referred to as 'Generation Bof', with 'bof' being a French expression for indifference, something like the English use of 'whatever'.)

What we are not is Baby Boomers. 'Baby Boomers' is the term used to describe the population explosion that followed the end of World War II. That boom started in 1946. That's my Dad (the Old Fart) and my Mum (the Old Bag). Did someone say we lacked respect for our parents?

Dad was born in October 1946, making him one of the very first Baby Boomers. Mum was born ... some time later. (Ha! Scared you, hey Mum!) But she's definitely a Boomer. Under the vast majority of definitions, the Boomer generation went through until at least 1959 or 1960. Then it becomes a little fuzzy. Some claim it didn't finish until 1964. Others say 1967.

And we're definitely not Generation Y. Where Generation Y starts, obviously, is dependent on where you think Generation X finishes. Depending on whose definition you use, Gen Y could start as late as 1983, or as early as about 1977.

The most common descriptors of Gen Y are that they are impatient and demanding. Some demographers say that they are the first generation in which it was standard for both parents to work and, as a result, they were spoilt rotten by guilt-ridden, career-driven parents. They haven't experienced anything but good times (particularly in Australia). It's been one long economic boom since any of them were old enough to remember. Xers, however, lived through the 'recession we had to have'. If we didn't find it difficult to get our own first job, there's a good chance that a parent lost a job (hand up here) or we definitely knew someone who did.

If demographers can't decide on hard and fast rules, then you're not going to get me to try to set them down.

I'm not going to pigeon-hole like that for the purposes of *Debt Man Walking*. That would be daft and limiting. There will be readers born in the late '50s and early '80s who will identify with Generation Xers and/or who will be able to benefit/profit from the advice in this book that is appropriate to them. Therefore, roughly, if you were born in the '60s or '70s, or just on either side, consider yourself on board Gen X for the purpose of this book.

What makes *Debt Man Walking* specifically for Generation X?

If we accept those rough dates, Generation Xers will be 28 to 48 years of age as at Christmas 2008, soon after this book was first published. You can make at least two broad assumptions about people in that age bracket. First, they've finished school/university and been out in the 'real world' for a while, with careers to consider and bills to pay. Second, very few of them are actively considering retirement.

As a result, *Debt Man Walking* doesn't cover the basics of how to start a savings program. It doesn't tell you how to reduce your mobile phone bill or buy the cheapest health insurance. And it doesn't ease your concerns about that nervous shift into retirement. I'm not going to tell you that you're crazy unless you're salary sacrificing the maximum into super or know that they serve great mutton chops on bingo night at the RSL. I'm not going to tell you that, because you already know the former (financial basics) and it's too early for you to care about the latter (retirement).

Debt Man Walking covers financial strategies that are neither for those taxiing to the runway to start their careers, nor for those who have contacted air traffic control and are awaiting clearance for landing (or have started their descent).

> Debt Man Walking is talking about learning what the next challenge is and deciding whether or not you want to take that risk.

It's for those who are taking off, are approaching, or have reached cruising altitude. It's for those people who have learnt the basics and want to know what's next.

Debt Man Walking is talking about learning what the next challenge is and deciding whether or not you want to take that risk. It's talking about shares and property. It's talking about potentially taking on investment debt, leveraging and margin loans. It's talking about taking out a million dollars or more of cover to protect yourself and your family and investment portfolios worth hundreds of thousands and, potentially, millions of dollars. And it's talking about those years when you've got the money to achieve long-term goals and enough of a working life left to see those plans through.

It doesn't matter if you're single, married, divorced, have one tin lid or a tribe, or have a *Brady Bunch*–style blended family. *Debt Man Walking* takes the *Seinfeld* oath — 'Not that there's anything wrong with that!' — if you're gay. It doesn't matter if you're a committed lifelong renter or have a mortgage you're dying to get rid of. This book is aimed at getting a generation to understand that they can achieve anything they want — because they have the time — so long as they understand the basic rules of finance.

Speaking of which … yes, sadly, there are rules. But don't despair. They're not complex; I've *Dumb and Dumber*-ed them down. And understanding them is absolutely critical, so they're near the start.

'Everybody Wants to Rule the World'

(Pub trivia … Q: Which band sang that '80s anthem? A: Tears for Fears. If you didn't get that, were you off at the toilet when we had the earlier roll call for this chapter? It's not too late to go back and join a more appropriate tour.)

Generation X, we're next.

The Boomers are coming to the end of their working life, their reign. And, despite them believing that we were never going to be trustworthy enough to leave in charge, it will be up to us to run the planet. Boomers will have to shuffle off into retirement.

What does ruling the world mean?

It means we'll have to make the laws as the next generation of politicians. We'll actually have to start voting for some of our own. Or we could just install Natasha Stott Despoja as Australia's first democratically elected president and be done with it. If she could just lean a little further right … into the middle … yep, thanks Natasha, that's it! Keep that up and we'll leave you there for the next decade.

We'll be running business. The big decisions will be made by us. Gen Y will have to learn some patience. And the Boomers will have to stay in the workforce to carry out *our* orders a little longer.

We'll have the biggest salaries. The highest average salaries currently are for those who are aged 45 to 50 (although it is believed this may shift higher, to 50 to 55, as we age). After that, the statistics say, workers start getting thrown on the employment junk heap. Of course, there are those who go on to become very senior executives, being paid squillions, but that's a minority and the maths says the highest average wages are earned in your late 40s.

That means Generation X has largely got that ahead of them. Our *peak earning ability* is still to come. That's a key point to this book—you need to understand that most of us are still to reach the peak of our career and therefore highest incomes. Even if you've done very little in the way of constructing a financial fortress for yourself up until this point in your life, you've still got plenty of time on your side. You can take what's in this book and make your fortune.

If we aren't making the most of it by the time we get there, what hope do we have? Hitting your mid-50s and being 'downsized' to make way for younger, cheaper up-and-comers is not the time to be starting a wealth-creation program.

Gen X's balls and chains

We face an uphill battle in many ways. For a start, we're not a big generation. The United States originally called us the Baby Busters. After the baby boom, naturally, came the baby bust.

But if those damned Boomers haven't saved enough money (including government coffers) for themselves, then we're going to have to foot the bill. The older Boomers have already started retiring early. They'll be retiring en masse from 2011, when the first of them hit age 65. That's going to create a constant employment vacuum until as late as 2030. That means fewer workers trying to support more on the age pension. This is a problem that was realised long ago and one of the reasons that compulsory superannuation was introduced. It was put into place too late to help Gen X's requirement to financially look after the Boomers, but is designed to make sure that we're not a drain on the generations to follow.

> ...you need to understand that most of us are still to reach the peak of our career and therefore highest incomes.

Don't forget their health. Boomers' health will start deteriorating soon after they retire. We'll be left with a very large medical bill to cover them. Not only will we be wiping the bums of our own children, but we'll be financially wiping the bums of Baby Boomers in nursing homes, too. So, we'd better learn how to build useful and functional retirement homes, because Boomers are going to fill the current ones to overflowing.

And it's not like we'll eventually get rewarded for all this by collecting whatever they leave in their wills when they die. Boomers' children (people like me are the exception rather than the rule) are generally Generation Y, so that big chunk of wealth is going to skip straight over the top of us. The wealth of those who listened to music on vinyl records will skip straight over the compact disc/MTV generation (my first music was tapes and vinyl, but the majority of it is CDs) and go straight to the iPod generation.

No point complaining about it. It's just going to happen. (Unless we legislate. And that could be justifiable payback against those who inflicted HECS on us.)

'Who the hell are you ... ?'

Me? I'm Gen X under anyone's definition, based on my birth date alone. I had a fairly regular childhood, with a Hills Hoist in the backyard (from which I strung a cricket ball in a stocking trying to channel Don Bradman's skills) and holidays by the beach near Ocean Grove, Bateman's Bay or south-east Queensland, swimming in Speedos (before they became uncool and then cool again) and hating wearing zinc cream (zinc cream didn't become cool again until the '90s).

My first bike was a Barracuda, followed by an Apollo (that got stolen from Woden Plaza in Canberra), which was replaced with an Apollo II. I played a lot of sports, ate Chiko rolls, worked part-time at McDonald's, rode a skateboard and watched *Countdown* every Sunday night. I wasted a lot of time and money in pinball arcades playing Space Invaders and Pac-Man, and just time at home playing Frogger on Atari. My main interest was sport, so I remember watching Trevor Chappell bowl the underarm ball and *Australia II* win the America's Cup (a yacht race that most Australians previously didn't know and couldn't have cared less about).

After studying at the University of Canberra, I started a journalism cadetship with the *Herald Sun* in 1992. I'm one of those people who stretched the concept of being a 'teenager' into the term 'adolescence'. Nothing more than an excuse not to have to grow up until I turned 30.

In the middle of 1999, I was 28 and things were going okay. I was happy enough. I'd done a bit of travel, backpacking through Europe and Asia. My relationship with my then girlfriend (now wife) was moving in the right direction. I had a great group of friends who shared my passion for a game of pool and a night out watching Melbourne's live bands covering great '80s Australian rock, such as Cold Chisel, Midnight Oil, INXS, Hunters & Collectors and those nearly Australian bands, such as AC/DC, or anything with a Finn brother in it.

Professionally … it was a different story. I was a bit frustrated. I really had no obvious direction. But while I could afford a cold beer with mates and to keep myself in packets of Winfield (that habit's long since gone), I wasn't concerned. Hell, I wasn't yet 30. There were plenty of people working far worse jobs and with less to be proud of.

Life was good, but not great. Journalism kept me out of trouble while I found out what I really wanted to do. Turns out that what I wanted to do was journalism anyway, just not the sort of journalism I had been doing.

'And what makes you qualified to write this?'

Then came my *Sliding Doors* moment. Actually, two of them.

The first was being thrown the job of covering the Goods and Services Tax (GST), which was due to be introduced on 1 July 2000 (the following year). Editor Peter Blunden wanted a yarn a day on how the GST would impact readers. What would the GST do to the price of a can of soft drink? The price of a computer, a child's toy, a house? We told people football tickets would go up and new cars would come down. That got me into trouble with two Peters—Blunden and Treasurer Costello. The government claimed I had wrongly scared the punters about the footy (which I hadn't—the GST *was* going to push prices up). And because we were telling people to delay buying cars (to save our readers money), car dealerships withdrew advertising.

I was now hooked on finance reporting, the politics of business and the 'rules' of money. Soon after, I moved to the *Business* section and became the paper's chief banking writer, which also opened up opportunities to write about personal finance matters.

The second sliding door was a property investment book that had been sitting on my bedside table for months. Bored on one particular day off, I began to read it. It wasn't a brilliant piece of writing, but it explained simply and clearly to me the case for property investment. I devoured the book in two days and set out to find out more. Within weeks, I'd applied for my first investment property loan, and within months I'd bought one.

Now I was in the finance section at Australia's largest daily newspaper and obsessed with the world of investment. And the best thing about being a business reporter and editor is that you have a licence to ask questions of anybody.

I spent thousands of hours reading the personal finance and business sections of every paper, magazine and book I could get my hands on. Property became a personal obsession, while my everyday gig was writing about shares and the stock market.

In the meantime, I'd gone back to school to gain the qualifications to become a financial adviser (an Advanced Diploma in Financial Services). I wrote a property investment book (*The Power of Property*, Wrightbooks, 2006). I eventually left the Herald Sun in 2006 and decided to try my hand giving specific financial advice to individuals as a financial adviser, rather than giving generic advice to millions as a journalist. I wrote another property investment book (*Investing in Real Estate For Dummies*, John Wiley & Sons, 2008).

I'm a fulltime financial adviser nowadays, but I haven't left journalism completely. I still write regularly for major publications (including *Eureka Report* and News Limited newspapers) and regularly appear on radio and TV to discuss personal finance issues.

> I spent thousands of hours reading the personal finance and business sections of every paper, magazine and book I could get my hands on.

Am I wealthy? Wealth is a relative concept. We (my wife and I—it's a partnership) have done okay, thank you very much. Could we be richer? Absolutely. But we've also spent money having a life. We've travelled a lot, we've spent a lot of money filling, emptying and refilling a wine cellar. And anyone who's been there knows that having kids is not a decision you make for financial efficiency. We're wealthy enough to be enjoying the life that we're living and hungry enough to realise the journey is a long way from finished.

Debt Man Walking—a financial planning concept

Debt Man Walking is not just a catchy title for a book. And, as already stated, it's not just a book about debt.

It is, I believe, an entire financial planning process that could be used for a generation of Australians. It's not just about gearing yourself to the max; it's about making sure that you have a plan. It's about making sure you understand what you're doing. It's about buying the right sorts of assets (with gearing, for those whom it is appropriate for). It's about understanding the importance of the implicit choice that you make when you decide to buy or rent. It's about accepting that paying for help will often make you more money and can protect you from very costly mistakes. It's about protecting your family in case any one of a very long list of unthinkable events happens. It's about putting some thought into some parts of your finances that could make an enormous difference to your future.

At the minimum, the least that I want Gen Xers to get out of this book is to understand that what was right for our parents is not necessarily right for us. Their attitudes to money don't need to be our attitudes to money. The next generation can do, *should do*, things much smarter than the previous generation.

Understanding the X-Flips

Our attitudes to money aren't always based on fact.

To that end, I've introduced a concept I've called the X-Flips.

The X-Flips are a sort of dyslexic version of *The X-Files*. Where the TV show had Fox and Dana having to 'believe' to try to explain the unexplainable, the covert and the covered up, the X-Flips similarly try to push aside conventional thinking that can hold people back.

There's an X-Flip at the end of every step of *Debt Man Walking*. They're designed to get you to flip your thinking on a particular issue — to understand that what may often feel natural, what you may have been taught at school, picked up by osmosis from your parents, or learned from your friends, the stuff that has sunk in so deep that it just seems like 'The Truth', might not be the best thing to do for your financial health.

> Why is it that we save our money, then invest? Why don't people actually invest to save?

For example … why is it that we save our money, *then* invest? Why don't people actually *invest to save*? Saving to invest can be a horribly slow way of achieving long-term financial targets. While some saving is inescapable and many shorter-term financial targets should be achieved through the physical act of saving money, everyone will have some longer-term financial goals where the opposite approach could be applied. That is, instead of saving your copper 1¢ and 2¢ pieces, you could ...

... hang on. Let's not get ahead of ourselves here. That X-Flip needs to be put into some context. So you'll have to wait until the end of step 2 for more on that.

The point is: the traditional rules aren't necessarily always right for every person. And they're certainly not right for every situation. Do you think that Kerry Packer (rest in peace, KP) got to where he was by playing the same money rules as everyone else? Not a chance! What most people understand is the money basics can be a little bit LCD — that's the mathematical lowest common denominator, not the Game Boy liquid crystal display. The traditional money rules are designed to be failsafe, idiot-proof rules that can't be proved wrong in any situation. They are good, solid rules. But they are the absolute basics.

Those who take an active interest in their finances, who want to understand how money is really made, can probably take a few more risks than the average punter. *Debt Man Walking* presupposes readers have mastered the financial basics. You want to move on to the next stage. You know there must be a better way. You understand that something bigger must be around the corner. You want to start on what's next.

Well, you've found it. It's here. It's *Debt Man Walking: A 10-Step Investment and Gearing Guide for Generation X*.

And what's next is step 1.

Bruce Brammall
October 2008

step 1

Q: Which band sang about Gen X's parents' drug and booze binges in their song titled 'The Generation Gap'?

A: Hoodoo Gurus

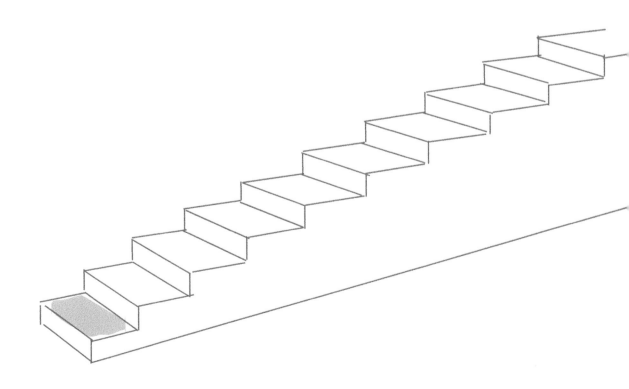

Write your own ticket

- Your lotto dream dollar figure
- Providing the incentive
- Fear and greed
- Nailing down some goals
- When plans change…
- A neverending money supply?
- The X-Flips: just…say…yes!

How much would you have to win in lotto to quit work forever?

It's a great discussion to have with any bunch of friends or in any workplace. What's the dollar figure and why? Would you keep working regardless?

I was talking about this with journalist colleagues one day many years ago (about 2000). Journalism is a great job for spending hours talking bollocks. Most of those conversations are considered 'research'. It's almost encouraged in a newsroom—the 'swapping of ideas'. In many other jobs, such frivolous discussions might be considered time-wasting. But not among 'reporters'.

One colleague said he'd quit work forever tomorrow if he won $1 million. He was one of the younger Baby Boomers and his mortgage (the non-deductible bit, at least) was gone and his kids were almost off his hands. He reckoned $1 million could get him through to accessing his super and see him shift into retirement.

Two Gen Xers in the group scoffed. They would still show up for work if they won $2 million or even $3 million on a Saturday night. They were late 20s, had

WASTED ON THE WRONG PEOPLE

How many times have current affairs shows run stories about people who win $1 million to $2 million, but are broke again within years? What they didn't give away to family and friends, they wasted on the frivolous. And then it's back to work. They didn't even pay off the mortgage! D'oh! It was their big financial opportunity and they blew it.

The problems for the jackpot winners who burn the lot are numerous. They clearly had no idea how to handle money. Even though they presumably dreamed about it for years, they had never given any consideration to how to make the most of it, if they *did* get it.

They'd planned on doing things such as buying a new car, getting rid of the mortgage, helping out the kids or grandkids, a bit of an overseas holiday. But they blew it on short-term gratification. Lump sums like that can create an income for life. A sum of $1 million is enough to get an annual income of, potentially, about $70 000 that will rise with inflation forever (see step 2).

above-average mortgages and one had two kids. Both of them said their absolute minimum to give up work forever was $4 million.

The chance that your numbers will come up to win division one is one in 2 million (if you play four games). Your chances don't get any better if you play once a week for 20 years, but at least you've had 1000 shots at it.

But lotto is not a plan to become rich. It's punting—a great, big gamble with impossible odds. If you added the money the average Australian blows gambling (such as lotto tickets, scratchies, pokies and the horses) each year, you'd have something that could really be turned into a serious figure.

Grasp this concept early—getting rich has nothing to do with luck. It's not about picking winners. It's not about a big bag with $$$ signs falling in your lap. Making your fortune is actually a process, or a recipe. And Generation X, led by Gordon Ramsay, has just arrived in the kitchen. (Move over Margaret Fulton. Off you go, Gabriel Gaté.)

What's your dream dollar figure?

Everyone can name their lotto price. The actual number is sort of irrelevant. What's important is what that number means to you and how you got to it. Why did the Boomer choose $1 million? Why did the Gen Xers choose $4 million? That's a pretty serious difference for people only about 10 years apart in age.

Your number should boil down to the minimum figure that would allow you to achieve all of your life's goals. It might buy you the home you want, in the neighbourhood of your choice, with leftovers that allow you to achieve other goals you've set yourself. Perhaps the annual rental of a ritzy holiday home, buying a beach house, new cars, being able to retire early, travelling the world following your favourite sporting team or having a personal masseuse, hair and clothes stylist, like you were one of the *Heathers*.

Is $1 million sufficient? Is $4 million just plain greedy? Maybe and possibly. In any case, it can be a fascinating conversation to have with friends. It will give you a great idea of what their dreams and aspirations are. They're effectively telling you what their dreams are and how much they need to fund them.

Everybody's dreams are different. The figure I named that day is still about the same figure I'd say is the amount that would get me to quit fulltime work forever. My dreams haven't faded with inflation (even if I'm substantially closer to reaching that goal).

But I've got less of a chance of winning the lotto than most. For a start, you've got to be in it to win it. And I've never, ever, bought a lotto ticket.

There's nothing necessarily wrong with buying lotto tickets. (Personally, I think you'd probably be better off buying shares in one of the big gambling companies.) So long as you understand that the technical mathematical term for the chance of you ever winning lotto is 'sod all' and that it's only spare cash that you're blowing, and that you understand that your real chances of picking the right six numbers are slim and lotto is therefore unlikely to pay off your credit card for you...

So what you need to take from this discussion is: *'What is it you want money to help you achieve?'* Don't answer that right now. Tony Barber will give you some *Sale of the Century* thinking music and time to write some answers later in the chapter.

'Can't Buy Me Love'

I can't remember where I first heard it, but it's stuck with me for life: 'Money doesn't solve all problems. And it creates new ones'. What sort of problems can too much money create? The worries of the wealthy are no less concerning—and just as likely to induce sleepless nights—as those facing people struggling to make ends meet (see table 1.1).

Table 1.1: the financial concerns of those who live…

Payday to payday	Comfortably
How will I pay this month's utility bills?	I've made my money, but I'm scared that I'm going to lose it.
If I give up buying a morning coffee, I could save enough for a house deposit or for an investment. But that will take forever.	How would I cope if the Australian or international stock markets collapse?
How can I get what my partner/ kids want for Christmas?	What if the property market implodes tomorrow?
Where can we have a cheap holiday this year?	How can I get back up to date with all this investment paperwork?
How will I get my credit card back to zero?	If interest rates fall, will I be able to survive on a lower income?
How am I going to meet the rent/ mortgage this month?	Where's the next big deal coming from?
What happens if I lose my job? We're so far in debt.	Will the kids be ready/want to take over the family business?
Interest rates have risen. I'll have to redo the home budget.	Is what I've got really enough?
	Should I say no to this investment opportunity?

Personally, I want my problems on the wealthy side to include: 'A customs officer of which country is going to be the next to put a stamp in my passport?' Which of the two groups has the more serious concerns? To each group, plus anyone who thinks they fit in between, their concerns are very real.

Don't think for an instant that reaching your chosen financial destination—whatever point you choose that to be—will be the day you get to cut loose. It's possible, but don't count on it. It's a rare person—rich or poor—who can claim not to be concerned about money. The few that I've met would actually be happy whether they were loaded or struggling week to week.

Being content is more a state of mind. That said, most of us would rather have the concerns of the wealthy than the poor.

Wealth can bring a fantastic boost to your confidence that can flow on to other aspects of your life. There's little more satisfying than the sense of achievement you get from putting in place a financial plan that delivers everything you want for yourself and/or your family. Think of the wealthiest friend you have. You've probably noticed that they have a higher level of self-esteem than others. They don't necessarily brag about money (some, obviously, can't help themselves), but they have an inner confidence that comes with the pride of having achieved financial security.

No incentive, no point

I've been playing indoor cricket since about 1998 with some mates. We're called the Tossers and I'm the wicketkeeper. I'd like to think I'm the Rod Marsh of the squad. However, they assure me that I'm only the 18th best keeper the team's ever had—a compliment that probably ranks alongside the 'as cool as Michael Bolton' variety. Thankfully, it's more about the beer after the game than being *Bodyline* serious. And that's not too hard to see from one look at our physiques.

Over the decade, we've tried to instigate several Tossers' *Biggest Loser*–style weight loss competitions. It goes something like this. Someone brings a pair of scales to the annual weekend away. On the Sunday morning, with enormous hangovers, we jump on the scales for the first weigh in. Names and the embarrassing starting weights are written down. Then we head off down to Sorrento for a greasy fry-up.

> If you're looking to achieve something yourself, then you need some form of incentive or motivation to do so.

But before we've scoffed down breakfast, the weight loss competition is all but doomed. Not because of the bacon and hash browns, but because no-one's committed anything to losing weight. We've never got around to collecting the $50 entry fee to give the competition some incentive. Unless the money has been committed for an eventual winner, there's no incentive and the idea is quickly forgotten. It's a shame, because we could safely shed enough kilos to power a small town for several months.

The point is this: commitment has to be more than just a passing thought. If you're looking to achieve something yourself, then you need some form of incentive or motivation to do so.

It's simple stuff, really. The people most likely to get off their butts and do something about their situation are those who sense one of life's *two great motivators*: fear and greed.

Fear—fight or flight

Fear is easy to understand. Fear evokes the response that is known as 'fight or flight' when it comes to a physical threat. When it comes to finances, fear can be a positive motivator if it causes you to focus on what scares you and what it is that you need to do in order to stop something from occurring.

The more you fear something (say, how you're going to fund the kids' education or how the family would financially cope if you were to die), the more likely you are to do something about it.

Greed—Gordon Gekko style

Greed, on the other hand, is a little harder to put a positive spin on. Greed has picked up a pretty nasty reputation, care of being immortalised by the Catholics as one of the seven deadly sins. It also wasn't helped much during our lifetimes by Oliver Stone's *Wall Street*.

Michael Douglas won an Oscar for his role as Gordon Gekko. The 1987 movie highlighted everything that was wrong with the excess of corporate America. (Later that year came the proof, with the global sharemarket crash.) Here is Gekko's famous speech, made to shareholders of Teldar Paper, a company he intended to take over:

> *The point is, ladies and gentleman, that greed—for lack of a better word—is good. Greed is right. Greed works. Greed clarifies, cuts through, and captures the essence of the evolutionary spirit. Greed, in all of its forms—greed for life, for money, for love, knowledge—has marked the upward surge of mankind.*

Over time, the line got shortened to simply 'Greed is good'. If you read the passage carefully, it makes sense. Greed is a motivating force for humans. And where can the harm be if the greed is for life, love and knowledge? It's only the money bit that's actually considered a bit evil.

Debt Man Walking does not condone full-blown greed. But, as we're told in regards to alcohol, greasy food and salt, everything in moderation is okay, isn't it? How hungry are you to achieve your goals? How worried are you about not achieving them? The stronger you feel, the stronger your commitment is likely to be.

Let's back up a bit now. It's come time for you to commit to something.

Write your own ticket

Generation X's goals are different. The decisions that Gen Xers are contemplating, and the ambitions they have, are targets already largely achieved by Boomers. And Gen X has largely passed those early life achievements that Generation Y is now grappling with.

John Farnham sang it in 'Reason'—if you've got one, you'll go running for it. It's time to name at least one practical goal, preferably several. You may already have one in your head—the financial concern that bugged you enough to decide to pick up *Debt Man Walking* in the first place.

It doesn't matter what your goal is. The following is a list to give you some ideas (most are, or were, on my own list):

- get a deposit together for a house
- pay off the home loan faster
- educate the tin lids, if they are on the way, or you've already bred a few
- own a property portfolio
- buy a holiday home
- build a self-funding share portfolio
- retire early
- create a passive income stream that will replace your own working income
- be able to buy the kids a house each.

These goals don't touch on cutting household expenditure or paying back the credit card. As was covered in the introduction, *Debt Man Walking* assumes you have some basic money skills and you're ready for the next step. The next step is wealth creation, or achieving big financial targets.

Some of the goals are pretty lofty and expensive. But they're not out of the reach of anyone in Generation X who has access to a steady income and a strong enough desire to achieve something. You don't even need to be earning the average wage. Achieving these sorts of targets requires only commitment from you and what you learn in *Debt Man Walking*.

List your goals below. If you're really serious, I'd like you to type this list up and have it somewhere where you can see it regularly.

1   _____

2   _____

3   _____

4   _____

What drives me?

I typed my goals on a piece of paper several years ago and kept them Blu-Tacked to the wall above my computer. My first real list was a fairly extensive one, where I wrote financial goals for one, five, 10 and 20 years. (Some of them were quite specific—we'll talk about those soon.)

They can be summarised as:

1   not *needing* to work much beyond 50

2   providing a good (possibly expensive) education for my children

3   owning a holiday home to create special memories for the family

4   travelling overseas every year.

I've italicised *needing* in the first goal, because of the difference between *need* and *want*. I want to be in a position where any income stream I create could, if I wished, allow me to retire without having to take a pay cut.

But plans change

Plans change like fashion. Anyone out there still wearing leg warmers, acid-wash jeans, bubble skirts or fingerless gloves?

Altering your plans because conditions change is okay. Ditching them without good reason is not. Let me give you two of my specific plans that have altered in recent years.

My wife and I wanted to live in a particular Melbourne suburb. My specific aim was to 'be able to afford the median-priced home' in that suburb. I'm not sure yet whether we'll end up living there or not. The goal has actually been met, in that we could afford to live there if we wanted to. However, in order to do so, we would have to make significant changes to some of our other priorities that we don't want to—that is, sell other assets we don't want to sell. After much consideration, we decided that changing those other goals wasn't acceptable.

Another was to have paid down the mortgage far enough that the interest portion of the mortgage was below our previous rent (because the principal repayment essentially becomes savings in reducing your loan). Again, that goal could have been achieved, but we made a choice to keep our debt structured as is.

Yes, a home mortgage is considered undesirable debt (but I'll refute that in step 6) and eliminating it is, in principle, a good idea. But it's not always the be-all and end-all. And *Debt Man Walking* will show you that a mortgage can play a big part in helping you achieve your goals.

If you've written a number of goals above, great. Don't make them too flexible. But don't make them inflexible. As you progress in your financial plans over the next five years, your goals will grow with you.

And give yourself credit for achieving goals. Don't meet them just for the sake of meeting them. If your lifestyle changes, or a more important goal rears its head (getting pregnant, or getting pregnant again, can change things dramatically and quickly), be prepared to be flexible.

'Money for Nothing'

Dire Straits' 'Money for Nothing' was a stab at music fans who believed rock stars got paid loads for doing not much. And the chicks were chucked in free.

I have no musical talent. Like most wannabes, I learned to use a guitar to play the first bit of 'Smoke on the Water' (duh, duh, duh…duh, duh du-nah) and a small piece of the soundtrack of *The Blues Brothers*. I can also play the one-finger version of 'Mary Had a Little Lamb' on a keyboard, which my children may one day enjoy. As I said, completely bereft of musical talent. So I've had to come up with my own attainable, substitute definition of 'Money for Nothing' that will allow me to at least retire one day without having to take a pay cut.

Passive income streams

Surely life's winners are the ones who get to wake up each morning to a job they really want to do, but who are financially settled enough that they don't *need* to keep working until they die. If that's the case, then passive income streams are the way that most of us—who aren't natural sportspeople, business leaders or Mark Knopfler—are going to get there.

> A passive income stream is an income stream that doesn't require you to have to work physically.

A passive income stream is an income stream that doesn't require you to have to work physically. The income stream could be provided by dividends or distributions from your shares or managed funds, rent from your investment properties or interest from your cash investments.

How does the prospect of cutting back to a four-day week when you turn 52, a three-day week at 56 and fully retire at 60, while never having to take a pay cut and never having to rely on the government age pension sound? Well, one of the aims of *Debt Man Walking* is to show you how you might be able to get yourself to that position (or even earlier, if that's your goal).

Passive income streams that will replace your own income don't eventuate without some sacrifice. You need to have a pool of assets that is capable of providing both enough income for you to survive on, plus be able to keep you one step ahead of inflation. If you can do that, you will have enough money to create a never-ending income stream.

The never-ending income stream

How much money do you need to create a never-ending income stream? Essentially, what we're looking for is a sum of money big enough to provide you with sufficient income to live off (plus have a bit more to add back to the investment so that the income will grow a little the next year).

There are three basic factors that affect how much money you need. They are: the long-term return from investments; the income you desire; and inflation. Dull, I know. But this is really, really simple, so just work with me for a sec.

Anyone reading this is probably too far away to know yet what the actual figure they'll need in retirement is. However, here's the equation to play around with. Start with the annual income you think you'll need in retirement: let's say $100 000, but it could be your family's current after-tax income. We'll also assume that inflation is 3 per cent and the long-term return on investments is 9 per cent.

$$\text{Lump sum needed} = \frac{\text{Income required}}{\text{Investment return} - \text{Inflation}}$$

$$\text{Lump sum needed} = \frac{\$100\,000}{9\% - 3\%}$$

$$\text{Lump sum needed} = \frac{\$100\,000}{0.06}$$

$$\text{Lump sum needed} = \$1\,666\,667$$

Assuming the return and inflation figures are correct, a lump sum of $1 666 667 will provide an income of $100 000 in the first year. There would be enough left over to cover inflation and make sure your income rises by 3 per cent each year. (See step 2 for more on insidious inflation and step 4 for investment returns.) Anyway, that's the theory. We'll show you how to achieve some of these really big targets in step 8.

The X-Flips:

Just ... say ... yes!

It's easier to say 'no'. Saying 'yes' often requires extra work, whereas 'no' usually means that something doesn't have to be done. It's almost as if we're conditioned to say 'no'. But how about you flip your thinking for a change?

Just say 'yes'. Because when it comes to your personal finances, it's often too easy to say 'no', or to put things off until next month or next year. There's a hilarious book by Englishman Danny Wallace, called *Yes Man*. Danny married an Australian friend of mine. (By the time *Debt Man Walking* comes out, *Yes Man* will, I understand, have been turned into a movie starring Jim Carrey.) *Yes Man* is ostensibly a true story about how Danny decided that he needed to turn his life around. He made a promise to himself (and a mate to help keep him honest) that he would say 'yes' to every proposal that was put to him for six months. Everything.

He was asked 'Do you want to buy my car?' when he didn't even have a driver's licence. A magazine he was reading asked 'Would you like a penis enlarger?' He was almost too drunk to talk in a nightclub and a large thug asked him 'Do you want a fight?' He said 'yes' to the lot, and it changed his life. I'm not suggesting that you do a Danny and say 'yes' to everything. Investing requires you to say 'no' probably 10 times as often as you say 'yes', as you try to find the right investments.

But the single most important thing about achieving anything in life is getting started. It's that 'A journey of 1000 miles starts with a single step' (or even a journey half as long, like The Proclaimers' '500 Miles') thing. Or 'In order to get to bed, first you need to stop ordering beers and exit the pub'.

It's going to take some sort of effort from you. Like Rachel Hunter said in those awful Pantene ads (with her New Zealand accent), 'It won't hippen overnight. But it will hippen'. I've been told I really shouldn't promise anything at all (damn liability reasons), but I will say that if you follow the steps in this book, you will achieve goals and impress yourself along the way.

Step 1 for Gen X

In the same vein that sees people claim that '78 per cent of all statistics are made up on the spot', I'm going to declare that '93 per cent of people who don't write down their goals fail to meet them'. Possibly a load of bollocks. But hell, it could be right. And if you want to prove me wrong—and you can be bothered with the expense and you're the first one to do so—I'll find some way of giving you public credit.

If you took the time to write down some goals earlier in the chapter, then you've already achieved step 1. Easy, hey? If you haven't, then humour me.

Go back and do one. At least one. I need you to have something to focus on, or think about, as we work through the steps.

Or, as teacher Richard Vernon (Paul Gleeson) says to Bender (Judd Nelson) in *The Breakfast Club*, 'Just take the first shot. I'm begging you, take a shot. Just one hit. Come on, that's all I need, just one swing...'

step 2

Q: Which Australian rockers wrote the '80s classics 'Everybody Wants to Work', 'Party' and '50 Years'?

A: The Uncanny X-Men

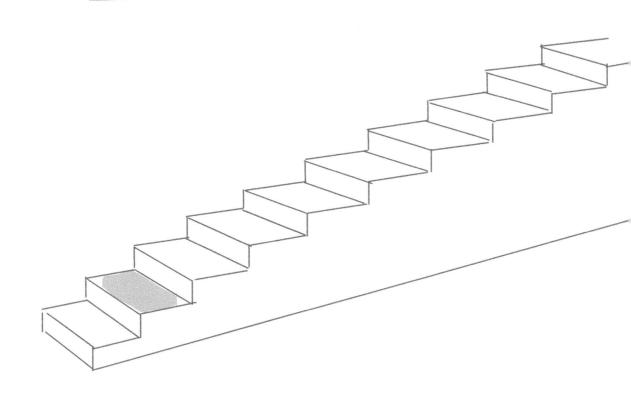

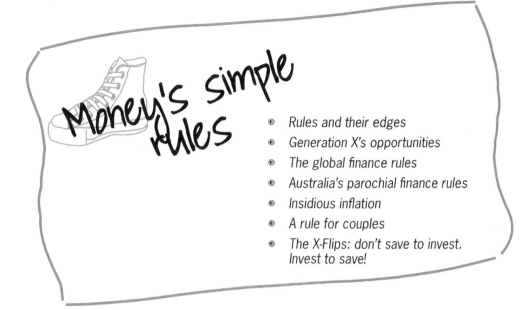

Money's simple rules

- Rules and their edges
- Generation X's opportunities
- The global finance rules
- Australia's parochial finance rules
- Insidious inflation
- A rule for couples
- The X-Flips: don't save to invest. Invest to save!

If I had five days spare—not that we need more than three when we're playing England—I could watch every ball of a Test Match, if they don't change ends too quickly and catch me still getting a beer from the fridge. But have you ever tried to explain the game of cricket to a foreigner? If you don't have a telly in front of you to show things as they happen, then you're going to need some terrific explanatory skills.

I've done it once and I didn't have a television. Bless the ABC, Kerry O'Keeffe and their amazing ability to turn six hours of playing time, where not a lot happens, into something worth listening to. It almost doesn't matter that there's a game being played. These guys are what non-music radio is about—insightful commentary scattered between bizarre, unrelated, personal conversations. On one annual Christmas holiday driving around between the families, my wife became a cricket fan.

If only the rules of cricket were a little more like the rules of soccer. The rules of soccer are considered to be among the most beautifully simple documents ever written. The same cannot be said for cricket. Try explaining the intricacies of LBWs when you're the driver, at 110 kilometres per hour, on the Hume Highway.

The money world has a lot of rules. Some are like soccer's rules—simple global rules that never change. They'll work everywhere, in every town, in every country. There's more lore than laws, if you like.

But every country also has its own set of rules—complex, cricket-like peculiarities. It often seems that they are known and understood only by the wealthy (it's partly why they're rich). That's because they've taken the time to understand them.

These local rules tend to be ones written by governments of individual countries for the purposes of … I have no idea. Honestly. For example, I can tell you how the laws as they relate to property investment differ between Australia and the United States (because I converted an American property investment book into an Australian one), but I can't tell you why two civilised Western countries came up with such different rules for making money through real estate.

What I can tell you is that learning the rules, and how to play them, is one of the keys to unlocking your financial freedom.

'Livin' On the Edge'

(Introducing … Aerosmith.)

I don't have a burning desire to set the rules. I don't hate many of them so badly that I want them changed. That said, there aren't too many rules that I love (although I've always been partial to offers from 'negative gearing').

> Once you learn the basics of any set of rules, you can find out how far those rules can be stretched.

I've got a fairly simple philosophy for life, whether it's finance, sport or the politics of survival in a workplace: 'Learn the rules. Then play them'.

Once you learn the basics of any set of rules, you can find out how far those rules can be stretched. The better a player knows the rules, the better they are able to interpret the game itself. Think European soccer players and their ability to take a dive and fake injury. Or five-time 500cc motorbike world champion Mick Doohan and his ability to slide, rather than drive, through corners.

Many people claim the rules are there to be broken, or that the rules don't apply to them. From my experience, these people play by the rules—they just know where the real boundary is.

The real boundary is the edge of the grey area, which is the bit that lies between what is definitely considered within the rules and what is definitely considered outside of the rules. In a non-financial sense, that could be the in-built leniency by police in some states, where they won't book you even if you're a little bit over the speed limit. (That's not to say I condone speeding.)

Rules have edges. The best people in any field of endeavour play in that grey area. The best comedians know the fine line between what's tasteful and what isn't. The best sports people know the limits of the rules about equipment (*Australia II* and the winged keel in the America's Cup).

The problem with most people's finances is that they've never bothered to learn, or understand, the rules. They learned what they needed to survive from their parents or friends and that was enough.

Plotting the path for Gen X

Generation X has arrived in the sweet spot for wealth creation. In the financial world, the age of 30 to 50 is commonly referred to as the wealth accumulation phase. The oldest Gen Xers are approaching the peak of their professional lives and earning capacity, while younger Xers are starting a long run of rising incomes.

The younger that money lessons are learned, the better. And, goddamnit, Gen X needs to do something about our own fortunes, because we've been told quite clearly that we won't be able to rely on an inheritance. The older generation intend to SKI (Spend the Kids' Inheritance). And neither should we be relying on the government age pension.

In broad terms, Gen Xers should have already learned to save. But it is still a long time before we will begin to consider (carefully) blowing our superannuation. Xers are not so young as to believe we are invincible and not so old as to be considering our own mortality. We know important financial decisions cannot be put off until next decade, but don't yet feel the need to go into financial protection mode. We are not so carefree as to want no boundaries or restrictions on our lives (Gen Y) and not so old as to feel trapped by decisions or mistakes made in our youth (older Boomers).

Rules are like the bricks on a path. So let's look at the important rules we need to know—the universal rules and the Australian rules—on Gen X's path to financial freedom.

Money's universal rules

The universal rules of money are as global as a Coca-Cola yo-yo being used to 'walk the dog' in the '70s and '80s. They will work in every country in the world and will be transportable to the rest of our solar system (as it opens up).

Understanding the basic rules of money is pivotal to creating mountains of it. People don't become wealthy by accident. People become rich *after* they have made a conscious decision to learn how money works.

You could take these first five rules on your travels to London, New York, Bangkok, Johannesburg or Buenos Aires, and they'll serve you just as well as they will in Brisbane or Broken Hill. They don't change depending on what stamp is in your passport.

Delayed gratification

Scientific experiments and animal testing—the fact that this might have been wrong didn't seem to occur to anyone much before Anita Roddick started opening The Body Shop all over the place, with its 'against animal testing' slogans. It only takes one. There's little likelihood that the following experiment would get past the psychologists' ethics board nowadays either.

One famous experiment by Walter Mischel in the late '60s used young animals with some reasoning and communication skills (human children) to test the theory of delayed gratification. One at a time, the children were left in a room by themselves with one marshmallow. The researcher told the child that if the marshmallow was still there when the researcher returned, they would get two marshmallows.

Most kids simply couldn't hold out. They tried their hardest, tried everything they could, but they just couldn't stop themselves eating the marshmallow. Some would try to fall asleep. Some would lick the marshmallow, then put it down. Some would sniff it. Some would pick it up, put it down and then lick their fingers. But 90 per cent would go on to eat it before the researcher came back.

Two marshmallows at some unspecified future time or one now. Right now. No waiting. What a conundrum for a kid.

This experiment was done in America on Gen Xers (that is, when we were children). And they've been able to follow those children into later life. They discovered—no surprise—that the 10 per cent who were able to delay gratification to get two marshmallows continued to do this in later life. They were more likely to have university degrees, not use drugs, become wealthy and have more friends.

Which one were you as a child and do you think you'd still tend to be that sort of person now?

Delayed gratification is the first universal law of money. And it's obvious. If you spend $1000 now, you don't have it for the future. If you don't spend that $1000 now, you will be able to turn it into $2000 to spend in the future. Or more, depending on how well you use all the rules.

Risk versus return

We're taught that risk means the chance that something bad will happen. But risk is really the chance that something outside of what is expected will happen, good or bad.

Universal investment rule number two is that risk and return are inextricably related. The less risk an investor is prepared to take with their money, the smaller return they can expect. The opposite also applies—the bigger the risk an investor embraces, the higher should be the potential for return (given enough time to overcome possible short-term volatility). That's because the higher the risk that an investor takes, the bigger chance that some, or all, of their money could be lost in the short term.

> *...risk is really the chance that something outside of what is expected will happen, good or bad*

Let's take Luna Park (or the annual Royal Show) and the 'puke test'. If you want safety, jump on the merry-go-round. The chance of having to hurl is fairly remote. But the excitement factor is non-existent. If you're prepared for an exciting, white-knuckled, stomach-churning ride, then the Gravitron, the roller-coaster or the Pirate Ship are probably for you.

With investing, like the Show, there are thrills and spills for everyone's interests in between.

Investment necessarily involves taking a risk—there is no such thing as a *riskless* investment. Even putting your money in the bank has a small element of risk. Investments will rarely perform exactly as expected and the higher the risk (particularly shares and property), the wider the likely fluctuations around the long-term averages.

What *Debt Man Walking* aims to show Generation Xers is that if you understand how time can smooth out some of those risks, it can make a major difference to your financial future. We'll go into detail on the different types of risk in step 3.

Compounding growth

Remember delayed gratification? Well, the rule regarding compounding growth is delayed gratification times 10…for grown ups (which we might even become one day).

If little Sarah was prepared to wait 30 minutes to get two marshmallows instead of getting one immediately, how many would she get if she was prepared to wait a week? Dozens, maybe hundreds. But that would be just too cruel an experiment to try.

That's compounding growth—except it's measured in years, not minutes and days.

If you put away money to invest, reinvest any gains and let the investment con-tinue to grow year after year, then it will start to earn growth on the growth. That is, if an investment of $100000 grows by 10 per cent in the first year it will grow to $110000. In its second year, 10 per cent growth would be $11000 (that's 10 per cent of $110000). By the time you hit year 10, it's growing at more than $23000 a year.

Compounding returns are one of the most powerful natural forces available to investors. And when it comes to larger investments (like property or large share portfolios), compounding growth can make the decision to sell a difficult one.

Consider what happens if you do delay. In figure 2.1, I show investors who have decided to put away $1000 a year. The first investor starts now and puts $1000 away per year for the next 30 years. The second investor doesn't start putting away his $1000 a year until year 10 and then puts the money away for years 11 to 30. I have assumed the investments are earning 9 per cent each year and all proceeds are reinvested.

Figure 2.1: the cost of time delay on an investment

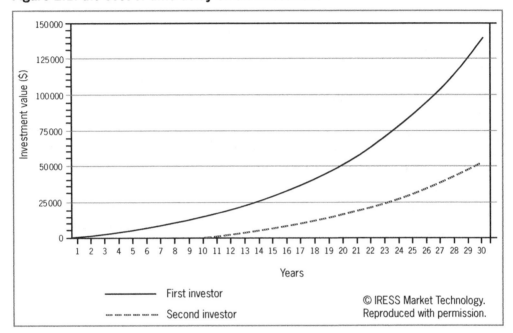

The investor who started immediately will have $142441 at the end of 30 years. The investor who delayed will have just $53462 at the end. The lesson is to start your investment plan early and add to it consistently. The cost of not putting in that $1000 each year for the first 10 years is not $10000, but nearly $89000.

Diversification — spread your risk

Diversification is traditionally explained via the eggs and baskets analogy. Don't put all your eggs in the one basket, because if you drop it, you're stuffed. Derrr!

But eggs on their own are a bit dull.

Remember back to your early 20s. Sunday morning. Major hangover. You didn't leave the club till 4am. You didn't stop at the hot dog caravan because you had only just enough cash for the taxi to get you about halfway home anyway. There's no food in the fridge because you went out for half-price drinks on Thursday instead of doing the shopping. And you rejected every offer you got last night, so you went home alone. Or there weren't any offers…

When you woke up, you were off to your favourite café. Eggs, bacon, toast, tomatoes and mushrooms, washed down with orange juice and coffee. Okay, so there's diversification on your plate, but that's not the diversification I'm talking about.

How would you pay for it when the cabbie got the last notes from your pocket?

> If your financial interests are diversfied and your money is spread across 20 investments (of about 5 per cent each), then the loss of one investment is the loss of only 5 per cent of your money.

Well, there's the money down the back of the couch. There's the $50 you loaned your flatmate last weekend. There's the credit card you (thankfully) left at home last night. There's the $20 note you left with your credit card for this exact purpose. There's the coin jar. There are your parents. Or there's the store credit a regular customer can get from an understanding café owner.

Diversification is simply that—spread the risk around. If your financial interests are diversified and your money is spread across 20 investments (of about 5 per cent each), then the loss of one investment is the loss of only 5 per cent of your money. This means having your money spread across different investments—in the four different investment asset classes of shares, property, cash and fixed interest—plus diversified within the asset classes themselves.

The power of leverage

I've saved the most powerful universal investment force until last. And it's the focus on this investment rule that I believe sets this book apart.

It's the *Debt* in *Debt Man Walking*.

Leverage is the addition of other people's money to your investment program. It's also known as borrowing (or gearing, or using debt) to amplify the returns you achieve. And by amplify, I mean it has the potential to increase your upside and your downside. And there's a cost, called interest.

Using debt in an investment portfolio (as I discussed in the introduction) is not for everyone. It can be used by anyone who understands the risks properly.

But, broadly, it's not for the really young, who haven't settled into their careers yet, and it's not for those who are at the end of their working lives, because of the risk that it could wipe out whatever stash they achieved through their working life.

If there is an age group, a generation, for whom debt-funded investing is appropriate, it's Generation X, which is largely settled into a working life and has plenty of time on their side to allow for the fluctuations inherent in geared investing.

Why do it?

- If you invest $50 000 of your own money and the investment increases by 10 per cent, you have gained $5000.

- If you invested $100 000 ($50 000 of your own and $50 000 that was borrowed), then a 10 per cent increase would result in a gain of $10 000, which is a 20 per cent return on your own $50 000.

- If you invest $500 000 ($50 000 of your own and $450 000 borrowed), and that investment rises by 10 per cent, the gain would be $50 000, which is a doubling of your initial $50 000.

I haven't factored in the cost of interest to these examples (I'll cover this in later steps). And the reverse of these examples is also true. If these were falls instead of rises, you would have lost 10 per cent, 20 per cent or 100 per cent, respectively, of your initial $50 000.

Property and shares tend to rise in value over time, rather than fall. For example, what did your parents pay for the family home? What would it be worth now? In 1988, the value of the All Ordinaries was below 1500 points. In 2007, it reached a high above 6800 points. The world's most watched index, the Dow Jones, was the equivalent of about 700 points in 1975 (and around 2000 points in 1988). In September 2008, it was trading around 11 000 points. Figure 2.2 (overleaf) shows these two indices over two decades.

Figure 2.2: growth in Australia's All Ordinaries and the US's Dow Jones Industrial Average over 20 years

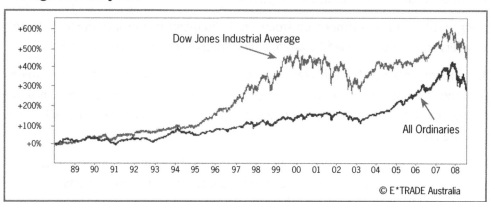

© E*TRADE Australia

Gearing is the most powerful force in investment. The people who understand the power of investment borrowing and have full respect for the risks will be able to get the most out of gearing. However, gearing is no guarantee of financial success.

Australia's unique money rules

The global rules of investing never change. Get a stamp in your passport and wander through the customs clearance of any member country of the United Nations and those rules will apply. Even in Fidel Castro's Cuba (where access to borrowed capital might be tough), the rules will apply.

But the Australian rules are so parochial that they probably wouldn't work across The Ditch with a New Zealand dollar in your hand. They go down a treat here—like finding the 'free Sunnyboy' or 'free Razz' on the inside of your iceblock wrapper— but don't expect to be able to use them anywhere else.

You won't get far without knowing the local laws. Governments pride themselves on the rules they make, no matter how bad they are. Investors work under different rules everywhere. Where governments initially imposed rules that were dumb, they'll often bring in even dumber rules to paper over the cracks.

Australia is no different. Successive Australian governments have created an investment framework that is as sensible as a show about a robot that can compute your compatability rating, à la Dexter on *Perfect Match*.

But it's important to know what Australia's main investment rules are. Like some Australian TV shows, when it comes to investment laws Australia has some classics (such as *Cop Shop* and *The Sullivans*) and some absolute stinkers (such as *Chances* and *Paradise Beach*).

Capital gains tax

Prior to 1985—when Prince still had a pronounceable name and a Revolution—Australians did not have to pay tax on the gains they made from investing.

Then Paul Keating gave us capital gains tax. Capital gains tax is only reasonable—if you make money from society, a sense of fairness states that you should contribute back to society. And since Keating introduced this 'scumbag' tax to the 'banana republic', successive treasurers have fiddled with it.

If you have a pre-1985 asset that you've inherited, then there is a different set of rules and you should see an accountant or a financial adviser before making any decision to sell. However, for simplicity, let's look at the rules as they stand now. The important differentiator is whether or not the investment has been held for more, or less, than a year. Hold it for longer than a year and you pay tax on only half the gain.

For example, if you buy an asset and sell it six months later for a profit of $5000, you will have to pay tax on the full $5000 gain. If you owned that asset for longer than a year, then you pay tax only on $2500, or half the gain.

Summary: there are tax benefits to holding investments for longer than one year.

Negative gearing

Australians are famous for their love of a tax deduction. We had the Bottom of the Harbour tax schemes of the '80s. We had the ostrich farms (managed investment schemes) and deductible film investments of the '90s. And we had the richest bloke in Australia, Kerry Packer, legitimise it all for us when he told a 1991 Government committee: 'If anybody in this country doesn't minimise their tax they want their heads read because, as a government, I can tell you, you're not spending it that well that we should be donating extra'.

Australia's favourite tax deduction is negative gearing. But what does it mean?

The 'gearing' means there's some investment debt involved. The 'negative' comes from the fact that the investor's costs are more than the income. If the dividends received from a share portfolio are $15000, but the interest (and other) costs on the margin loan funding that portfolio are $20000, then the investor has technically 'lost' $5000. The investor gets to reduce his or her other income by $5000. This will save him or her tax based on the marginal tax rate. (While I've used negative gearing with shares, it is most commonly associated with property.)

Why would an investor want to be negatively geared, if that means losing money? To continue with the above example (where the investor has 'lost' $5000), if the value of the portfolio has risen from $400000 to $450000, the investor is still well ahead. She has lost $5000 in cash for the year, but the investment has increased in value by $50000, making her a net $45000 ahead. And don't forget that the loss is also creating tax deduction savings.

> Negative gearing allows an investor to claim a tax break if the costs of the investment are higher than the income the investment generates.

As debt, particularly investment gearing strategies, is a central theme to *Debt Man Walking*, I'll spend the whole of step 6 going into detail about the role of borrowing in your investment portfolio. I'll also challenge the common perception that debt is either good or bad. There are actually three types of debt: Dumb, Okay and Great Debt.

Summary: negative gearing allows an investor to claim a tax break if the costs of the investment are higher than the income the investment generates.

Franking credits

Like most other entities, Australian businesses pay tax on profits. If they make a profit of $100 million, then they'll have to pay tax of approximately $30 million (Australia's corporate tax rate is 30 per cent), leaving them with $70 million. Those companies often then pay out a portion of their earnings as dividends to shareholders. The government has acknowledged that it should not double-tax those dividends—first as profits from the company and then as income to the shareholder.

Franking credits were born. Where companies have paid tax on the portion of the dividend that is awarded to shareholders, the shareholder gets a tax imputation credit. (This doesn't happen with all dividends paid in Australia, due to other complexities in Australia's tax law. Check out the Tax Office's website for more details on franking credits, at <www.ato.gov.au>.)

If a company pays out a fully franked dividend of $700 to a shareholder, it means that the Tax Office accepts that $300 of tax has already been paid on that dividend. (It is accepted that it is a $1000 dividend on which $300 in tax has already been paid.)

The average income earner in Australia pays a marginal tax rate of 31.5 cents in the dollar earned. Therefore, because that $700 dividend has already had 30 per cent tax paid, most Australians would pay further tax of only 1.5 cents in the dollar (an extra $15 to take the total tax on the $1000 dividend to $315). Workers on lower tax rates—that is, earning below $34000 in the 2008–09 financial year—will actually get a tax return from that dividend, because their marginal tax rate is less than the 30 per cent corporate rate.

Workers on higher marginal tax rates (those earning in excess of $80000 in 2008–09) will pay no more than $165 in further tax because the top tax rate in Australia currently is 46.5 cents in the dollar.

Summary: franked dividends are tax-effective income.

Property depreciation

It wouldn't be Australia if there wasn't something similar for property investors. Australians' fascination with property is an abiding love affair (like that of Scott and Charlene, who are still, apparently, happily married on *Neighbours* to this day).

The tax bonus for property investors is called the building depreciation write off. The costs of any residential building used as an investment (so it doesn't include your home) and built after September 1985, or any extensions or additions built after then, can be depreciated against the owner's personal tax position. (Commercial properties have slightly different rules.)

For example, if the cost of building a house was $150000 in 2003, the investor could claim 2.5 per cent of the cost of that building for 40 years. That would reduce the investor's income each year by $3750 ($150000 × 2.5 per cent) until 2043, if they continued to own it until then. That would save an investor who earns $100000 a year approximately $1556 a year ($3750 × the investor's marginal tax rate of 41.5 per cent) in tax.

That sort of tax deduction for newer properties can go a significant way to helping reduce the cost of holding the property and increase the investor's cash flow. We will cover this in more detail in step 7.

Summary: property built after 1985 can give investors depreciation tax breaks that, in turn, can improve cash flow.

Superannuation

Saving for retirement is still something that not too many Gen Xers are getting excited about yet. While older Xers will be able to access their super when they're 55 (and are, therefore, within a decade of being able to spend it), anyone born after July 1964 will have to wait until they're 60 years old to be able to touch their super. That's most of us.

What is super really? Super is a tax haven for your money to help it to grow for when you retire. It's your money sunning itself in the Bahamas waiting for you. It's Tom Cruise waiting to serve you 'Cocktails and Dreams' in your retirement.

What makes it a tax haven? Special low tax rates apply to superannuation as an incentive for people to save for their retirement. While ordinary income is taxed at anything up to 46.5 per cent in Australia, the highest tax rate for superannuation is 15 per cent. Under changes introduced in 2007, when you turn 60 and turn your super fund into a pension, everything you take out of super is tax free.

The problem with super is that governments just can't help themselves. Like *Home Improvement*'s Tim 'The Tool Man' Taylor, governments tinker with super even when they know they don't need to. So, while super is currently an appealing retirement savings proposition, there is no guarantee that it will stay that way. And it's not that appealing yet to make big contributions to it unless you're within about 10 years of being able to access it (except that you lose some compounding; however, I believe Gen X can do more with their money outside of super).

For Gen Xers, there are a couple of reasons to pay attention to super now. I've devoted an entire chapter to superannuation (step 10), where I'll demonstrate how many Xers could double their super in retirement with 15 minutes' work now.

Summary: super is a government-sanctioned tax haven, designed to help you provide for your own retirement.

Insidious inflation

What we've covered now are the most important rules of the game. Now to introduce you to your main opponent—inflation.

Saving is made all the more difficult by the silent termite of inflation that eats away at the value of money. If inflation is running at 3 per cent and you've managed to earn 7 per cent in your savings account, your savings have really only grown by about 4 per cent.

How does this work? Your $100 has grown to $107 with interest. However, what used to cost $100 a year ago now costs $103 due to inflation. So, really, your $100 has only grown in value by $4 ($107 − $103).

Cue Tim Shaw, the Demtel man, waving a set of steak knives: 'But wait, there's more!'

It gets worse than that. Because of the way Australia's tax system works, you will have to pay tax on the whole $7 that you earned. If you are on the top marginal tax rate of 46.5 per cent, this means your $7 in interest is worth as little as $3.75 after inflation takes its bite out. For those on the average wage (with a marginal tax rate of 31.5 per cent), there would be $104.80 left after tax and therefore real growth of $1.80.

> Saving is made all the more difficult by the silent termite of inflation that eats away at the value of money

Let's look at that again. You've earned $7 on your $100. But, after tax and inflation, *it might be worth only an extra 75 cents*. If the interest rate is only 6 per cent, and inflation is still 3 per cent, there would be just 21 cents left after tax and inflation for those on the top marginal rate. There would be $1.11 left for average wage earners.

That's hard to believe and it sounds like madness. But it's true.

So, what of those normal bank accounts that pay 0.1 per cent interest? You were literally going backwards through inflation, even if you weren't paying much tax.

A rule for couples: talk about it

In virtually every household, someone tends to take control of the finances. That person will be in charge of paying the bills, budgeting for big events (such as

Christmas or birthdays) and making sure some savings are accessible to pay for special things when they need to be paid for.

How couples' finances are put together is a constant source of interest to me. Many couples have 'my' money and 'your' money. They may have separate budgets and if one runs short one week, they might have to effectively borrow money from the other partner until they are paid next. Others simply pool their money—it all goes in to one account and it doesn't matter who earned it or who spent it. There are endless possibilities between those two extremes. Managing the home finances can be tough work for the person who takes it on and can be the source of a lot of arguments in a household, especially if one tends to make decisions that the other disagrees with: 'Honey, whaddya mean the Tigers membership didn't get paid this year because the kids needed new school shoes?!'

When it comes to investing, it is even more important that you talk things over before anyone makes any financial commitment. In every investment strategy, some level of sacrifice has to be made and it's inevitably for an extended period: whether it's to *not spend* the initial sum you were thinking to invest (perhaps $20000 or $50000) on a new bathroom, or whether it's to *forgo* $100 or $300 a week to pay the ongoing cost of an investment.

That doesn't mean that both individuals have to agree on every aspect of each investment that's made, but you both have to at least agree on the overall strategy. It's a good idea to put this strategy in writing so that both of you can go back and re-read it when required. This should cover the point of the investment. Is it to upgrade the home? To prepare for your retirement? To buy a holiday home? To put the kids through private school? Talk it through before you end up in the divorce courts, like Dustin Hoffman and Meryl Streep in *Kramer vs Kramer*.

If you're serious about your wealth creation intentions, you need to sit down and talk about longer-term investment issues with your partner. A financial adviser can help you talk through the relative costs of your various ideas. But the discussion is crucial. For a start, you need to find out if you're both comfortable investing in similar sorts of assets. If one of you wants to buy investment property or shares and the other says they wouldn't be able to sleep at night if they owed a bank $400000, then you need to come up with a workable solution. (For a start, you should both take the risk profile test in step 3.)

If necessary, set aside time on a weekend afternoon, or after the kids have gone to bed, to have the initial chat. If there is a general agreement to begin doing something, then set another time to follow it up a few days later, which will give both of you time to come back with further questions. After that, it might be time for further research (or time to call a financial adviser).

The X-Flips:

Don't save to invest.
Invest to save!

One of the first finance rules that we all learn as kids is about saving: 'If you save enough, you'll be able to buy that bike'. That's a great lesson for children to learn. It teaches them about going without, or sacrificing, to reach goals. That approach is usually used again later in life. Most advice in newspapers and books recommends people put something away each week/month to build up a sum of money that can *then* be used to invest.

There's nothing wrong with this. It's a slow and steady way of reaching a target. But as we'll show in greater detail in step 8, how do you save really large amounts of money? Hundreds of thousands of dollars?

There are some goals—life's really big financial goals—where, perhaps, the right people (which I believe Gen Xers are) should take the opposite approach.

That is, instead of deciding to *save to invest*, why not *invest to save*? If you save $300 a week, you'll have about $32000 (including some interest) to invest after two years.

However, if you used your $300 as your interest cost (or at least partly for interest repayments) for an investment, you could have a far larger investment to start with.

As it is investment growth that tends to provide the majority of investor returns over the *long term* (see step 4), the larger the investment, the larger your chance of reaching your targets.

For example, for a net cost of less than $300 a week, you could potentially:

◉ invest in a geared savings program (that is, with a margin loan), where you could have an investment of $60 000 to $125 000 at the end of a two-year period

- buy $200 000 to $300 000 of capital-protected investments that have a five- or seven-year time frame (see step 6)

- buy a $300 000 investment property (see step 4).

There are dozens of possibilities and these are just three. (Step 8 of *Debt Man Walking* covers five different ways to reach long-term goals, showing how different risk levels can help you achieve set savings targets.)

The point to consider in relation to the above three scenarios is that you have a far larger asset at the start of your investment program. A sum of $32 000 that increases in value at 10 per cent a year for the next 10 years will be worth nearly $90 000. However, a $300 000 share portfolio appreciating at 10 per cent a year for 10 years will be worth more than $778 000.

(There are many things that this simple example does not take into account, such as interest costs, rental income, income tax and capital gains tax. This will be expanded on in steps 6 and 8.)

The risks are obviously higher. But if your goal is big enough and you've got a long investment time frame — and at least a part of everyone's investments should be long term — a strategy like this could make a phenomenal difference to your wealth.

Step 2 for Gen X

In any game I play, the first thing I want is to know what the rules are. That's been my modus operandi since birth, apparently. My parents said I always wanted to know where the boundaries were so that I could stay within them. My brother, Dirk, wanted to know where the boundary was so he could jump over it and find out how serious the trouble on the other side really was. He *usually* ended up okay. We were two very different boys.

Love them or loathe them, rules are a part of life. Some people like to follow them to the letter, some people like to operate in the grey bit, and others like to push the envelope and create new boundaries.

Make the time to learn the basic rules of investing. Starting off with even a basic understanding will allow you to study how the best investors exploit them.

step 3

Q: Which ABBA song was about having to go to Las Vegas or Monaco to bag a rich dude and money being perpetually humorous in a wealthy bloke's domain?

A: 'Money, Money, Money.'

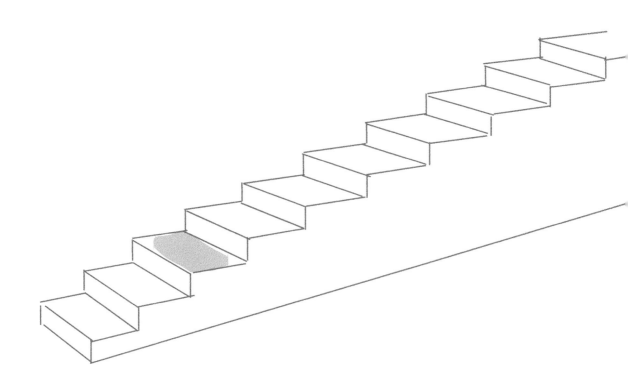

Risky business

- The biggest risk of all
- Risk, reward, age and time
- Take the risk profile test
- Stepping out of your comfort zone
- Investment insomnia
- Gambling versus investing
- The X-Flips: stop worrying about today

Everybody's idea of risk is different.

In *Working Girl*, Melanie Griffith played Tess, the impressionable heroine from the wrong side of the tracks. She'd do anything to achieve her dream of climbing the first rung of the corporate ladder. She bent the rules, deceived her boss, lied and went the double-cross. She ended up getting what she wanted. At the same time, in her personal life, Mel was playing Russian roulette with a cocktail of drugs and booze that nearly killed her.

Earlier that decade, Tom Cruise got his first lead role as Joel in *Risky Business*. Joel screwed a hooker, invited the wrath of her violent pimp, drowned his dad's Porsche, became a pimp himself, and sang Bob Seger's 'Old Time Rock and Roll' in his underpants. Tom hadn't yet started on the really dangerous stuff—messing with Scientology, toying with *our* Nicole and unrehearsed dance routines on Oprah's couches. Nearly career-killing stuff, that lot.

I own a sand-blasted brown leather bomber jacket (bought in 1992). It sits at the back of a cupboard, hidden, and I haven't worn it in more than a decade. Every time that jacket even crosses my mind, my wife threatens to throw it out. It adds a constant element of danger to my marriage, but I've sworn to protect it with my life. One day, I swear, I'll be the best dressed at an '80s party, with the only authentic *Top Gun* getup in the place (complete with Ray Ban black metal aviator glasses). Pencil me in as Tom 'Maverick' Cruise or Val 'Iceman' Kilmer. Just loads fatter.

Danger is a relative concept. And people have an amazing abitity to compartment-alise risk-taking for different aspects of their lives. They might not think twice about starting up their own business (even though more than 90 per cent of small businesses fail in the first year), but they'll be too scared to invest some money in the stock market. *Debt Man Walking* can't help junkies with the risks their drug problems pose (if Ronald Reagan's war on drugs failed, what hope do I have?), or your business enterprise with how to better manage cash flow, but I can help you understand investment risk.

Dangerous Liaisons

The potential dangers in the world of finance are many. Front page headlines that scream about $100 billion being lost in a single day (as they did in January 2008) do more to stop people starting an investment plan than a dozen headlines talking about how much money is made in the markets will encourage them. And that fear stops some people from even making it to the starting line.

The big Australian property crash of 1989–90 burnt more potential investors than possibly any other event in our lifetime. It took years for investors to get back into the black from some purchases made just before that balloon burst.

Investing has its dangers. There's no hiding that. While long-term investing returns show that those who are patient will make plenty of money, sometimes it can be a white-knuckle ride.

But there is a far bigger risk than having the occasional bad year in investment markets…

The biggest risk of all

…and that's not doing anything at all.

Not doing anything at all means that you believe you'll be right. Ultimately, that when you can no longer work, the government will still be paying the age pension, that the pension will be sufficient to live on and that the 9 per cent super your employer pays will be enough to make up any shortfall.

Good luck with that plan. While governments appear committed to continuing the age pension, they have made no commitment as to how sufficient it will be. And there is general agreement that the 9 per cent Superannuation Guarantee is well short of what would really be required to cover anyone in retirement. If we were to be real about it, it would need to be something like 15 per cent (but at least 12 per cent).

To have picked up *Debt Man Walking*, you must have been thinking about your financial future. By now, it has hopefully sunk in that Gen X's big opportunity is now. And acting now could stop you getting stuck in a money rut and have you achieving important financial goals.

As the opening credits of *The X-Files* said, 'The truth is out there'. Good news: the truth is

OH, THE HUMANITY! Alfred Lord Tennyson said 'Tis better to have loved and lost than never to have loved at all'. With due apologies comes this investment variation: 'Tis better to have invested and won, and lost, and won again, than never to have invested at all'.

Psychologists claim that people feel losses twice as strongly as they feel gains. That is, the pain of losing $1000 is as intense as the joy of making $2000.

Twice in my investing life, I've watched the equivalent of a year of my own salary disappear in paper profits. Ouch. And I remember those months far more acutely than I do the fact that markets inevitably bounce or climb back and those losses are recouped. Or the fact that I'd made those 'profits' in the first place.

But when things look a little shaky, I run through my strategy again. I might make minor adjustments, but generally things will be left as they were, as the initial reason that I made those investments hasn't changed.

Of all the risks in the world, the biggest is being paralysed and failing to invest out of fear that something will go wrong. Things will go wrong. Markets will turn down. But they will come back again—they inevitably do.

in here, too. As *Debt Man Walking* will show, making money is not about being a financial genius; it's about having a plan, understanding a few rules and taking a few calculated risks. The risks are likely to be looming larger in your head than they are in reality.

What's the number one problem facing people who are thinking about beginning an investment strategy? Inertia—moving from non-investor to investor. It is far easier to put off doing something about your finances, or seeing someone about organising your finances. If you are surviving, it's something that can be put off until later.

Investment's Yin and Yang

Remember the old 'Confucious say' jokes of the '70s and '80s?

- Confucious say: Person with finger up nose should not jump up and down.

- Confucious say: Don't drink and park. Accidents cause people.

- Confucious say: Man who put face in punchbowl, get punch in nose.

We got many important life insights from Confucious (a Chinese philosopher) and films such as *They Call me Bruce?* and *Karate Kid*. But Gen X's other exposure to Chinese philosophy was Yin and Yang, which in its simplest form can be described as 'two mutually correlated opposites'.

Yin and Yang are opposites that complement, or complete, each other. Like sunshine and darkness, north and south, masculine and feminine, positive and negative ... or Renee Zellweger's 'You complete me' to Tom Cruise in *Jerry Maguire*. A health warning Yin and Yang: 'The more red wine enjoyed on Saturday night, the less Sunday morning is enjoyed'.

In the world of investing, Yin and Yang are omnipresent, represented through the concepts of reward and risk.

Yin—reward

Reward is the whole point of investing in the first place. Why else would you do it if there wasn't a payoff down the road?

Investment reward is what you expect to receive for not having access to your money for a while. Like the experimentation on little children in step 2 (delayed gratification), if you are prepared to forgo access to your money for a while, you will expect a reward or a return for doing so.

The size of that reward is a function of several elements, including how long you're prepared to go without it and how much risk you're prepared to take.

Yang—risk

Risk is a very individual concept. Some people will cross a busy street from wherever they're standing, while others will walk to the relative safety of pedestrian lights. Some kids showed no fear doing tricks on skateboards, BMXs or trampolines. Other kids weren't concerned about doing well at school. (Happy with your choices there?)

Every investment comes with a different level of risk. And when it comes to investment risk, the higher the risk, the higher the potential reward and potential loss (and vice versa).

Some people will feel uncomfortable with some risks and completely comfortable with others. Some people only feel comfortable knowing their money is in a bank. Others aren't concerned by having nearly all of their money in the stock market.

Mutually correlated opposites

'Love and Marriage', the Frank Sinatra classic that we got to know as the theme song of *Married… With Children*, summed up Al and Peggy Bundy perfectly. Al could never have survived without Peg, but that didn't stop him dreaming of his perfect life from the couch.

It's also perfectly true of the dynamic between risk and reward—the Yin and Yang investment principle. You can't have high growth without high risk. And if you want low risk, you'll have to accept low returns. They are inextricably linked.

> Some people will feel uncomfortable with some risks and completely comfortable with others.

Time—the Oil of Ulan

Time adds wrinkles. Just ask Rod Stewart, Jamie Lee Curtis or Keith Richards. It's no friend to our looks. Time makes us (comparatively and increasingly) ugly.

But time has the opposite impact for investors. Time flattens out the bumps, removes the wrinkles, wipes away a lot of the risks. It's one of the best friends an investor could hope for. Time muffles volatility. Time is Oil of Ulan for investors.

Sharemarkets can move substantially in short periods—occasionally markets move more than 10 per cent in a single day. But most countries' sharemarkets would see, on average, a dozen days a year where there are movements of more than 2 per cent in a day (up or down).

Over the course of a year, the average daily movement will be a fraction of 1 per cent. Even if the stock market is 25 per cent higher or lower—which would be a very good or very bad year—the average daily movement is about 0.1 per cent (there are about 250 trading days each year).

Therefore, it is far less danger-ous to be in any sort of invest-ment market for a year than it is to be in it for one day. And if a market doubles over the course of seven years, how much has it increased on average each day? Answer: 0.0057 per cent. So slowly you wouldn't notice. Bruce Willis would be ecstatic if his hairline receded that slowly. But you've *doubled* your money!

Averages make it far safer to invest for 10 years than to invest for one year, which is safer than

AUSTRALIA YOU'RE STANDING IN IT

(Remember Chunky Custard, the Dodgy Brothers and the 'amaaaz-ing' Tim and Debbie?)

The best ever 12-month period for the Aus-tralian stock market was between July 1986 and June 1987 when it rose 86.1 per cent (just before the October 1987 crash). The worst year was between September 1973 and August 1974 when it lost 39.2 per cent (figures courtesy of Fidelity International). That's a pretty big difference. You'd be less than happy if you put in your life savings—for one year only—in August 1973.

However, if you take 10-year averages, the Aus-tralian market is very unlikely to have a negative run. According to Fidelity again, the worst 10-year performance by the Australian market was 2.9 per cent a year and the best was 28.7 per cent a year.

one month. (If we could have averaged out Billy Ray Cyrus over a decade we wouldn't have even noticed 'Achy, Breaky Heart'.)

So, why invest in stock or property markets? Because, *given enough time*, you can be confident that shares and property will outperform cash and fixed-interest investments.

Table 3.1 shows how much $10000 would be worth if it was invested for one year in each of the asset classes listed (based on historical figures back to 1990).

Table 3.1: one-year investment performances

Investment	Minimum	Maximum	Average
Cash	$10 400	$11 700	$10 660
Australian shares	$6 100	$18 600	$11 080
International shares	$6 700	$19 300	$11 080

That shows the volatility from being in a market for one year. However, if you invested your $10 000 for a decade, table 3.2 shows the range of what it would be worth.

Table 3.2: one-decade investment performances

Investment	Minimum	Maximum	Average
Cash	$17 900	$21 600	$19 000
Australian shares	$13 300	$124 700	$28 000
International shares	$14 100	$108 300	$28 000

The spread of possible results, particularly for Australian and international shares, is vast. However, if you invested $10 000 in:

◉ cash for a decade, you are likely to have about $19 000 at the end of it

◉ Australian or international shares (or property for that matter), your likely return would be about $28 000.

What these figures really show is that the average decade-long performance from shares is multiples of the returns for cash. However, even the bad decades for shares aren't much worse than the bad decades for cash.

That's why it's important to invest in shares (and property, whose average performance is similar) for longer-term investments.

Gen X: youth is on your side

The wrinkly Rod Stewart reminded his young lovers in 'Young Turks' that they had plenty of time up their sleeves. This from a man who, no matter how much older he gets, manages to trade in one leggy blonde every few years for a younger model (literally).

Generation X—and I mean all of us—has enough time to take advantage of the fact that shares and property are better long-term performers. By long term, I mean a minimum of seven to 10 years, because investment cycles tend to work in lengths of about that long.

The oldest Gen Xers are in their mid to late 40s. If they are talking about planning for their retirement after age 55 or 60, then they certainly still have enough time to invest in growth assets (shares and property). If they are thinking about investing to take them into their *old age*, perhaps 65, 70 or 75, then they have up to 30 years, which is perfect for growth asset investments.

Mid-Xers and younger Xers won't have retirement on their radars yet. But they will have some longer-term targets they could be aiming for.

It is, therefore, a well-accepted principle that the longer the time you have to invest, the bigger the investment risks you can afford to take.

People who are close to or have reached retirement are less likely to want to take big risks with their money. Losing 10 or 20 per cent of their money in a short period would have a significant impact on their retirement plans.

A RETURN TO MORE NORMAL MARKET CONDITIONS

There is an interesting phenomenon to watch in the media every year.

The December/January period is a quiet time for business news. It's a good time for journalists to call experts to get their predictions for the year ahead. But no matter how good or bad the previous year was, experts seem to predict 'more normal market returns' for the year ahead. If there's been a 20 per cent plus year, then the prediction will be for gains in the year ahead of 8 to 12 per cent. If the market has a dreadful year and is down 8 per cent, the predictions will still largely be for...'more normal market returns' of about 8 to 12 per cent.

Why? Because they're guessing. Nobody knows for sure what the year ahead will bring. And it's safer to have a punt on the average. It's a similar story with property.

Short-term targets

The opposite also applies: don't throw large amounts of money at risk-based investments unless you have a time frame to match. If you have $20 000 that is the start of your savings plan for a home that you intend to buy within two years, then a cash-based investment is probably the best option. Putting that into shares could see your $20000 fall in value to $15000 or less. Two years is not long enough for a stock market to recover (if it falls soon after you invest).

Younger investors, however, would not face the same devastating impacts if they lost a similar amount of money. If they have a few bad years, there is literally plenty of time to recover.

Volvo engineer ... or Evel Knievel? Take the test!

More importantly, what sort of risk-taker are you?

The simple age-based test (see right) is only a rough guide that plants the sensible idea that younger people should have more invested in growth assets. But it does not take into account your personality. It does not take into account your financial situation, nor what sort of risk you might need to take in order to reach your goals.

AGE AND RISK: A SIMPLE TEST

An investment plan should be as individual as a fingerprint. No two people's situations are the same when you take in age, income, risk profile, presence or lack of a partner, interest in saving, goals, children, career prospects, and so on.

Given that big disclaimer ... here is a calculation used around the world that gives a quick indication of how the average person's risk profiles should change over time.

Classic investment theory states that you should subtract your age from 100. That is, if you're 38, then your score is 62 (100 − 38). This is the percentage of your investments that should be invested in shares and property. The older you get, the more your assets should be switched into cash and fixed interest.

But I think there's something not quite right — like a half-frozen Chiko Roll — about that calculation in today's world, given the fact that we are living longer and longer. Gen X should be using 110, or even 120, as the starting point. That is, a 40 year old should have at least 70 per cent (110 − 40) of their long-term investment money (including super) in growth assets.

By the time today's 40 year olds hit 60, the average age of death may well be over 90, thanks to medical advancements. If an investment cycle is about seven to 10 years, then today's 40 year olds have at least four, but perhaps six, full cycles through to age 80.

Some people are naturally the safety-first types. They would have felt right at home working in '80s Sweden in an office full of Volvo engineers, who ranked safety first, second, third and fourth. At Volvo, sophistication, glamour, ease of driving, street cred, looks and comfort took (pardon the pun) a back seat.

At the opposite end of the scale are the true daredevils—Evel Knievel soaring on his motorbike over double-decker buses on his way to breaking more than 40 bones.

In between lie the majority. Some are Richie Cunningham (just very, very average), others more your Arthur 'The Fonz' Fonzarelli ('He-e-e-e-y!').

Profiler—by the numbers

This is the one and only exam you'll have to take in this book, I promise.

This simple test will rank you into one of six different risk categories and will help you get an idea of your own attitude to risk. Circle the number next to the answer that most closely suits you.

Question 1: *How far away is the next major financial goal you're working towards achieving?*

1   Less than one year.

2   One to three years.

3   Three to seven years.

4   More than seven years.

Question 2: *Keeping in mind that achieving higher returns requires higher risks to be taken, approximately what annual rate of return would you feel comfortable seeking?*

1   Less than 5 per cent return (minimal risk).

2   Five to 10 per cent return (medium risk).

3   Above 10 per cent return (high risk).

Question 3: *Assuming you have an amount of money to invest today, how would you invest it?*

1   The safety of my money is my primary objective. I would rather have a low rate of return than risk the loss of any part of my capital.

2   I want my investment to produce the current income I need and my capital should remain relatively stable.

3   I am willing to accept some fluctuation in my capital over the short term in exchange for higher returns over the long term.

4   In order to receive the maximum return on my investment, I am willing to accept a higher degree of risk.

Question 4: *Which statement best describes your attitude to tax when it comes to the effect it has on meeting your goals?*

1   I do not want to derive tax savings by purchasing investments that may put my capital at risk.

2   I would prefer stable, reliable capital value and returns with some tax savings if possible.

3   I can accept a small reduction in value from time to time in exchange for tax-advantaged income.

4   My main aim is to minimise tax and I am prepared to risk my capital to achieve this aim.

Question 5: *Inflation lowers the value of $1 from one year to the next. How concerned are you that your investments/savings earn more than the rate of inflation and therefore maintain their purchasing power?*

1   Not concerned.

2   Slightly concerned.

3   Moderately concerned.

4   Highly concerned.

5   Very highly concerned.

Question 6: *Have you ever invested your own money (not superannuation) in shares, property or managed funds before?*

1   No, but if I had, the fluctuations would make me uncomfortable.

2   No, but if I had, I would be comfortable with the fluctuations in order to receive the potential for higher returns.

3   Yes, I have, but I was uncomfortable with the fluctuations despite the potential for higher returns.

4   Yes, I have, and I felt comfortable with the fluctuations in order to receive the potential for higher returns.

Question 7: *How would you feel if your long-term investments declined by 10 per cent in one year?*

1   Awful. I can't accept declines in the value of my investments.

2   A bit unsettled, but if the income I received didn't change, I wouldn't be too concerned about my capital declining in the short term.

3   Okay. I generally invest for the long term but would be a little concerned with this decline.

4   Fine. I invest for the long term and would accept that these fluctuations are due to short-term market influences.

Question 8: *Which of the following statements best describes how you would choose your investments if you had to choose them yourself?*

2   I would select investments that have a low degree of risk. I could not accept negative returns in my portfolio.

4   I would prefer to diversify with a mix of investments that have an emphasis on low risk. I would have only a small portion of the portfolio invested in higher-risk assets. I would accept a negative investment return of one in nine years.

6   I prefer to have a spread of investments in a balanced portfolio. I would accept a negative investment return of one in seven years.

8   I would place an emphasis on investments that have higher returns, but still have a small amount of low-risk investments. I would accept a negative return of one in five years.

10 I would select only high-growth investments and understand this would come with higher volatility. My aim is higher, long-term returns. I would accept a negative return of one in three years in order to achieve this goal.

Add up the numbers next to your answers and match the total with one of the following risk profiles.

9–13: Conservative (1)

A conservative investor does not want to take any investment risk. Your priorities are the safeguarding of your investment capital. You are prepared to sacrifice higher returns for peace of mind. The most appropriate investment strategy is 100 per cent income-based investments.

14–18: Cautious (2)

Cautious investors are prepared to accept a small amount of risk. Your priority remains preservation of capital over the medium to long term. You may have some understanding of investment markets; however, you don't want to take unnecessary chances with your capital. The recommended investment strategy is 80 per cent income, 20 per cent growth.

19–23: Judicious (3)

Judicious investors have some understanding of market behaviour. You do not wish to see all of your capital eaten away by tax and inflation and are prepared to take small short-term risks in order to gain longer-term capital growth. An investment strategy of 60 per cent income, 40 per cent growth would be suitable.

24–28: Prudent (4)

Prudent investors seek a greater growth component from their investments to protect capital from tax and inflation. You remain cautious towards taking high risks; however, you feel comfortable with some short-term risk. Your priority is consistent capital growth with some income to smooth your returns. You should have 60 per cent of your investments in growth and 40 per cent in income-based investments.

29–33: Assertive (5)

Assertive investors understand the volatility of investment markets. You are most interested in maximising long-term capital growth, although you do not wish to make unbalanced investment decisions. You are happy to sacrifice short-term safety in order to maximise long-term capital growth. Your most appropriate investment strategy would be 80 per cent growth, 20 per cent income.

34 and over: Aggressive (6)

Aggressive investors have long-time horizons for investment capital, because they are pursuing the highest returns reasonably possible. You have an understanding of the behaviour of investment markets and are interested in reducing your taxable income. The most appropriate investment strategy is 100 per cent growth.

So, where does this lead us? Table 3.3 shows how these risk profiles play out into an investment strategy. We will go into further detail in step 4 about what each asset class is, so you'll need to refer back to this table. The column labelled 1 is for conservative investors and the column labelled 6 is for aggressive investors.

Table 3.3: risk profiles and investment

Asset class	Style	1	2	3	4	5	6
Cash	Income	10	10	5	5	5	0
Fixed interest	Income	90	70	55	35	15	0
Australian shares	Growth	0	10	20	30	40	50
International shares	Growth	0	5	15	20	25	35
Property	Growth	0	5	5	10	15	15
Growth/income	–	0/100	20/80	40/60	60/40	80/20	100/0

I will show how these investment profiles relate to long-term investment performance in step 4.

Understanding your risk profile

It's a simple test. It's not designed to be a psychological masterpiece. Your result in this test shouldn't surprise you.

It's a snapshot of who you are now, and should change over your lifetime. Early in your investing life, you may be a little more conservative, as you lack investing experience. With some experience under your belt, your tolerance will probably rise a little. But as you approach retirement, classic investment theory says that your risk appetite tends to decrease, as you move into a protection phase. This should not always be the case, as the average person will live for 17 to 20 years after the retirement age of 65, will live through several investment cycles, and should still be taking on some higher risks.

Should my risk profile rule all my investment decisions?

Not unless you used to let Athena Starwoman horoscopes rule the rest of your life.

A risk profile is a guide, a starting point. And you shouldn't have the same risk profile for *all* of your investments. For example, you might have a few goals that you're seeking to achieve in two or three years, while others are eight- to ten-year goals. The former should be in investments that are more defensive than the latter.

And then there's superannuation. If you're 35, you've got 25 years until you can touch your superannuation. That, surely, deserves its own special investment rules.

'Push It'

Salt-N-Pepa and *Debt Man Walking* join forces with a single message to help you achieve some long-term goals:

Whatever your risk profile, consider pushing yourself one step further.

If you're a judicious investor, make some prudent choices for your long-term investments. If you're prudent, then consider shifting up one step to assertive. If you're assertive or aggressive, then you might be a candidate for a move into Debt Man territory (see step 6).

(If you're conservative or cautious, then check your birth certificate and your pulse. You might be too old or simply too early. *Debt Man: Flatliners* is scheduled for release in about 2024.)

Taking that extra step can make an enormous difference over a lifetime of investing. Based on historical numbers, if you invested $100000 in a prudent-style portfolio for 20 years, your portfolio would have grown to around $490000. In an assertive portfolio, that would have grown to around $560000, and an aggressive portfolio would have grown to around $614000. (We'll explain how we get to these figures in step 4.)

> Whatever your risk profile, consider pushing yourself one step further.

There are no guarantees. But history shows that shares and property appreciate in value faster than cash and fixed interest, so having a higher weighting to them in your investment portfolio should deliver better long-term returns.

Avoiding a War of the Roses

If both parties in a couple have the same risk profile, that's a great start. Hopefully, there won't be any spats, à la Kathleen Turner and Michael Douglas in *The War of the Roses,* over the initial investment plan. If their risk profiles are only one profile apart, it can also be fairly simple to tailor an investment program that is halfway between each style.

The problems will start if there is a gap of two or more profiles between individuals in the couple. In that case, some education might be required, or somebody might have to give. Perhaps investment monies should be split in two and the two should pursue different strategies.

But it's not an excuse not to invest. Perhaps start with the person with the more cautious profile, with the understanding that over the years, risk profiles will be re-evaluated.

'Highway to the Danger Zone'

(Kenny Loggins…*Top Gun*, *Caddyshack* and *Footloose*. Has there ever been a movie soundtrack lyricist to whom Gen X has a deeper gratitude?)

Step 3 aims to give you a better understanding of risk—how it works and how to take advantage of it. Because we Gen Xers have the best of our careers and earning capacity ahead of us, we can use time to remove much of the risk/volatility involved. Time and considered risk-taking will allow you to achieve more than you thought was possible with your finances.

Extending yourself by learning about investment is more likely to get you to where you want to go than *not* investing, or simply trying to save your way to a fortune.

Investment insomnia

But everyone has limits.

Having a large diversified portfolio of quality stocks and a couple of investment properties is the sort of wealth creation strategy that is bound to see you achieve wealth targets, if you have the conviction to stay the distance. These sorts of strategies are often backed, if structured for the best tax outcome, by investment debt—often hundreds of thousands of dollars worth, but possibly quite a bit more.

But making extra money through investments is not worth it if it comes at the cost of your health.

Financial advisers call this the 'sleep at night' test. If your investments, or the debts associated with them, worry you so much that they keep you awake at night, then there's something wrong. You need to do something to make yourself more comfortable—reduce the risk in your portfolio, or pay down some debt.

If you invest according to your risk profile, you really should be fine. Your investments might still fall in value in some years, but the falls shouldn't be outside your comfort zone.

If you invest one step more aggressively than your risk profile says, as I suggest you do for longer-term investments, then you will obviously have a little more money in riskier investments than you would have if you stayed within your own risk profile. If the more aggressive investments have you sleepless (in Seattle, or anywhere else), or if you find you're continually worrying and checking stock or managed fund prices, then do something about it.

In most cases, investing slightly more aggressively than your natural risk profile suggests shouldn't push you into investment insomnia. But it could. And you need to be aware that if that happens, nothing is more important than your health.

Don't let fear paralyse you. It shouldn't be an excuse to not start your investment strategy.

That's not an investment!

'That's not a knife. *That's* a knife', said Mick Dundee, drawing the distinction between a play thing and the real thing in the original *Crocodile Dundee*.

Similarly, the difference between gambling (play thing) and investing (real thing) shouldn't be confused. The most common decisions that some people try to pass off as 'investment decisions' include:

- share tips received from a mate
- your weekly lotto ticket
- trying to buy the next big thing through an IPO, float, or penny dreadfuls on the stock market

- punting on the horses

- pushing coins through the pokies.

That's not investing. That's gambling. Yes, they could make you rich, but the chance of any doing so is remote. Roughly the same chance that Fags, those '80s cigarette-shaped lollies (now called Fads), will ever again become socially acceptable for kids to have.

Gambling and get-rich-quick seminars pander to humanity's innate hope that we will just wake up one day and the bank balance will read $4 million. Getting rich the lazy way is a one-in-a-million chance. There's nothing wrong with having an occasional punt, if you accept the fact that it's gambling.

The X-Flips:
Stop worrying about today

It can be hard to stop worrying about today. It really can, while there's bills to pay, rent or the mortgage to meet, mouths to feed and bods to clothe, a car that needs updating, the desperately needed holiday, the credit card to pay off, and so on.

But you won't be able to stop worrying about *today's* money problems until you've done something about *tomorrow's* finances.

And by tomorrow, I don't mean the day after today. The day you should be worried about is five or 10 years from now. Or 20 years from now. Or the day that you turn 55. Or when your kids are due to begin school. Or the date you've set yourself to buy a beach shack, or a ski chalet. It's about the big financial targets you've set yourself.

Today's financial woes will never go away if you don't have a plan to stop them being a problem at some point in the future. Following the steps in this book will get you there. And that is a thousand times more likely to make you rich than any method of gambling.

But it won't happen overnight. Hugh Grant didn't get back onto the winner's list (after Divine Brown *and* getting dumped by Liz Hurley) overnight. A girl by the name of Bridget Jones and two films made over a period of three years did help. Three years is a long time in the movie world, but not long enough in the money world. Nevertheless, the point is that a plan, backed by a long-term horizon, makes sense.

Stop worrying about today. Start focusing on how you're going to pave your path with the major income years you have ahead of you. They will eventually make today's problems disappear.

Step 3 for Gen X

You won't get rich just by *reading*. You need to act, but not act blindly. You need to understand risk, get comfortable with risk and be prepared to take some risk. Generation Xers should be prepared to take on a little more risk because of the long-term nature of their horizons.

Start by sitting the risk profile test earlier in this chapter. It might not be a highly scientific risk-profiling questionnaire (and there are some very detailed ones around), but it will give you a good indication of what sort of financial risk-taker you are.

step 4

Q: In *The Meaning of Life*, who played the waiter to Mr Creosote, who was left with nothing but a beating heart when he exploded after being coerced into going one step too far with a 'wafer-thin mint'?

A: John Cleese

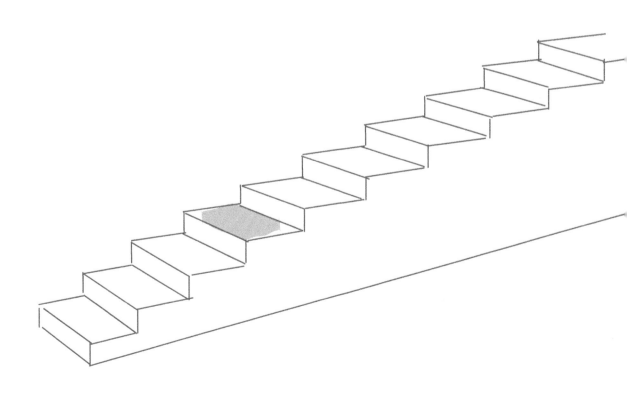

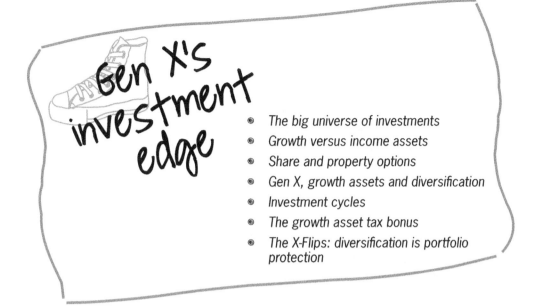

Gen X's investment edge

- The big universe of investments
- Growth versus income assets
- Share and property options
- Gen X, growth assets and diversification
- Investment cycles
- The growth asset tax bonus
- The X-Flips: diversification is portfolio protection

My brother and I loved to play Monopoly. We'd play from sun-up to sundown and some games lasted for days. We allowed others to play, but the matches would inevitably become just the two of us. Our friends would either get bored, get wiped out, or they would have to go home for dinner.

The games would go on so long that we would get to the stage where we had to lend the bank money because it had run out. The Monopoly economy had to keep going, so private enterprise would step in and provide liquidity to keep the financier running (just like Kerry Packer did for Westpac in the early '90s).

While some would hesitate over whether to buy a particular property, Dirk and I never would. If we had cash available, we'd snap it up. If we didn't have cash available, we'd mortgage something. All property was worth having. To us, the rule of Monopoly was simple—the guy with the most property inevitably won. He'll collect the most rent, put up the most houses and build the most hotels.

It was about 15 years after my last game of Monopoly with Dirk before the real lessons of Monopoly began to sink in. Many of the rules of how to win at Monopoly can, as it turns out, be used in the real-life version of investing.

LESS BUFFET...
MORE BUFFETT

I hate buffets.

A buffet is an open invitation to make a pig of oneself, which I inevitably do (if the food is any good). Every time I eat a buffet, I can't help but think about *Monty Python's The Meaning of Life*, where John Cleese gets the morbidly obese Mr Creosote a 'wafer-thin mint' to finish off his evening meal. Mr Creosote eats the wafer and explodes, with his insides splattering all over the restaurant's patrons. It's one of the most disgusting scenes ever made for film.

The world of investment is too much like a buffet—the volume of information to wade through is overwhelming. You need a method to help you find the gems.

Start by adding a 't'. Now you've got Buffett.

Warren Buffett, one of the world's richest men, runs Berkshire Hathaway, a business that invests in other businesses. Buffett looks for good investments that have fallen out of favour, buys them at fire-sale prices, then waits for people to come to their senses again. He does it far more successfully than anyone else on the planet. And he is the king of boiling down complex principles into simple philosophies, like the following thoughts:

- There are only two rules: 'Rule No. 1—never lose money. Rule No. 2—never forget rule No. 1'.

- Don't make things unnecessarily hard: 'I don't look to jump over seven-foot bars. I look around for one-foot bars that I can step over'.

- Don't let go of a good thing: 'Our favourite holding period is forever'.

- The majority can often be wrong: 'We simply attempt to be fearful when others are greedy and to be greedy only when others are fearful.'

- He can also be a little bit Confucius: 'Only when the tide goes out do you discover who's been swimming naked'.

Reading more on Buffett and his investment style is recommended and easy. His success has meant that there are more Buffett followers, biographers and investment copiers around than for anyone else in the solar system. Any decent bookshop will have several books on him.

An impossibly wide choice

There are only 30 properties to buy on a Monopoly board—that's a fairly easy range of investment opportunities to get your head around. Out in the real world, the investment opportunities are endless.

Look at the daily newspapers, magazines, the business section at a bookshop, or turn on a television and you'll see there are endless ways to put your money to work. There are thousands of different managed funds to invest in, as many different shares, real estate opportunities, investment seminars, billboards advertising high rates of returns for your cash … and that's without considering the ads for superannuation.

The array of investments can be utterly confusing for the novice. It's not as simple as choosing which member of ABBA you wanted to be (or date).

Making the decision that you're going to change your future by committing to an investment strategy is one thing. Choosing your first few investments is something else.

Keep it simple, stupid (KISS)

(Now, seriously, who thought those makeup-wearing glam rockers would still be around and kicking ass today?)

To help your cause, *Debt Man Walking* is going to simplify the options as much as possible. Let's boil down the world of investment opportunities to their most basic.

There are really only three different types of asset. All the thousands of different investment opportunities on offer can be classified as:

- an income asset
- a growth asset
- or a mixture of both.

Income assets are those where the majority of the investment's return will be income (such as interest, distributions, rent, dividends, and so on). **Growth assets** are those where the investor's return will largely come from an increase in the value of the investment (such as a share price or property value increasing).

A simple example of an income asset is cash in a bank account. The initial sum of money will grow only as interest (income) is paid. A growth asset is something like shares in BHP Billiton. BHP doesn't pay much of a dividend, but investors stand to benefit if the shares rise in value. See table 4.1 for more examples of income and growth assets.

Table 4.1: styles of income and growth assets

Income assets	Growth assets
◉ Savings accounts	◉ Australian shares
◉ Term deposits	◉ International shares
◉ Cash management trusts	◉ Residential property
◉ Loans	◉ Commercial property
◉ Bonds	◉ Your own business
◉ Fixed-interest investments	

Income investments—a bit of interest

Income investments are essentially loans to banks, governments or businesses. In essence, you lend your money to another entity. In return, the borrower pays interest, until such time as the initial amount is repaid.

That's what a bank account is. The money in your bank account is a loan to the bank. Banks gather money from many depositors and lend that money to others, predominantly to buy houses or invest in businesses. Banks pay interest because they on-lend your money to others. They lend this money to others at a higher rate of interest than they are paying you. They might pay you 5 per cent, but they're lending that money to someone else at 9 per cent.

Bonds are a loan to the government, who in return would pay interest (which, in the case of a bond, is known as a coupon). Bonds are becoming increasingly rare in Australia as governments pay down their debt.

More common nowadays are fixed-interest investments. These are loans to businesses and therefore carry a higher risk than bonds or bank accounts. As a result, to win over investors, businesses need to offer a higher interest rate. Fixed-interest securities pay a nominated amount of interest each year. The initial investment, known as a security, behaves partly like a share, in that the value of the security will fluctuate a little, related to moves in general interest rates.

Growth investments—a capital strategy

With shares and property, capital growth is the main aim of the game. That is, your returns are expected to come from the value of the house or shares increasing, rather than from receiving a set income.

For example, the share price of BHP at the start of 1989 was about $3.50. In mid 2008, BHP was trading at about $40. BHP does pay relatively small dividends. The upside has been the more than 10-fold increase in the company's value.

Ask your parents or an uncle or aunt what they paid for their first home. Then ask what that house would be worth now. For example, my parents paid about $25 250 for our first family home. They sold it 17 years later (in 1991) for about $147 000, after spending about $30 000 on an extension. At the start of 2008, the house would have been worth in excess of $450 000.

A BET EACH WAY

Not all share and property strategies are purely about capital growth. Many properties, particularly commercial properties, are bought for the income they generate rather than capital growth. And many shares—such as property and bank stocks—are bought by some investors for their big dividends rather than their growth.

In general, however, shares and property are viewed as growth assets, and cash and fixed interest are income investments.

Gen X and growth assets—the perfect mix

One of the key strategic messages behind *Debt Man Walking*—that Generation X can create the financial future they want—is based on mixing time and the right assets, possibly with a bit of investment debt.

So what are the right assets for Generation X? Need you ask? They're…GROWTH ASSETS!

While everyone has short- and medium-term financial needs and goals, and those are being juggled everyday, keeping on top of them is not what will make you wealthy. Creating real wealth requires thinking and planning beyond today and making some plans for years down the track.

MONOPOLY'S LIFELONG LESSONS

There were several life lessons for me to learn from Monopoly:

- The guy with the most property will probably win.
- Property provides income through rent.
- My brother can be stubborn.
- Rents rise as you improve the property.
- No matter how hard you work, some of the best opportunities come by chance.
- Sometimes you'll get an asset for a steal — you'll pay peanuts compared with what it is really worth to you.
- Other times, a property you bought, but aren't in love with, will make you a fortune, because someone else *really* wants it.
- Dirk can be really stubborn. Sometimes I want to strangle him.
- Property can have an extra, strategic, value that is based on its location.
- It's not always the most expensive property that produces the best return.
- When there's no land left for sale, land's underlying value improves dramatically.
- Some non-core assets (utility companies and train stations) can be profitable sidelines to the main game.
- Some property moguls are destined to spend some time in gaol.
- Dirk can be a really stubborn bugger. But even he will hand over Vine Street for the right price.

These are largely valuable lessons for all sorts of investing. (And for those who know Dirk, the rest of them will be valuable also.)

Growth assets are the right assets for Generation X's longer-term dreams because they do provide better returns (see step 3 and later in this step). The reason that they provide better returns is because they are higher-risk assets. And the reason that the risks associated with growth assets shouldn't overly concern Gen Xers' wealth creation plans is that they should have long-term horizons for those goals.

Growth assets, like Shane Warne, are prone to the odd indiscretion, but they've got the better record over the longer period, like Shane Warne.

Cash and fixed-interest assets have a place in almost every investment strategy. I'm not arguing that any single investor should have all their money in growth assets. Your personal risk profile (from step 3) will determine roughly what you should have in each asset class. However, for your longer-term investments (seven-plus year goals and investments, plus superannuation) you should consider taking a more aggressive investment profile.

Risk profiles—the theory

Let's take a deeper look at the role growth assets play in financial strategies. How does the mix of growth investments in your portfolio affect the amount of money you are likely to make from your investments?

Table 4.2 is typical of the returns that could be expected, on average, for each of the risk profile types (covered in step 3). It shows the lower returns likely for cash and fixed interest compared to shares and property. So, as more money is invested in shares and property, higher returns are expected.

Table 4.2: performance of a $100000 investment over 10, 20 and 30 years

Risk profile	% growth/ % income	Performance expectations	10 years	20 years	30 years
Conservative	0/100	6	$179084	$320714	$574349
Cautious	20/80	6.75	$192167	$369282	$709637
Defensive	40/60	7.5	$206103	$424785	$875495
Prudent	60/40	8.25	$220942	$488155	$1078542
Assertive	80/20	9	$236736	$560441	$1326767
Aggressive	100/0	9.5	$247823	$614161	$1522031

The performance expectations figures are from research house Lonsec. They are long-term expectations for each investment profile and take into account risk and the historical returns from the various asset classes.

If you look at how the investments would perform over 10 years, the difference between each risk profile is fairly small. The impact of small changes in performance expectations, however, becomes quite significant over 20- and 30-year periods.

Risk profiles — the practice

However, theory and practice can be very different things. Take everything we were ever taught in those awkward high school sex education classes. Seriously. How much of that information was actually useful when you lost your virginity, apart from, hopefully, the contraception?

It can be said, with dozens of years of statistics to back it up, that property and shares will outperform cash and fixed interest over the longer term. But let's take a look at an actual $100000 investment and show how it would have panned out, using actual figures from 1990 to 2008 (see table 4.3).

Table 4.3: performance of risk profile portfolios over 10, 20 and 30 years

Risk profile	% growth/ % income	Actual performance	10 years	20 years	30 years
Conservative	0/100	7.56%	$207256	$429552	$890274
Cautious	20/80	8.57%	$227561	$517841	$1178407
Defensive	40/60	9.46%	$249919	$609690	$1505540
Prudent	60/40	10.47%	$270672	$732634	$1983036
Assertive	80/20	11.48%	$296462	$878899	$2605606
Aggressive	100/0	12.38%	$321285	$1032240	$3316430

The figures in this table are from research house Lonsec. I've used averages tallied by Lonsec for the past 18 years (to 30 June 2008), then extrapolated them to 10, 20 and 30 years.

Even following the radical shakedown of the financial markets (particularly property and shares) during the 2007–08 year, these figures show that portfolios made up of higher amounts of growth assets in a portfolio (Australian and international shares, plus property) have performed the best over an extended period. Over that period, Australian shares have been the best performer (with an average of 14.3 per cent), followed by property (13.4 per cent), international shares (9.2 per cent), fixed interest (7.75 per cent) and cash (5.8 per cent). Again, these are from Lonsec's figures.

Shares or property?

Is property or shares the better performer? Now *there's* a neverending argument. Backers of real estate argue that property is the better performer. Champions of equities will argue that shares are the superior investment. And both sides can pull out reams of statistics to back their case. Would a stockbroker argue anything other than shares? Would a real estate agent argue against property?

But statistics show what the user wants them to show. Most people only pull out the statistics that prove their point. As a result, I no longer enter the debate over whether property or shares is the better performer. The truth is that shares and property are used for different purposes and shouldn't be directly compared.

In absolute terms, shares and property are likely to provide average returns of 8 to 12 per cent a year over the long term. In some decades, property will be the better performer, in others it will be shares. Sometimes one of them will go backwards, sometimes for several years in succession. Very occasionally, both will go backwards together.

Arguing which is the better performing asset class is a pointless fight, like the live punchup between Normie Rowe and Ron Casey on the *Midday Show with Ray Martin* in 1991. So, *Debt Man Walking* has no intention of weighing in to that debate.

What property and shares have in common is that they can both offer spectacular returns, but they rarely perform in the same way at the same time. That is, their performances are not *correlated*. If property's hot, shares could be doing just okay or even poorly. If shares are running strong, property could be so-so, or even in the doghouse. That said, they can also perform well or poorly at the same time.

Both asset classes also allow investors to leverage into them, and I'll come back to that in step 6. Apart from those similarities, they are very different assets (see 'Showdown: shares versus property' on p. 102).

Shares and property!

It is exactly because shares and property don't perform in unison that smart, long-term investors will have both assets in their investment basket.

Because they don't necessarily move in unison, there will always be value in diversification—the 'don't put all your eggs in the one basket' mantra (see step 2). Having your money spread across both means that if the market for one slows for a while, the investment party might be happening in the other. And if you've got both, you won't be missing out.

Imagine if you had all of your money in the sharemarket on 30 October 2007. Just nine months later, you would have lost more than one-quarter of your money. Worse, if you'd invested with rogue entrepreneurs Alan Bond (Bond Corporation) or Christopher Skase (Qintex) in the '80s, you'd have lost almost every cent of your investment.

Property, too, has off years. If you bought your first property (home or investment) in Sydney in early 2004, in late 2008 the property might still not be worth what you paid for it. And back in the '80s, there was the Gold Coast's 'white shoe brigade' in Joh 'Don't you worry about that' Bjelke-Petersen's Queensland, when overdevelopment caused chaos for a decade.

Property and shares. Yes, they do have hiccups, but proper diversification and a long-term horizon will see you come out on top.

Owning small bits of big companies

A share is a partial ownership of a business. You could be one of a handful of owners of a company, or you could be, potentially, one of up to a million or more part owners.

There are hundreds of thousands of businesses in Australia. Only a few thousand, really, have more than a handful or two of owners. Most businesses are owned by individuals, a few family members or a fairly small group of employees. Small business ownership usually includes having some control over how the business is run.

When *DMW* discusses shares, we are talking about really big businesses—those that are listed on the Australian Securities Exchange (ASX). Even then, we're only really talking about the biggest 200 to 300 stocks on the ASX. These are businesses whose shares you can buy or sell on almost any day. When you're a passive investor—that is, you are not involved in the day-to-day decision making of the company—being able to get in and out of an investment is important. If you want to take a profit, you can sell. If you change your mind and don't like the company any more, out you get. Simply, cheaply, quickly. (This is called liquidity, which we'll return to later in this step.)

When we're talking about small pieces of large companies, how small is small? Even if you owned $20000 of BHP Billiton shares (in early 2008), then you owned approximately one millionth of the company. That is, at that time, BHP Billiton was worth approximately $200 billion.

Direct shares

The simplest way of buying companies is through direct shares. This involves investigating a company in which to become a shareholder and buying some shares in that company. This can be done either through a stockbroker or over the net through an online broker.

There are approximately 2000 companies listed on the ASX. The options of companies and industries to choose from are vast. You could choose banks, resource companies, retailers, phone companies or insurance groups, to list a few. But to do it yourself requires a lot of research (which can also be done online).

DIRECT SHARES AND DIVERSIFICATION

Should you buy shares directly? It depends on how much money you have to invest and how much time you can devote to keeping an eye on your shares. The answer could be yes if you've got enough money to be able to spread it over a number of companies. The answer could be no if you don't have enough money to buy a broad selection of companies (diversification again).

Even if you buy your shares cheaply, through an online broker, it will cost about $30 a trade. If you have $15 000 to invest and you're going to buy $1000 worth of 15 companies' shares, then it will cost you $450 (15 times $30) to buy those shares. That's 3 per cent of your investment. If you need to sell them at a later stage, there is another $450 to get out (hopefully the value of the investment will have grown so it will be a smaller percentage to sell the shares).

I believe that it is best to buy shares in lots of more than $3000. At $3000, brokerage of $30 is 1 per cent (this cost becomes a part of your cost base for the investment, so will reduce any tax to be paid on sale). Below this figure, it would make more sense to buy a listed investment company (see overleaf) or use managed funds, particularly as this also gives you instant diversification.

The main advantage of direct shares is the investor's control. You can choose exactly which company you buy shares in, when you buy them, how much you pay and when you sell.

There are several ways to build a direct share portfolio if you don't have a lot of money with which to start:

◉ Use your capital to buy a smaller number of shares.

◉ Borrow some extra money so that you have more to invest.

- Use some equity from elsewhere (possibly your home) to increase your initial investment funds.

There are increased risks with all three of these strategies. The first option would be higher risk because of the lack of diversification. The other two options have higher risks because of the gearing involved. However, the increased risks of the last two are risks that Generation Xers should be open to. We'll return to this in step 6.

It is not easy to invest directly in international shares from Australia because it is harder to get to know the company and its competitors.

Listed investment companies

Listed investment companies (LICs) are businesses listed on the stock exchange that invest in other businesses. They aim to add value by picking shares that will perform better than the rest of the market. LICs are a nicely wrapped bundle of diversification — a bit like the Village People.

They might choose to invest in 20 to 30 Australian companies. Those investment holdings will change over time as the LICs make investment decisions.

An advantage of LICs over buying your own shares directly is that you can buy them like you buy a share, but you will get instant diversification. One investment strategy, for those with a relatively small amount of money, would be to buy a couple of LICs, giving you diversification in both the shares you own and the management styles of your LICs.

Two of the largest LICs in Australia are Australian Foundation Investment Company (AFIC) and Argo Investments, but they are not the only ones available. The main advantages of LICs are that they are very low cost and they also tend to track fairly closely the movement in the overall stock market indices. They are low cost in the sense that the management fee for running an LIC tends to be a small fraction of 1 per cent.

Managed funds

There seems to be more managed funds in Australia than there are companies listed on the ASX. There are thousands of them. And just like Castrol's famous 'Oils ain't oils' advertising campaign, managed funds ain't managed funds.

'Managed funds' is a term that takes in a broad array of investing. Managed funds may invest in anything, but usually stick to cash, fixed interest, shares and property. They may specialise in just one of the asset classes or they may invest across each. Their product disclosure statement sets out what the fund will invest in.

Even with funds that invest in Australian shares, there's plenty of room for specialisation around themes. And the themes only get wider when it comes to international managed funds. These may include China, the US, Europe, emerging markets (such as Eastern Europe, and South and Central America), BRIC (Brazil, Russia, India and China) or particular industries, such as biotechnology, media, IT or Asian property.

Managed funds offer some diversification in a one-stop shop. You can choose the style of investment you want to make and let the fund managers do their thing. Fund managers assess themselves by a stated benchmark, which they try to match or beat. Some will beat their benchmark, some won't. If your fund manager repeatedly falls well below their target and the bad news each year seems to be a little *Groundhog Day*-ish, that's as good an indication as any that it's time to move your money somewhere else.

> Managed funds may invest in anything, but usually stick to cash, fixed interest, shares and property

The management costs for managed funds are typically about 1.5 to 2 per cent of the funds being managed. Therefore, if you have a $20000 managed fund invest-ment, the manager will charge a fee of about $400 a year to look after that investment for you, which comes out of your investment.

Index and exchange-traded funds

Index funds and exchange-traded funds (ETFs) are essentially a variety of managed funds with all the glitz and glamour taken out. While fund managers set themselves benchmarks to beat, index funds and ETFs don't try to beat anything—they try to match exactly the return of a particular sector.

Index funds and ETFs work similarly. They offer a range of funds, usually based on indices (such as the S&P/ASX 300, the Dow Jones Industrial Average, the FTSE 100, or other index-like benchmarks that cover international shares, property, cash and so on) and will invest proportionally in that index. If it's the S&P/ASX 300, then they will buy the 300 companies in that index in the amounts that make up the index;

that is, if BHP Billiton is 10 per cent of the index, then an index fund will have 10 per cent of their money in BHP. If a little manufacturer sneaks into the list at 297 and is just 0.02 per cent of the index, then they will buy enough of that stock so that it makes up just 0.02 per cent of their fund. As there are no sophisticated investment strategies to be worked out and paid for, index funds charge much lower fees than most managed funds.

Sheltering the needy

Property became my first investment love. I found a book that just explained it clearly to me and…bang! It was like cracker night in Canberra in the '70s, when explosive fireworks were still legal. Suddenly, property investment made sense. I'd bought my first investment property within about four months and it was joined by others in a few years.

> Australians are obsessed with property, both living in it and investing in it.

Australians are obsessed with property, both with living in it and investing in it. When it comes to living, we love our quarter-acre blocks, we love our holiday homes and, increasingly, we quite like living in high-rise apartment buildings. We've got a big country and we haven't been afraid as a nation of a bit of urban sprawl. Property is, however, much more than just places for people to live. Businesses need homes, too.

A major drawcard of property is leverage—few people buy investment property without a loan. And, in most circumstances, buying property with debt is what makes the most sense. In the right circumstances, banks will lend the entire cost of a property, plus the costs. When it comes to property, the concept of negative gearing is not just well understood, it's almost an expectation.

If you own a $300000 property and it increases in value by 10 per cent, the increase in value is $30000. If you have $50000 of your own savings invested and that increases by 10 per cent, the increase is just $5000. It's that higher return that property investors are generally seeking.

The advantages of directly held property investments include:

◉ rent—a generally reliable income stream

◉ gearing—banks are comfortable lending for property

- volatility—property values fluctuate far less than shares

- tax—while negative gearing applies to shares and property, people tend to be far more comfortable with the concept in regards to property

- control—owning an investment property allows you to exert far more control over the property's value than owning shares.

The disadvantages of directly held properties, as compared with shares, include:

- high entry costs—anyone who has ever paid stamp duty will attest to how much it costs to buy a property. Factor in about 4 to 7 per cent to purchase

- high exit costs—ditto. It can cost about 2 to 3 per cent of the property's value to sell it

- high management costs—rental agents tend to charge around 5 to 9 per cent of the rent for collection. Then there are annual council rates, insurance costs, gardening, maintenance, and so on

- time consumption—from a maintenance perspective, direct property investment can, with no warning, require a significant investment of your time

- paperwork—there's plenty more of it than collecting share dividend or distribution statements

- lack of liquidity—it's much easier and faster to turn shares into cash than it is for property (which takes, on average, three to four months to sell)

- diversification—owning one investment property does not give you much diversification

- understanding—while many people believe they know property, they often misunderstand the complexity of owning and maintaining properties.

A home for everybody

Residential real estate makes up the majority of the direct ownership opportunities in real estate and is an investment that most feel comfortable with, and may understand more than the sharemarket. Almost everyone has spent time being a tenant. And quite a few—perhaps half of Gen X by now, but that figure is likely to rise as our generation ages—have also experienced the joys and pain of having a mortgage.

Everyone needs a home. It's just a matter of whether the monthly payment to live there is rent or a mortgage. There are really only three options:

- you rent a place from someone else
- you have a mortgage on a place that you bought
- you own a place outright after having paid back the bank.

However, *Debt Man Walking* accepts that there are many Gen Xers still mooching off mum and dad (nice one!).

One important point to note, however, is that *your home is not an investment property*. I will explain this in more detail in step 5.

As approximately every third home in Australia is rented, there are tens of thousands of investment property owners in Australia. Most hold just one or two properties. Others build up a portfolio over time.

Banks lend for property. Lots. It's the cornerstone of banking and where they make most of their profits.

They are usually happy to lend up to 80 per cent of the value of residential real estate. In reality, they will often lend more for individual properties. This will allow someone with, say, $50000, to buy a $300000 investment property. This would cover the 10 per cent deposit ($30000) plus all the legals (stamp duty, conveyancing, and so on), which might be up to $20000.

If your $300000 property rises in value by 10 per cent a year, then the value of the property will have risen by $63000 in two years, or more than your original capital outlay of $50000. This does not, however, include your interest costs, which we will go into more detail on in steps 6 and 8.

If you owned that property for 10 years and it grew at a compound rate of 10 per cent, your initial $300000 property would now be worth approximately $780000, leaving you with a net investment of approximately $510000. Based on your initial investment of $50000, that's an annual compound return of more than 26 per cent (again, less interest costs). This is one of the major appeals of geared investing and is something we'll return to in step 6.

A home for everything

Pretty much all other property comes under the broad banner of commercial property—providing homes for businesses. All but the smallest operations need somewhere to exist. These include offices, factories, shopping centres, restaurants, manufacturing plants, business parks, airports, retailers and sports centres.

Commercial property investors provide all this. In fact, commercial property investors also invest in homes for businesses which provide a home for the stuff we can't fit in our homes. It's called storage.

While many businesses choose to also own the home that the business lives in (that is, being their own landlord), most businesses realise that property investment isn't their core competency, so they tend to rent their premises from investors.

Commercial property can be bought in the same way as residential property. Individual investors can buy small shops and lease them to small businesses. Over time, you could buy larger properties that house larger businesses, or properties that house larger numbers of businesses.

The basic differences between investing in residential and commercial property are:

* it can take a longer time to find commercial tenants than residential tenants

LIQUIDITY: NOT AN AMBER FLUID How quickly can you turn an investment into cash? This is known as liquidity, and is an important consideration when thinking about an investment.

Cash in your wallet is perfect liquidity. Cash at the bank is pretty liquid also.

If you have shares, it takes about three to four days between selling your investment and receiving the cash. Most managed fund providers will take one to two weeks to process and redeem your request.

But what if you buy your own investment property? From making the decision to sell, you are still looking at months before settlement.

Liquidity can be a good and a bad thing from an investment perspective. Knowing that you can get your cash quickly can be a positive if you think you might need to get it quickly. But if you're the sort who acts on impulse, then it might almost be better to have an investment that you can't access quickly. Selling an investment such as property is a big and costly decision. You don't just get in, get out and get back in to property.

Not being able to buy and sell the investments quickly can be an aid to wealth creation if it stops impulse actions. Some investors might find that they are better suited to investments without easy liquidity.

- commercial property returns tend to be more about the income (rent) than the growth (capital gain). It's the opposite with residential property

- banks are generally willing to allow investors to borrow only 70 per cent of the asset value, versus about 80 per cent for residential, without further collateral

- businesses tend to sign up for leases of many years (while residential tenants tend to sign one-year leases).

Because commercial property tends to lend itself to professional management, much more so than residential property, the options to invest in commercial property tend to be much wider, including real estate investment trusts, property managed funds and unlisted/direct property funds.

Real estate investment trusts

Until March 2008, real estate investment trusts were widely known as listed property trusts or LPTs, which are listed on stock exchanges. Australia virtually invented LPTs, but has decided to follow the rest of the world in calling them real estate investment trusts (REITs). REITs can only invest in commercial property.

PROPERTY EXCHANGE-TRADED FUNDS Property ETFs are a hybrid between a direct equity (such as an A-REIT) and a managed fund. They are listed on the stock exchange in Australia and give diversification benefits, because they invest, like index funds, in a broad cross-section of companies that make up a particular index.

ETFs, for both shares and property, tend to be very low cost from a management expense perspective and are growing in popularity in Australia. They are already very popular in the US.

Australian REITs (A-REITs) are companies such as Frank Lowy's Westfield Group, the largest shopping mall owner in the world. It owns shopping centres in Australia, the United States and Europe. (Another example is Centro, which got itself into trouble in late 2007 and was working its way through its issues during 2008.)

A-REIT businesses manage the properties, find tenants and do the administration, repairs and maintenance, and the investors themselves get income in the form of distributions. Under the trust model, the investor tends to get tax-advantaged income in the form of income and distributions, which allows the investor to delay paying a portion of their tax.

Property managed funds

In the same way that you can buy managed funds that invest in shares, you can buy managed funds that deal solely in commercial property investments. Because they invest in commercial properties, and because the performance of commercial and residential property is not highly correlated, property managed funds can be a good means of diversifying property holdings.

Most Australians with superannuation will have a portion of their money (5 to 15 per cent) invested in property managed funds.

Unlisted/direct property funds

There are also a number of developers and investment managers who market direct property funds straight to investors. This style of investment will often have a defined investment life in years. Investors buy units in a fund and the fund's managers buy and manage commercial properties, hold them and rent them out to commercial tenants. Still other property businesses will develop properties from scratch with investors' money.

These investments are not to be confused with the style of property investments that fell apart so spectacularly between 2006 and 2008. These investments (particularly Westpoint, ACR and Fincorp) were actually fixed-interest investments, where investors lent money to property developers, who generally couldn't raise the money from primary funding sources like banks.

How sheltering the needy can make you rich

But, really, *The Power of Property* (subtle plug for previous title by your author) is the ability to compound your returns.

And you'll never get loaded by owning just one investment property. Owning many investment properties could, however, make you rich. This is complicated, and the intricacies of property investment are not something that we can go into great detail about in this book. (Perhaps you could read *Investing in Real Estate For Dummies*. Yep, it's by me, too. You'll never get rich writing just one book!)

What would happen if you had not one but six investment properties? What if you had a portfolio worth $2 million and *then* property prices doubled? Then we would be talking about some serious money.

We'll go into the details of big portfolios in step 6, when *Debt Man Walking* goes for a stroll into investment debt.

Time for a reality check

When it comes to investing, you can have too much of a good thing. From a risk perspective, one of the most dangerous things an investor can do is fall in love with one asset class. Diversification is what stops everything turning sour at once. You've got to spread the love a little.

I need to bring up diversification again, not so much to remind you of the dangers of falling in love with a single asset class, but to ram home the advantages that being properly diversified can bring, particularly as they relate to growth assets.

Spread your wings

Few people start out with a large, well-diversified investment portfolio. It's something that needs to be worked towards, built over years. Even those with a large sum of money to invest immediately are unlikely to be comfortable enough to buy a properly diversified portfolio (without a professional adviser or invest-ment team).

> Diversification is what stops everything turning sour at once. You've got to spread the love a little.

What would happen if you had decided that your first investment was a property in Melbourne or Sydney in late 2003? Or if you'd heavily invested in the stock market in late 2007? You'd have watched your own personal investment version of *A Nightmare on Elm Street*, that's what. Carnage. Your investment would have gone backwards, possibly for several years, before anything started to go your way.

For example, if you poured $50000 ($30000 for equity and $20000 for purchase costs) into a $300000 investment property in Melbourne in late 2003, your entire $50000 would have been wiped out just 15 months later. House prices, on average, fell about 10 per cent in value. This would have reduced your $300000 house to approximately $270000, and the other $20000 (as we discussed earlier in this chapter) was already blown on purchase costs.

The property's value would have briefly broken even three years later, before property prices fell again and put you back to square one (see figure 4.1). By this stage, you've held the property for nearly three-and-a-half years and you haven't made a cent. However, if you were negatively geared, you were also footing an interest bill every year (even if you were getting some tax breaks).

Figure 4.1: Melbourne's median property price (June 2003 to March 2008)

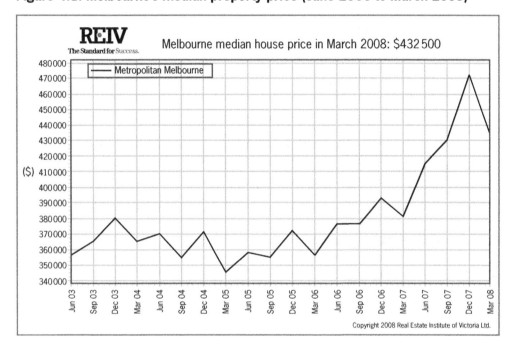

During that time, however, the Australian sharemarket performed very well, while international sharemarkets didn't. The commercial property market was doing very well. Had you put an equal investment into each of these four asset classes, the worst performer would have been your residential investment property. Your lack of diversification meant you'd placed a big bet on residential property and lost.

You need to have a plan to build a diversified portfolio over time. If you've come up with a figure of how much you plan to invest (or how much you can afford as repayments on loans), then spread those purchases over a couple of different investments.

Depending on your risk profile, you could use a portion of a lump sum that you have saved to buy a few diversified managed funds (or index funds) that have the corresponding percentage of your funds in growth assets and the remainder in income investments.

Constant contributions

There's little worse than the fear that as soon as you buy into an investment, the price starts to fall (as in the example above). There is a way of managing this risk also, called dollar-cost averaging.

Dollar-cost averaging is the regular purchasing of an investment, so that you pick up an average purchase price over time. It is often used to describe how, when prices fall, you'll pick up more of your investment with the same amount of money.

For example, you have decided to invest $200 into a managed fund every month for six months. In January, it had an entry price of $2. The market experienced a rocky time over the six months and you ended up buying your units at a variety of prices (see table 4.4).

Table 4.4: dollar-cost averaging

Month	Investment	Managed fund price	Number of units bought
January	$200	2.00	100
February	$200	1.90	105.3
March	$200	1.80	111.1
April	$200	1.90	105.3
May	$200	2.05	97.6
June	$200	2.00	100
Totals	$1200	1.942 (avg.)	619.3

You've spent $1200 on your investment over the six-month period. Over that time, you have picked up 619.3 units, which are worth $2 each again. There are two things to note. First, your investment, even though it spent most of that period below what you'd initially paid, is now worth $1238.60. Second, the average price you have paid for your investments is $1.942 rather than $2.

Dollar-cost averaging is also a good way of ensuring you don't overpay for your investments over time. Your average price will never be the top price. You might buy some at the very bottom of a cycle and some at the very top. But if you commit to investing more money each month or year, it's unlikely that you will end up purchasing one overpriced dud.

Some years you will pick up assets at lower prices than you did the year before. Most years you will pay more for them, but with each year that you invest, you will be reducing the risk of overpaying for an asset.

Dollar-cost averaging is how most people's superannuation is invested. Your employer puts money into your superannuation each month and it gets invested at that time.

Riding the cycle

As has been covered previously, the *Debt Man Walking* philosophy requires long-term investment horizons when it comes to shares and property. Given enough time, growth assets will outperform income assets. But in the short term, they are capable of having a few bad years.

Let's have a look at some more figures compiled by Lonsec. Table 4.5 and figure 4.2 (overleaf) show the performances of each investment class since the 1991 financial year.

Table 4.5: investment performance by asset class (based on Lonsec statistics for the 1990–91 to 2007–08 financial years)

	Worst performance	Best performance	1991–2008 average
Cash	4.6%	8%	5.8%
Australian fixed interest	−6.2%	20.1%	7.3%
International fixed interest	−2.5%	20.6%	7.3%
Australian shares	−17.8%	56.7%	14.3%
International shares	−33.1%	57.2%	9.2%
Australian property	−36.3%	40.8%	13.4%
International property	−24.7%	54.8%	15.4%

Figure 4.2: investment performance by asset class (based on Lonsec statistics for the 1990–91 to 2007–08 financial years)

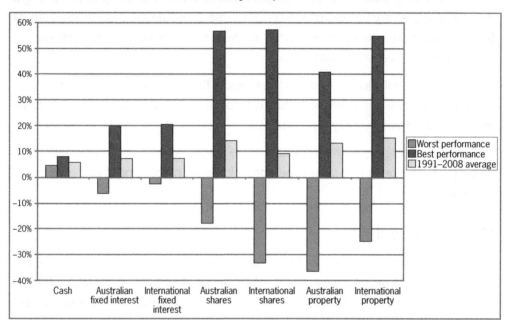

If you had invested in anything and that was the year that asset class had its worst performance, you'd have been as livid as John McEnroe after a questionable line call ('You CANNOT be serious!'). But if you'd diversified your investments, you'd have rarely been too unhappy. And the long-term averages for each asset class are none too shabby.

All investment asset classes have cycles. But even the best brains in the business struggle to pick them. So, as a novice, why would you try? Invest regularly and invest for the long term.

Holding on for a return

This leads us to another rough guide. Because of the risks involved in various asset classes, there are recommended minimum investment time frames for each risk profile. Table 4.6 is based around the fact that the low-risk profiles are largely in cash, which doesn't fluctuate dramatically, while the higher-risk profiles are invested in the more volatile asset classes of shares and property.

Table 4.6: holding periods for risk-based investments

Risk profile	% growth/ % income	Annual performance expectations	Recommended minimum investment period
Cautious	20/80	6.75	1–2 years
Defensive	40/60	7.5	2–3 years
Prudent	60/40	8.25	3–5 years
Assertive	80/20	9	5–6 years
Aggressive	100/0	9.5	7+ years

What do these time frames mean in practical terms? If your life savings are $50000 and you are intending to use that money as a deposit for a house in one or two years, you should not be looking to invest those savings aggressively—in all shares and property—which really needs an investor to have a seven-year time frame. You should probably have the money in cash, or only a small portion of it in shares and property.

Similarly, if you are only starting out trying to save for a big target (like buying a house in five to seven years) and you want to start a savings plan (or even a geared savings plan), then you can probably afford to take an assertive or aggressive approach to investing.

Speaking of long time frames, how long is it until you will get access to your super?

Halve your tax

Paying tax is generally a good thing—you don't pay tax unless you've made money. We will cover tax implications in more detail in step 7. But there is one point to understand now, while we're talking about investing in growth assets. *You pay tax on only half of the gains made through the growth in value of an asset held for more than a year, but you pay full tax on any income you receive from it regardless of the time frame.*

This is a deliberate bias in favour of long-term investors. If you own an investment for longer than a year before selling it (which should be most property and share investments), the Tax Office makes you pay tax on only half of your gain. For example, if you make a $100000 profit on the sale of a property you've had for five years, you will add only $50000 to your other income that you have to pay tax on.

However, if you make $100000 on an investment you've held for less than a year, then you'll pay tax on the full $100000, just as if you had earned it as salary.

Showdown: shares versus property

I'm often asked which is best—shares or property—and why.

As I said earlier, I'm not going to enter the debate about which is the better performer. Over the long term, both will provide similar sorts of returns in absolute terms.

However, as investments, they are very, very different. And those differences might turn some investors off property and on to shares, or vice versa.

So, I've put together what I hope is a fairly exhaustive list (table 4.7) comparing the two. This is *Debt Man Walking*'s 'showdown' of shares versus property.

If you've got a question about the differences between direct property and shares and managed funds, then hopefully this table answers it. For the purposes of this exercise, I've separated property. The direct property column relates to directly held residential or commercial property, while I've included managed fund property with shares and managed funds (because they are investments managed by others).

Table 4.7: showdown—property versus shares

	Direct property	Shares/managed funds (including property managed funds)
Volatility	May vary considerably over a quarter or a year	Can fall or rise sharply in a day or a month
Control	Almost complete control over your investment	Almost no control over the investments
Individuality	Every property is unique	A share in one company is exactly the same as a share in another company and the same applies for units in managed funds

	Direct property	Shares/managed funds (including property managed funds)
Diversification	Difficult to get diversification, because you are buying only one (expensive) property at a time	Easily done, because small parcels can be bought
International investment	Very difficult	Simple through managed funds
Gearing (non-homeowner)	Up to about 95% with many lenders	Up to about 75% with margin loans (100% with some structured products)
Gearing (homeowner with equity)	Up to about 106% (whole cost plus legals)	Up to about 75% with margin loans (100% with some structured products)
Purchase what you want	No. Can really only purchase what's available for sale	Yes. Shares in most big companies are on offer every day
Liquidity	Difficult. Usually takes months to sell	Easy, can usually be converted to cash within days or weeks
Size of individual investment	Large. If bought individually, usually hundreds of thousands of dollars	Can be as little as a few hundred or a few thousand dollars
Ongoing operating costs	Expensive. Agent fees, insurance, stamp duty, gardening, maintenance, and so on	Little to no direct cost for shares; ongoing fees of an average of 2% for managed funds
Effort to run investment	Requires ongoing decision making and monitoring of agents and/or tenants	Little to no decision making for managed funds. Constant monitoring of direct shares portfolio required
Building portfolio	Difficult, because of large nature of individual purchases	Easy, can be added to at any time
Valuations	Irregular. Expensive to get valuations	Up-to-the-minute with shares, daily or weekly with managed funds

Table 4.7: showdown—property versus shares *(cont'd)*

	Direct property	Shares/managed funds (including property managed funds)
Entry costs	High. Up to 7%	Low. As little as 0.1%, up to 4%, with an average of about 2%
Exit costs	High. About 2%	Usually quite low
Paperwork	Loads. You'll have to be a good manager, or pay someone else to do it	Can be complex for direct shares, but usually very simple with managed funds
Borrowing funding costs	Usually at standard home loan rates	Margin loans are a few per cent above home loan rates. Other options will mostly be more expensive
Value add opportunity	Investor can extend, renovate, subdivide or take advantage of other opportunities	No ability to add value
Downsize capacity	Not possible. Can't just sell off a kitchen for extra cash	Easy, partial sale possible. Except some funds have long redemption periods (some direct trusts, hedge funds, etc.)
Income	Known as rent. Commercial property yields tend to be high-income investments	Known as dividends and distributions, which can vary dramatically depending on the type of investment

The X-Flips:

Diversification is portfolio protection

Too many people make one or two investments—buy one investment property or shares in a couple of companies—and hope the investment will produce for them untold riches down the track. It might. It could. But let's face it, it probably won't.

Sure, you may pick *something* that performs spectacularly. But, unless you're very closely related to someone stupendously lucky—Cosmo Kramer or Ferris Bueller—what's the chance a novice will strike it rich with just one investment?

Proper diversification removes the risk that you'll make a major, costly mis-take. The secret to investment riches is not necessarily being an investment genius, but making regular small sacrifices (for investment purposes) for longer-term gains. That goes hand in hand with diversification—both of asset type and timing—and means you don't have to worry that you'll buy an investment just before everything plunges.

Seasoned investors understand that some investments simply don't work out. Some might go bust, while others might go backwards over a 10-year period. Some might perform spectacularly. But it's actually far more danger-ous to pin all your hopes on the one investment than it is to have a dozen or so.

Step 4 for Gen X

Growth assets are where the action is at. They are where Generation X investors should have their investments (super and long-term investments), or a portion of their investments. Given time, they are going to produce a superior return to having money in the bank or other low-risk investments.

Plan to move a larger portion of your longer-term investments into the high-er growth asset classes of shares and property. If you have already collected a few assets, start by listing where they all are (cash, fixed interest, property or shares) and determine whether your assets are invested correctly.

Step 5

Q: Which loud, colourful female rocker did well with a cover of The Brains' 'Money Changes Everything' and was the musical director, as well as appearing in the hit movie *The Goonies*?

A: Cyndi Lauper.

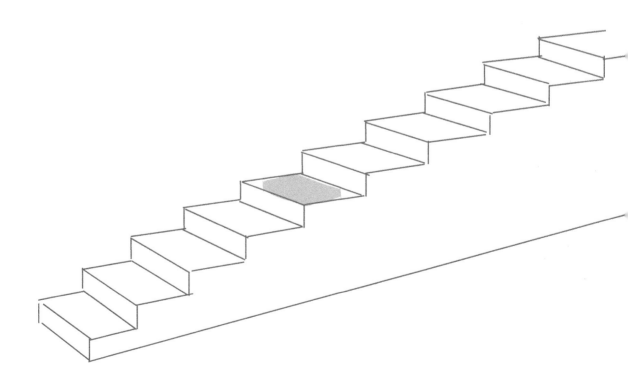

Home: investment central

- Making the decision to buy or rent
- Renting and investment strategies
- Investment central—making your home your investment base
- Home is not an investment property
- Equity—your cheapest source of investment finance
- Don't panic about property prices
- The X-Flips: manage your mortgage, then manage your wealth

The worst form of punishment as a kid was being grounded. That was a disaster, particularly from a social perspective. Being stuck at home with mum and dad was a form of punishment far worse than a teacher's cane (corporal punishment is an experience future generations will sadly miss out on), having your pocket money cut, being denied dessert, or being put on detention.

As a teenager, all you really had on your hands was time—it's not like we couldn't afford to give some of it up. But being grounded seemed a cruel and unusual punishment. Thankfully, my parents weren't big believers in it. We got a thwack! on the bum with the feather duster handle instead. Hated it, but at least Dirk and I knew that it was over in a second or two and the pain lasted only a minute. But a grounding gave you days or weeks to consider whatever evil you'd allegedly done.

But we're not kids anymore. Damn it. As much as Generation X tried to avoid it—we elongated growing up from a teenage thing to an adolescent thing which we stretched to about 30—we eventually accepted the need to mature. Now, being grounded is a good thing—it means being balanced, stable, reliable and settled.

Home is usually a big part of that. Being unsettled at home can be very troubling. My 20s were spent moving house about every 12 months. When I finally shacked up with my first home mortgage, it was my 12th address in 10 years. But I haven't had to pack a moving box now for nearly eight years.

Your choice of home is usually a major part of your finances. It's something over which you have some choice. You pay rent or a mortgage to live there. You have a choice about how much you pay to buy a property. Renters generally have a choice of places on offer. Buyers' choices extend to how much of a deposit they have and how much they pay for a home.

A place to stash your stuff

You do have a choice about where you live. You could hang out with mum and dad (or considering our parents' rising divorce rates, possibly mum or dad) until they, or you, have had enough. You could take your chances renting in a share house—and end up with Neil, Rick, Vivian and Mike from *The Young Ones* as your housemates.

You can rent your own place. You can live in the 'burbs. You can live inner-city. House, flat or unit. Each comes with a price tag. And you have a choice over which living arrangement you put in your shopping trolley.

The same goes for buying a pad to live in. You have a choice about how much you save before you start looking, how close to the action or the city you want to live and whether you want land for any kids or animals.

Many people argue they don't have a choice about where they live. They are forced to rent or buy in a particular area because it is all they can afford. You've always got *some* choice. You can move. The new situation might not be much better. In fact, it could be worse. But you do, inevitably, have a choice—unless you're doing time. Schapelle Corby doesn't have a lot of choice about where she's currently stashing her stuff. (And to any others serving time at Her Majesty's Pleasure, I hope this book, and AC/DC's 'Jailbreak', are providing some mental distraction.)

Till death do us part?

The basic choice most people face is whether to buy or rent.It's a discussion that occasionally plays out in the media. Newspaper articles run a table based on variables such as the cost of rent, the cost of a mortgage, the returns on property, the returns on stocks (if you invest the savings from renting over the cost of a mortgage) versus the return on property.

The argument in favour of renting can be boiled down to this:

⦿ Rent is cheaper than a mortgage. You can usually rent for less than the cost of a mortgage on the same property.

⦿ If you invest the savings you make from renting and not buying, you'll be way ahead by the time the mortgage is paid out.

In one article that ran in a metropolitan newspaper in 2007, the author assumed that property prices increased with inflation (3 per cent), but then allowed the renter to get a return of 8 per cent on the money they invested in managed funds and extrapolated that over 30 years. They were serious! How was that a fair fight for an argument of renting versus buying? That's like putting Iron Mike Tyson in the ring against Lewis *and* Gilbert from *Revenge of the Nerds*. And then giving Mighty Mike 'the green light to bite'. The figures they came out with were astounding...ly bad.

I've read loads of these arguments in favour of renting. Inevitably, there is one thing missed/ignored by those who push the rent-for-life-and-invest-the-difference line over buying a home.

And that is...*renting is forever*.

I've never seen a pro-renting article take into account that after 25 or 30 years, the mortgage will be paid off. The renter, however, will still be paying rent. Forever. And ever. Amen.

Want the message as a catchy jingle that says it all?

If you decide not to buy,
you will rent until you die.

(Okay, it's not brilliant but despite years of trying to be Jimmy Barnes in the shower and at karaoke nights, I'm a musical moron—that includes songwriting, singing and instrument playing. However, I can take solace from the fact that that puts me one step higher on the musical talent scales than Milli Vanilli, those famously fraudulent fakes.)

Mortgages are designed to be paid off, usually over 25 to 30 years. It may seem like a lifetime, but it isn't. If you buy at age 30, then your home is paid off by the time you're 60 (but probably 55 or 50). You've still got rates and maintenance bills that the renter won't have, but the renter has another 25 years, maybe more, of having to pay rent. (And if Gen X is going to be the first generation to live forever, as Australian science guru Dr Karl Kruszelnicki believes we might be, the renters might have a few hundred years of rising rents to look forward to.)

I believe buying a home is the cornerstone for wealth creation. That's my bias. (I'll show you why with my own numbers later in this step.) There are dozens of reasons I believe that buying a home makes long-term sense. Here are a few more:

- You can access the equity in your home for further investments.

- Home loan interest rates are the cheapest form of financing for future investment.

- Paying the mortgage is a much easier discipline to stick to than investing the money, each and every month.

- You won't get kicked out of a home you own because your landlord has sold.

- You have more control over a home that you own. If you don't like something, you can change it. You can extend it.

- You can (generally) have pets if you want to and hang pictures where you wish.

- Your mortgage will, in real terms, decline over the years, while rents will continue to rise with inflation.

- You can increase the value of your home by improving it.

Choose your strategy

But that's just my opinion. I believe people should buy when they can afford to. Some disagree on economic grounds. Others are happy to rent because they don't want the responsibility that comes with home ownership.

Whether your home is subject to rent or a mortgage, you need to understand the financial ramifications of the choice that you've made. A mortgage can be quite painful financially for the first few years. Rent, by comparison, should never really be painful. Many people will rent a place that is comparatively more expensive than they could buy (but that's another choice).

The decision you make is important. Whichever decision you make needs to be built into your investment strategy.

If your decision is to rent, but you're committed to developing an investment strategy, then you need to make the most of that decision. You need to make it work for you. Here's how I suggest you do that.

Ask a real estate agent in the area what the selling value of your rented home would be. (Agents will make the time to talk to any potential client.) Once you've got a value that seems about right, jump on the internet and find out how much it would cost to service a loan the size of the value of your home. Then you need to invest the difference between what you're paying in rent and the cost of that loan.

Introducing Adam Renter

Let's go through an example. Adam Renter is a musician paying $450 a week rent on a nice, inner-city apartment. The local real estate agent values the apartment at about $450 000. Assuming an interest rate of 8.5 per cent, the repayments on a principal and interest loan would be approximately $835 a week.

There's a $385 a week difference. This is how much Adam needs to put away each week.

If Adam can't afford to put away that much money on top of his rent, then he's 'renting above his budget'. Adam is living in a place that he couldn't afford to buy (which is obviously a clear advantage to renting).

> Whether your home is subject to rent or a mortgage, you need to understand the financial ramifications of the choice that you've made.

This is nothing to be sneezed at. A sum of $385 a week is $20 020 a year. That's a powerful sum to be putting towards an investment strategy. However, rents rise with inflation. In year 10, his rent has risen to $605 a week ($31 460 a year) and he can now put only $11 970 away that year (this is the amount that he's still ahead on an equivalent mortgage).

If he was getting an average return of 8 per cent on his growth assets (shares and property), he will have a lump sum of approximately $265 000. (Assuming he was

35 when he started, Adam is 45 and has only another 40 years of paying rent ahead of him, assuming he drops dead at 85.)

And FYI... if Adam is still paying rent when he's 85, the rent will be approximately $1970 a week (assuming rent rises with inflation of 3 per cent).

Introducing Anna Buyer

Anna Buyer is paying $835 a week on a 25-year mortgage.

As a portion of that $835 is paying off her loan, after 10 years Anna will have knocked off $82000 from her $450000 mortgage. But the longer the mortgage continues, the less interest Anna pays on her home loan and the more principal she pays. Anna's home, if it has increased in value by only 3 per cent a year, is worth $605000. She's picked up equity of a further $155000, taking her total equity stake to $237000 (at the same time, Adam Renter's non-home investments are worth $265000).

Adam is ahead of Anna by less than $20000 at the 10-year mark. Within a few years, he will be behind, and it will only get worse for Adam and better for Anna from there.

Adam's rent will continue to rise with inflation and Anna's mortgage won't. (Anna's mortgage repayments will fluctuate, up *and* down, with interest rate movements, but the size of the mortgage itself will continue to fall.) If Anna Buyer was 35 when she started, she's just 15 years off owning her home outright. After that, she can expect about 25 years of being mortgage free in retirement.

> ...in order to rent and make that decision work, you'll have to be more disciplined than someone with a mortgage.

Anna will be in a position where she can be quite confident that in a few years she will be able to use the equity she has built in her home (from paying down the mortgage and the value of the house going up) to make further investments. She might not be able to make many investments in the first few years because her mortgage is much bigger than the cost of renting an equivalent home.

Adam, on the other hand, will have some investments in his personal name. And he will be able to use those investments to leverage into further investments. But banks have a preference for bricks and mortar investments when it comes to security for lending.

Being disciplined

Think about 1980s fitness guru Richard Simmons. Or don't. I don't think that he's aged all that well. But his enthusiasm was infectious.

If your decision is to rent, that's perfectly fine. But if your goal is long-term wealth creation, in order to rent and make that decision work, you'll have to be more disciplined than someone with a mortgage.

You need to be more determined because you can cancel your investment plans on a whim. Just for a couple of weeks or a couple of months: 'It's a big year, so we'll need to cancel it just for this year'. If you do, you will lose much of the early advantage that you have.

You simply can't do that with a mortgage. A person who fails to meet mortgage repayments will soon find themselves kicked out by their bank and they will be back renting again.

Renting is forever

Let me just repeat that ditty again:

If you decide not to buy,
you will rent until you die.

Other sayings about rent aren't necessarily as accurate.

'Rent money is dead money.' No, it's not. It's a relatively cheap way to store your stuff. And it is cheaper than a mortgage in the short and medium terms.

'Renting is just paying off a mortgage for someone else.' That's not really true either. Most of the time, your rent isn't covering the cost of the mortgage. Not even the interest component. On a cash flow basis, the landlord is usually losing money for many of the early years of ownership of a property (that's negative gearing and it's the risk they take as they try to make money from rising capital values).

Renting is cheaper in the short and medium terms. However, if your $450-a-week rent bill rises in line with inflation (let's assume 3 per cent a year), then in the 21st year, your rent will have risen to $837 a week. You're now paying more each week than the person who bought is paying for their mortgage. And the person who bought is just four years away from having no mortgage left to pay.

Renting allows you to live in a better place than you would otherwise be able to afford if you had to buy. If your budget for accommodation (rent or mortgage) is $700 a week, then you could buy a home in a middle-ring suburb of most capital cities, or you could afford to rent an excellent place in the inner city. However, renting at this level wouldn't allow you to save money for your investment plan.

While there are advantages to renting, I don't believe that renting is the better long-term option if your aim is wealth creation. Renting never ends. If you choose not to buy, you choose to rent forever.

Investment central

So, it's settled. You're going to buy. Or you're going to rent. Up to you.

Either way, hopefully now you understand the ramifications of your decision. Your home, whether you rent or buy, is investment central. It's a decision pivotal to your wealth creation plans.

Home versus investment property

I want to get something else straight.

Your home (if you own one) is not an investment property.

That might not sound too difficult to understand, but many people struggle with the difference between the two. Many people buy a home believing that they are really buying 'a good investment'. They're not.

It's important to understand that a home isn't an investment property for some really fundamental reasons, which largely relate to tax and include the following:

- If you make a profit when you sell your home, there is no tax to pay.
- If you make a profit on an investment property, you will have to pay capital gains tax.
- There are no ongoing tax breaks/deductions to owning your own home.
- The interest you pay on an investment property is tax deductible.
- Maintenance on your home isn't tax deductible.
- Maintenance on an investment property is tax deductible.

- Your home won't ever give you a passive income.

- As the mortgage on your investment property is paid down and the rent increases with time, you will begin to receive a passive income from your property (see 'Money for Nothing' in step 1).

- A home is a place to live. It fills an emotional need.

- An investment property is for someone else to live in. It's about making money.

But there is a more important, non-financial, difference: a home is about a lifestyle.

The primary reason for buying a home is to buy somewhere to live. It's about lifestyle. But with an investment property, making money—not lifestyle considerations—should be first and foremost in your mind.

While almost all homes will appreciate in value like an investment, homes should never be thought of as an investment.

Home equity financing

The interest rates charged on home loans are generally the cheapest source of financing available to individuals.

There are two reasons for this. The first is that banks know that property tends to maintain its value, and will actually grow in value over time. If a bank lends someone $280 000 on a $350 000 property, the bank can be *reasonably* confident that if it needs to sell the home because the home buyer can no longer meet the repayments, the bank will at least get its $280 000 back.

If the bank lent $30 000 for a car two years ago and the borrower can no longer meet the repayments, what is the car worth? Probably about $20 000. Banks charge for this uncertainty by having higher interest rates and shorter loan terms (usually five to seven years) so that the principal is paid back faster. As a result, car loan rates are considerably higher. And when it comes to credit cards, there is no security, which can lead to obscenely high interest rates.

Secondly, banks know that people will do whatever they can in order to stay in their homes. They will sacrifice spending in every other area of their lives rather than get behind on their mortgage and risk the possibility that they will be kicked out of their castle.

Home equity loans earned a bad name in the 1990s and early 2000s because of the way they were marketed. Banks were advertising that home buyers could withdraw equity from their home for consumable items, such as cars, holidays, caravans and plasma TVs. It's certainly cheaper than taking out a personal loan, or a car loan, or whacking the purchase on a 20-per-cent-plus rate on the credit card.

But let's not underplay the danger of using a home equity loan. You are adding to your home mortgage to purchase whatever investments/goods you are buying. If the car that you've bought with home equity tips you over the financial edge, then you might lose your home as a result.

A good rule of thumb for finance is that you should pay cash (savings) to purchase depreciating assets, such as cars, home theatre systems or holidays. But you should use borrowings, such as home equity loans (and lines of credit, which we'll discuss next) for appreciating assets. We go into much more detail on debt in step 6.

WHAT IS HOME EQUITY?

If you've had a home for a few years, it's likely that you've built up some equity, or ownership, in your home. Imagine you bought a home seven years ago for $335 000, with a loan for $310 000. Over the period of seven years, you paid down your home loan to $250 000 and your home has increased in value to $574 000.

When you took out the original home loan, you owned just 11.4 per cent of your home. After seven years, you now own 56.4 per cent of your home. You now have equity, or ownership, in your home of $324 000.

Why is this important? Because if you're looking to use borrowed money to invest, your home is probably going to be the best source of collateral for bank funding. Because of the security that banks get with a mortgage, there is rarely a cheaper source of funding than equity from your home.

Line-of-credit financing

A line of credit is a form of home-equity financing, under the terms of which the bank agrees to let the homeowner borrow up to a certain percentage of the home's value, usually 80 per cent.

If your property is worth $500 000, the bank may approve a total loan of $400 000 (80 per cent of $500 000). If you already owe $250 000 on your home mortgage, the bank might approve a 'line of credit' loan of $150 000. Once approved, you can draw on the loan up to $400 000 at will.

The same dangers apply here as they do to normal home-equity loans. You can use this $150 000 for anything, and the temptation will be there to use it for consumable items. The warning still applies—you should pay cash for depreciating lifestyle assets. Your line of credit should be for investment assets to create wealth.

If you do use it for household goods and investment purposes (investment property or share-based investments), keep records of exactly which portion is being used for investment, because the interest on the investment portion will be tax deductible.

'I'd buy, but homes are unaffordable!'

I've outlined most of the reasons that people with a wealth-building program should aim for home ownership already in this chapter. But when the decision to buy or rent is being made, it is as much about lifestyle as it is about anything else. The characters of *Friends*—the show that most closely defined Gen X's lifestyle—and *The Secret Life Of Us* certainly showed no interest in buying. They were perfectly happy with the rent-forever, inner-city life.

I doubt I'll change many minds, but I hope to have got you thinking about it again.

But then comes the argument that 'property prices are just too high!'

Here's a fact: property prices are cyclical. Sometimes excitement pushes them too high. At other times, the nation falls out of love with property and it is consigned to the bargain barrel. It appears both property and shares in Australia reached a cyclical peak at the end of 2007.

Don't get uptight about the 'home affordability crisis'. When everyone is squealing about the price of housing being too high—particularly the media—house prices probably are too high. Bargains are probably just a few years away. You can almost guarantee that at some stage in the next five to ten years, you will be able to find a graph that says that they were dirt cheap for another period. That's the nature of cycles.

The basic rules of economics—about when demand and supply are out of whack—always prevail. *If people can't afford to buy property, then property prices will fall.*

The X-Flips:

Manage your mortgage, then manage your wealth

For most people, the first few years of the first mortgage are about keeping up with the repayments and doing up and/or furnishing the home. Most people have bitten off a very big mouthful and the chewing can be a struggle.

It tends to be that people buy their home when they're on the way up the career ladder. A few years after they buy, they've earned themselves a pay rise or two, they've paid a little extra off the mortgage and earned themselves some breathing space on the loan.

What next? The options are:

1   use the excess money to reward yourself for the hard work and sacrifice with a more expensive lifestyle

2   use the excess cash to fund other parts of your expenses that are growing, like paying for the children's education

3   trade up and buy yourself a bigger home with a bigger mortgage

4   accelerate your repayments and pay off the home loan in just 15 to 20 years, instead of 25 to 30

5   use that extra savings potential to start an investment program

6   a combination of all of the above.

There is no wrong option. It's all about personal priorities. However, too many people decide to spend too much of their excess spending money on option 1.

You deserve a reward, no question. But, as we discussed in step 2, the first universal rule of money is delayed gratification, and the less you reward yourself now, the more you can do so later. So try to remember how much easier life is going to be when you don't need to work because of the passive income derived from the portfolio you built with delayed gratification. Surely that's going to feel much better than the fleeting reward you're about to buy.

Once your mortgage is under control (which only you can decide), it's time to move from managing your mortgage to managing your wealth. You've got to decide to tip a portion of your excess savings capacity into another wealth creation strategy.

(Those renting might find that the rent becomes a less significant portion of their income over time also. They might rent nicer digs, increase the amount they are investing, spend more on lifestyle, or a combination of all three.)

For example, let's say that your mortgage repayments were $2000 a month. After a few years, you realise that you could afford to raise the repayments to $3000 or $4000 a month. That extra $1000 or $2000 a month will take large chunks off your mortgage quite quickly. It would also pay for a very comfortable overseas holiday every year. But it would also go a long way to building a portfolio of investment assets.

Let's take $1500 a month, which is $18 000 a year. A figure like $18 000 a year can fund significant investments. Depending on a few factors, it could be used to fund a negatively geared investment property, a geared-savings investment program, or it could fund the interest payments on a debt-funded share portfolio.

Yes, it will slow down the rate at which the home loan is paid off. But the benefits include the potentially higher long-term rewards of having started an investment program, diversification of the asset base outside of the equity in your home and getting a start on that path to creating passive income streams that will provide an income for you (and your family).

Home ownership—as in paying off the home loan—is an admirable goal. But waiting until the home loan is paid off before investing elsewhere means potentially missing out on the opportunities to create the sort of asset base that will provide income as you get older.

Step 5 for Gen X

A home is primarily about meeting emotional needs. You should feel comfortable and safe there. Whether it's the perfect bachelor pad (Gary and Tony's place in *Men Behaving Badly*), a happy home for a couple (such as *Mad About You*'s Paul and Jamie Buchman) or a family's fortress (the Kerrigan's house in *The Castle*), the best homes are also where the best memories are made.

Feeling grounded at home should be the primary consideration. Secondary is whether the price paid is rent or a mortgage.

Step 5 for Gen X (cont'd)

But you have to make your decision—whether that's buying or renting—an integral part of your future financial plans. If you're renting, go back and find out how much it would be costing you for a mortgage on the house. The difference between that and what you're paying in rent is what you need to invest.

If you've got a mortgage, is it under control? If it is, then you should try to direct some amount of money towards an investment strategy that will eventually provide you with an income stream. There will be big benefits to getting started now, rather than waiting until the mortgage is nearly, or fully paid off.

step 6

Q: Who played Vivian, a prostitute who lands a 'whale' in loaded businessman Richard Gere, in the movie *Pretty Woman*, ?

A: Julia Roberts

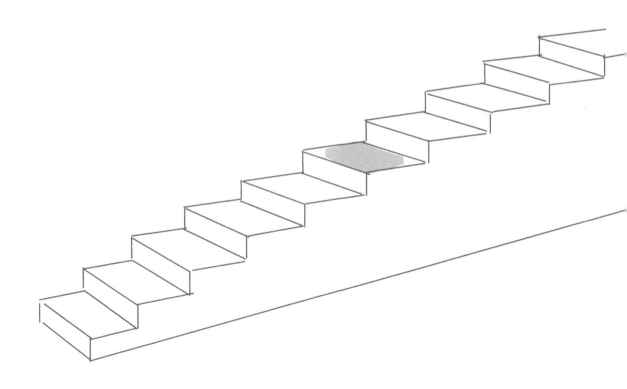

Investing: the debt mantra

- Gearing—investment's secret ingredient
- The truth about borrowing
- DOG debt: Dumb, Okay and Great debt
- Why gear investments?
- Building a geared investment portfolio
- Investment debt and knowing your limits
- The X-Flips: going green—recycling your debt

The way some people and sections of the media talk, you'd think that debt was the Grim Reaper from the AIDS ads in the 1980s.

Some people have learned a pathological fear of debt from friends and family. To some people, all debt is bad and you must not sleep easy at night unless you're debt free. Owing someone money is akin to a sin, like coveting your neighbour's wife (even if she is Demi Moore and you know she likes younger guys).

Some debt is pretty stupid. Some debt is pretty pointless. Some debt is just about being a little bit greedy—allowing you to buy something that you really should have saved for.

Some debt is inescapable (who pays for their first home with cash?). Some types of debt are better than other types of debt. And, despite what many people say, some types of debt can actually be good for your financial health.

Not all debt is evil.

Not that any of this is particularly obvious now. As I write this, the financial world is going through a process of de-leveraging—a term that is supposed to describe systemic debt reduction around the globe.

This de-leveraging is occurring because of the sub-prime crisis of 2007 and 2008. The sub-prime crisis occurred because banks in the United States went through a period where they took leave of their senses (like Angelina Jolie and Billy Bob Thornton both seemed to when they were married to each other), ignored their usual borrowing standards and loaned money to people who, under normal circumstances, would struggle to get credit to buy a couch. These poor saps were known as sub-prime borrowers. In other words, there were other people banks would prefer to lend money to. But those other people didn't want any more money.

> Sub-prime loans were also known as NINJA loans – 'No Income, No Job, no Assets'. Any wonder it led to a global mess?

Sub-prime loans were also known as NINJA loans — 'No Income, No Job, no Assets'. Any wonder it led to a global mess?

Occasionally, markets do stupid things. These lending arrangements were one such time. As a result, borrowing came to be 'on the nose'. Banks were less willing to lend. People were less willing to borrow. Businesses struggled to get loans. Banks were struggling to get money to lend to them. The world was de-leveraging because they had too much debt. And too much of anything can be a bad thing. But, as a result, debt, leveraging, borrowing and gearing became — at least temporarily — dirty words.

They shouldn't be. Not for Generation X. Not for any truly long-term investors.

Mission Impossible

There would be few people who get through life without ever borrowing money. Show me a 60 year old who has never had a car loan, a personal loan or a credit card.

Most Gen Xers probably borrowed a few thousand dollars for their first (second-hand) car — a Holden Torana, Ford Cortina, Honda Civic or Volkswagen Beetle — or had a credit card by the time they were 25. (I got a loan in 1992 for my second car, a 1984 Ford Laser I bought from my parents, and got my first credit card in 1993, aged 22.) Others might have taken store credit to furnish their first flat. I've never met anyone who has bought their own *first* home by plonking down the entire purchase price in cash. What's the average house price in your area? Know anyone in their 30s with that amount sitting in a bank account?

It's almost *Mission Impossible* to save your way to a fortune. Because of the insidious nature of inflation (see step 2), the inbuilt biases towards growth assets in Australia's tax laws (also step 2) and the traditionally low interest rates on bank accounts, saving your way to a fortune is tough work.

Think about how long it would take to save for the average Australian home — about $400000. Even if you could save that amount of money in 10 years, how much would the average house price have risen by then? All your saving to that point might have, *really*, only got you half way to owning that house.

Debt—the secret investment ingredient

The advice contained in the rest of *Debt Man Walking* stands on its own, without step 6. Whether it is about understanding rules, buying growth assets, your home's place in your investment strategy or what's coming in future steps, it is all reliable wealth-creating advice for investors.

But step 6 is what makes this book different from others on the shelf. Step 6 shows how a powerful four-letter word can be used by Generation X to create for ourselves a better financial future. It is about how leverage, or debt—used conservatively and correctly—is the secret ingredient to wealth building.

Borrowing to invest is not necessarily dicing with death or a recipe for disaster. Leverage is a magnifying glass. It enhances an investment's movement. The aim, of course, is to magnify your returns.

A world in black and white

If you think the banks are bastards now, you should have dealt with them prior to the 1980s.

Australians used to have to beg to borrow. Previous generations had to frock up to see their bank managers to get a home loan. Banks wanted to see a consistent savings pattern. Customers had to earn the right to go into debt. Times have changed. And hey, did you notice, TV's no longer black and white!

Debt is far easier to get—many argue too easy. A steady income is all you need to get a credit card (then the offers for increased limits start). There's plenty of credit available for cars. You no longer need to show a long pattern of savings to get a home loan.

However, debt can be trouble to some personality types. Debt will send *some* people bankrupt. Despite the way the media reports it, sometimes it will be the customer's own fault. Perhaps they should have bought a second-hand car instead of a new one. Or they shouldn't have filled their house with no-interest-for-three-years furniture deals when their job was looking shaky. Or they didn't have a big enough deposit, but didn't want to get locked out of the property market. Or they went with an organisation that they'd never heard of because they were the only ones who would lend them the money.

> Debt deserves respect, but it is not something to be feared. It can be a powerful investment force, but it can also work against you.

Debt deserves respect, but it is not something to be feared.

It can be a powerful investment force, but it can also work against you. Some people simply don't use debt properly and end up not being properly rewarded for the extra risk they have taken on.

The big lenders aren't stupid (even if sometimes the media makes them out to be Jim Carrey's character in *Dumb and Dumber*, Lloyd Christmas). They have spent decades honing their lending criteria. At any given point, they know how many of their customers are in trouble. They know how to deal with it. And, what's more, they had a fairly good idea how many of these clients would end up unable to repay their loans when they first offered the finance (well, Australian banks do). They just didn't know exactly which clients.

'Mum, where does cash come from?'

When you put money into a bank account, you are essentially lending the bank your money. The banks bundle up customers' cash and lend it to others who don't have enough of their own savings to get what they want. They might pay someone 5 per cent interest for their deposits, but charge 9 per cent to the people who borrow it.

So why borrow? People borrow for all the reasons we've already discussed (to buy homes, cars, or other goods for their home). Businesses borrow because they need capital to buy equipment and premises and to manage their cash flow.

But there is another reason for borrowing—investment. This is inevitably what businesses are borrowing for. They borrow because they believe that they can use that money to make more money than the cost of borrowing this money from a bank. For instance, the bank charges them 10 per cent, but they believe they can use that money to make a 20 per cent return.

Individuals borrow to invest for the same reason. They believe the cost of borrowing the money will be smaller than the money that can be made from the investment itself. If the cost of borrowing $100 000 to invest is $8000 a year, the investor believes that he or she will make far more than the $8000 interest cost.

Only growth assets allowed!

As a result, there is no point using borrowed funds to invest in cash assets. Most of the time, you would be borrowing money to invest at, say, 9 per cent, to get a return of 7 per cent. That's a loss of 2 per cent a year and doesn't make sense.

Investment gearing is really only for shares and property—assets that are designed to give total returns (rent/dividends, plus capital growth; see step 4) that outstrip borrowing costs. And because growth assets can have periods where they fall in value, borrowing is only ever for assets you intend to hold for a longer period.

Not all debt is bad—the DOG of debt

Sure, some debt ain't so great. In fact, some debt is stupid.

But other debt is actually not so bad. And there is, as I'll explain, debt that is great. This is the sort of debt that, when used wisely, can help you build wealth. Despite what some say, how can debt that helps make you wealthy be wrong?

You might have heard about the good debt/bad debt principle. For those who talk about debt in this way, the only differential is whether a tax deduction can be claimed (good debt) or cannot be claimed (bad debt) on the interest.

That's a clean distinction. But I believe it fails to classify debt properly. It's missing something—it's just not quite that simple.

I believe there are actually three types of debt. They are the DOG of debt:

- Dumb debt.
- Okay debt.
- Great debt.

The differences between them are summed up in whether they answer yes or no to the following questions:

1 Is the item purchased likely to increase in value?

2 Can you claim the interest as a tax deduction?

The first question is quite obvious. Items (or assets) that increase in value are clearly good for your wealth. But why does it matter if the interest is a tax deduction? If you can claim the interest on a loan as a tax deduction, then it decreases the real cost of borrowing for that item. If you pay $100 in interest, then claim that interest as a deduction, you could end up getting up to $46.50 (on Australia's highest marginal tax rate) of that money back on tax, reducing the cost of the $100 interest to as little as $53.50.

> Dumb debt includes almost all consumer goods...it is usually for the sort of items that you could afford if you saved for a little while.

If the debt answers no to both questions, it's dumb debt. If it answers yes to both, it's great debt. And if it answers yes to one, but not the other, it's got to be somewhere in the middle.

D is for dumb debt

Dumb debt includes almost all consumer goods—furniture, white goods, cars, groceries, holidays, and so on. You might find some of this debt is inescapable. But it is usually for the sort of items that you could afford if you saved for a little while.

Assets in this category fall in value. You buy them for, say, $30000 and take out a loan for $30000. Two years later, the asset is worth $15000 and you've got a loan for about $20000. On top of that, these are items for which you can't claim a tax deduction.

O is for okay debt

The most obvious okay debt is a home loan. The interest you pay on your home loan is not a tax deduction. But the home is an asset that will increase in value over time.

Another related okay debt is using money to improve your house. If you borrow $150000 to renovate your home and you increase the market value of your home by $200000 or $300000, that can't be all bad. That won't happen with every renovation. But not every renovation is about adding value—it is often about making the home more functional for your family. Again, you can't claim a tax deduction, but it does increase your wealth.

A less obvious example is a car or a computer that is a partial tax deduction because it is a work expense. Cars and computers rapidly depreciate in value. But in some cases you will be able to claim the interest, which decreases the real cost to you.

The good debt/bad debt principle doesn't allow for the distinction here. A home loan is bad debt and a car/computer loan is good debt. How can a home loan really be classified as bad?

G is for great debt

Great debt is *Debt Man Walking* debt.

Great debt answers yes to both questions—it is both a tax deduction and should help to increase your wealth. It needs to be used to buy the right sort of assets. And it needs to be given an appropriate amount of time to do its work.

But great debt is a powerful tool used by investors the world over to leverage returns from their investment strategies.

Great debt should be used to buy quality *investment* assets. By quality, I mean well-researched property and share assets (see step 4). Other assets may appreciate in value (including artwork and wine), but shares and property are where the majority of the investment opportunities are.

So, what about the tax deductions? The tax law states that

PRIORITISING DEBT

If you have a variety of debt, there is a definite order in which the debts should be repaid. Let's assume that you have $200000 of debt on your home loan (at 8.5 per cent), $20000 debt on your car (at 10.5 per cent) and a line of credit of $100000 on a share portfolio (at 8.5 per cent).

Which debt should be paid off first?

It will come down to the home loan or the car loan. If the car is a tax-deductible expense (perhaps for work), then it might make sense to pay down the home loan first. If the car is not a deduction, that loan should be paid down first, because of the higher interest rate. Because the line-of-credit loan is tax deductible, this loan should be on interest only—you shouldn't be paying off any principal there.

if a debt is held for income-generating purposes, the interest on the loan is tax deductible. If the interest is tax deductible, it essentially reduces the net cost of that interest.

If you have $100 000 of debt at 9 per cent (interest only), it will cost you $9000 a year to service that loan. If that debt is not deductible, then it will cost you the full $9000.

However, if the loan is tax deductible, the effective cost of that $9000 interest bill will be reduced by your marginal tax rate. Someone earning $70 000 a year in Australia in 2008 will get 31.5 per cent (including the Medicare levy) of that interest back, or $2835. That reduces the net cost to $6165. The higher your marginal tax rate, the larger the tax return you will get (or the less tax you will pay) and the lower the average cost of that debt.

Table 6.1 shows the real cost of servicing debt at various marginal tax rates in Australia in the 2008–09 financial year.

Table 6.1: marginal tax rates, including the Medicare levy, and their effect on interest costs

	No deduction	31.5%	41.5%	46.5%
Interest cost	$9000	$9000	$9000	$9000
Tax deduction	$0	$2835	$3735	$4185
Real cost	**$9000**	**$6165**	**$5265**	**$4815**

The real cost of a loan is considerably lower if the loan is for investment purposes. The higher the investor's marginal tax rate, the lower the real cost. If it seems a little unfair that the biggest earners get the biggest deductions, well they're the rules. They also pay the most tax. And, remember, if you know the rules, you can plan around them (step 2).

So, why borrow?

The real point of borrowing to invest is to control a larger set of growth assets that will appreciate in underlying value faster than you could own with only your own savings.

Borrowings should be used to buy assets that are going to increase in value at a faster rate than the cost of borrowing the money. If you are borrowing at 9 per cent and the investment has a total return of 8 per cent, you're generally unlikely to make any money. (However, Australia's tax rules mean that it is still possible to turn a profit when returns are equal to, or even slightly lower than, the interest rate.)

If you have $10000 in cash and you put that in the sharemarket and the sharemarket returns 15 per cent for the year, then your $10000 is now worth $11500. Not bad, and probably well above inflation. (This and the following examples are shown in table 6.2.)

If you use your $10000 and borrow another $10000 to have a $20000 investment and the market improves in value by 15 per cent, then the $20000 will be worth $23000. You've made $1500 more than when you'd invested only your own money. A 15 per cent return has been turned into a 30 per cent return. And, if we assume a 9 per cent interest rate for your borrowing, you've paid approximately $900 in interest. This gearing strategy has put you $600 ahead of the no-gearing investment.

If you take your $10000 and borrow $90000 to have $100000 to invest, a 15 per cent return will see your investment funds worth $115000—a $15000 profit. Here the higher debt ratio has magnified the return even further, from 15 per cent to 150 per cent. The interest will be $8100 ($90000 × 9%). Your net return is $6900. That's four times higher than the $1500 you would have made investing only your own money.

Table 6.2: gearing and the impact on gains

	No gearing	50% gearing	90% gearing
Your money	$10000	$10000	$10000
Borrowed money	$0	$10000	$90000
Total investment	$10000	$20000	$100000
15% return	$1500	$3000	$15000
New total investment	$11500	$23000	$115000
Interest on borrowings (9%)	$0	−$900	−$8100
Net return	**$1500**	**$2100**	**$6900**
Net return %	**15%**	**21%**	**69%**

How much of the net return you get to keep will depend on your personal marginal income tax rate. But don't forget: you don't have to pay capital gains tax unless you sell.

A smooth Gere change

Gearing doesn't always have romantic happy endings like *Pretty Woman*, where the deserving hooker, Julia Roberts, is 'rescued' by the rich and cool Richard Gere.

Unlike Vivian's (Roberts) comment about Edward's (Gere) chances being a dead certainty that night, there are no sure things when it comes to geared investment strategies.

Gearing can work the other way as well—*a gearing flirt can lose her shirt*.

Using the previous example, a 10 per cent decrease would have seen your $100000 investment become $90000 (see table 6.3). You still owe the bank $90000, so in this case you have lost your entire $10000 initial equity. And, after a year, you've had to pay $9000 in interest. Further,

LOVE YOU LONG TIME Rob Lowe tried to have a one-night stand with Demi Moore (again!) in *About Last Night*. But he couldn't stay away.

Investment borrowing is not for the impatient. If you're considering getting into gearing, there is absolutely no such thing as a one-night stand. You have to be prepared to go in for the long term.

Hundreds of years of history have shown that, given time, shares and property will increase in value. There can be short-term downward fluctuations and there can be medium-term periods of stagnation. But you can't have a short-term, get-rich-quick relationship with investment gearing—you have to be prepared to be in there for at least seven years in order to ride out asset cycles. That's a minimum. Gearing really should be a relationship that goes on for decades.

for the $90000 to increase to over $100000, it needs to increase by 11.12 per cent, which is known as price decay. And the bigger the fall, the worse it gets. A 20 per cent loss requires a 25 per cent increase to get back to even, and a 25 per cent loss requires a 33.3 per cent increase.

You will get an immediate tax deduction on the interest you have paid ($8100). The amount of your return will depend on your marginal tax rate. However, you would only get a deduction for the capital loss if you sold it.

Table 6.3: gearing and the impact on losses

	No gearing	50% gearing	90% gearing
Your money	$10 000	$10 000	$10 000
Borrowed money	$0	$10 000	$90 000
Total investment	$10 000	$20 000	$100 000
10% fall	−$1 000	−$2 000	−$10 000
New total investment	$9 000	$18 000	$90 000
Interest on borrowings (9%)	$0	−$900	−$8 100
Net return	**−$1 000**	**−$2 900**	**−$18 100**
Net return %	**−10%**	**−29%**	**−181%**

With regard to capital losses, an investor can offset losses only against capital gains. For example, if you make a capital loss of $10 000, you could offset future capital gains against it. If you made a $20 000 gain on another investment, you could reduce your $20 000 gain by your $10 000 loss, leaving you with capital gains tax to pay on just $10 000.

If you don't make a capital gain in the year that you made a loss, then you can carry forward the loss to a future year when you do make a gain. While capital losses can be carried forward, capital gains cannot.

Time and money, money and time

Because gearing increases the risks of investing, it necessarily requires those contemplating debt-funded investment to have two extra ingredients available to them—income and time.

In step 4, we discussed how investing in shares and property requires investment time frames of at least seven years. Gearing magnifies returns, either on the upside or downside, so it's necessary to extend your investment time horizon to ensure that the markets have sufficient time to go in the right direction. Gearing strategies require a minimum of seven to ten years. You should never go into a geared investment strategy planning to be out in just a few years. It is possible to make a reasonable profit within a short period and get out. But gearing strategies, because they can magnify the downside, can require more time to make them work. Your plan should always be to ride out more than one cycle, and although history does have instances where an entire cycle lasted three years, it's very rare. Don't chance it.

RAISING THE RISK BAR   Two risks that apply to geared investments that don't apply where only your own capital is involved have to do with interest rates and losing someone else's money.

Interest rates aren't static—they rise and fall. Gearing strategies work better when interest rates are low and markets are performing strongly. If you're borrowing money at 7 per cent, it's obviously going to be easier to try to beat that as an investment return than if you were paying an interest rate of 12 or 15 per cent.

As a result, there must come a point with interest rates where it doesn't make sense to invest with borrowed money. The tipping point is difficult to know exactly. Certainly, the investment case using borrowed money to invest when interest rates reached 20 or 21 per cent, as they did in the late 1980s during 'the recession we had to have', would have been much more difficult, if not impossible.

There is little point using borrowed money for investments unless you believe that the total percentage return from the investment (dividends or rent, plus capital gains) is going to be more than the interest rate.

The other risk is losing someone else's money. If you borrow $100 000 for an investment and the value of that investment falls to $80 000 and you are forced to sell, then you've lost $20 000 of the bank's money (although you haven't actually lost any money unless you sell). But if you do need to sell, you will still owe them $100 000. (See later in this step for information on the dreaded margin calls.)

As so many borrowing strategies tend to involve negative gearing, people considering gearing generally need to have an income that can fund the annual income losses. If you have an investment property that is losing $10 000 a year before tax (but hopefully appreciating in value by at least twice that), then you need to be able to fund those losses on a monthly basis.

Gen X: we've got the time and the money, honey

Older Baby Boomers have got the money, but they don't have the time. A strategy involving significant gearing is not something that is best started at 55 or 60, even if you're still earning a reasonable salary, because of the danger gearing can pose to what you have spent your life working towards. Those approaching retirement would generally be better off salary sacrificing into super and making the most of superannuation rules. Younger Boomers don't necessarily fall into this category.

You're never too young to start. But while Generation Y certainly has the time, they don't have the money (income) yet. As a broad generalisation, they're still coping with mobile phone and credit card debt and are a long way from reaching the peak of their careers and salaries. Generally, Gen Ys are learning how to save their still relatively small wages. However, older Gen Ys might have reached a stage where they should consider gearing.

That leaves Generation X. We've got the time and the money. As we are aged in our 30s and early 40s, we have approximately 15 years, and up to 35 years, until the current retirement age of 65. The eldest are entering their peak earning period, during our mid to late 40s. The youngest of Gen X will be starting to rise up the corporate ladder and the eldest of us are probably there. The stats say that this period of a working person's life is when they experience rapidly accelerating wages.

This is why Generation X can and should *consider* geared investment programs. It's not right for everyone. *But if gearing is appropriate for a generation, then it's Generation X.*

Shifting up a gear

Before *Debt Man Walking* goes any further, I'll cover the different gearing strategies—what they mean and where they might be appropriate.

This might seem as obvious as the sighting of a boob job on *Baywatch*, but there are three different types of gearing—positive, negative and neutral. They are differentiated by the after-tax cost of the investment (or the portfolio).

Clearly, in order for something to be positively, negatively or neutrally geared there must be an element of borrowing. (Hey! Was that Pamela Anderson?)

Positive gearing

A positively geared investment is one where the income is higher than the costs of the investment (predominantly interest, but it must include all other costs). This can happen in a number of ways:

- The income (rent, dividends and occasionally your tax refund) from the investment itself can be higher than the interest cost of the loan.

- Only a small amount (say, 50 per cent) was borrowed for the investment and, therefore, the interest costs were lower.

- The income from the investment might rise to the point where it exceeds the interest costs.

- Interest rates may fall so that the interest costs are lower than the income.

As an example, let's assume David has made a $200000 investment in shares. Interest rates are 9 per cent and he is receiving dividends of 7 per cent.

When David bought the investment, he used $100000 of his own savings and borrowed $100000. His dividends total $14000. The interest on the $100000 loan will be $9000. That leaves a positive income of $5000 a year.

In this instance, even if David borrowed $140000 of his initial investment, he would still be positively geared. The interest component would then be $12600, which would still leave him $1400 a year ahead of his $14000 income.

Assuming this is David's only investment (and if we assume that franking credits have already been included in the case of franked dividends), he would have to add the income from this investment to his other ordinary income and pay tax on it.

Positive gearing is more appropriate for those with lower incomes, or those wanting a passive income (see step 2) to supplement their other income.

Negative gearing

Negative gearing is the opposite—where the costs of the investment are higher than the income received (obvious, like Tori Spelling's enhancements).

Back to David and his $200000 investment. This time, let's assume that it is a property investment. Interest rates are still 9 per cent, but he's only getting a rental yield on a property investment of 5 per cent. He has another $3000 a year in other costs (agents, fees, insurance, rates, and so on), plus he borrowed $180000 for this investment.

His total costs are now $19200 and his rental income is just $10000. Each year, he is going to have to fork out $9200 to cover the gap between his expenses and his income. David is negatively geared to the tune of $9200.

In Australia, this $9200 can be used to reduce his other income. If David earned $90000 from his regular job, he would now have to pay tax only on $80800, saving David $3818 in tax (at his marginal tax rate of 41.5 per cent). The net cost of his negative gearing is now $5382 ($9200 minus $3818). (We've ignored property depreciation, for simplicity's sake, here. See step 2 for more details.)

Negative gearing is more appropriate for higher-income earners, or for younger people who either don't spend their full income or are prepared to sacrifice a portion of it for longer-term gain.

Neutral gearing

No investment is ever perfectly neutrally geared. It would be sheer fluke if the income from an investment exactly matched the expense to the cent (like Danny and Sandy—John Travolta and Olivia Newton-John—meeting on holidays and ending up at the same American high school in *Grease* when Sandy's family change their plans).

Neutral gearing describes a rough balance. In general, an investment that is within $1000 of being cost neutral could be considered neutrally geared. Bigger investors might feel that a $2 million investment is neutrally geared if it's within, say, $10000 or $15000 of being square. It's a relative thing.

Neutrally geared investments can move to positive or negative depending on interest rates and investment income. If your interest cost suddenly falls, a neutrally geared investment may suddenly become positively geared. If rates rise, it could become negatively geared.

Even though there is no net income coming from a neutrally geared investment, the profits will hopefully come from the asset itself appreciating.

Neutral gearing can be appropriate for anyone who doesn't need income from their investments, but wants to have control of a larger amount of assets to help them build longer-term growth.

Gearing: it's not just about property

The first thing that comes to mind about Arnold Schwarzenegger is his monosyllabic character in *The Terminator*. But, as Arnie likes to remind people, he is so much more versatile than that. He played *many* one-word-sentence characters in films such as *Conan the Barbarian*, *Total Recall* and *The Running Man*. Plus, he is also a legendary body builder. And nowadays, he's The Governator—the politician in charge of America's most American state, California.

Australians understand borrowing when it comes to investment property. The vast majority who buy property do so with a loan. Borrowing and negative gearing for property to maximise the tax benefits is almost an expectation. But, as Arnie is not just about *The Terminator*, gearing is not just about negatively geared property.

What is far less well understood is that gearing—and negative gearing—is equally applicable to share-based investment strategies. The same rules apply even if the processes are a little different.

Investment loans are usually secured against the asset that was purchased, or other assets, such as the investor's home. In the case of property, the house or unit will be held by the bank as security. If the investor fails to maintain the loan, the lender can sell the house to get back the money they're owed.

When it comes to buying shares, borrowed money will generally come from a margin loan, a line of credit against the home, or a combination of both. With a line of credit, the lender has the security of a mortgage against the investor's home. With a margin loan, their security is generally restricted to the shares owned. The lender holds the right to sell the shares to pay down the loan if the shares fall in value.

THE DREADED MARGIN CALL

For the biggest companies, known as blue chips, a lender might lend up to 70 or 75 per cent of the value of the portfolio. For example, with a $100 000 portfolio of blue chip shares, the bank might lend $70 000. The bank might allow a 5 per cent buffer (to 75 per cent).

If the value of the shares fall to $90 000, the $70 000 loan will now be 77.78 per cent of the value of the portfolio. This would trigger a margin call from the bank to the investor. The investor will then usually have 24 hours to restore the loan to 70 per cent. There are four options:

1   put in cash to pay down the loan

2   sell some shares

3   add new shares as security for the portfolio

4   leave it to the bank, which will sell some shares.

In this example, the investor could contribute $7000 cash to pay down the loan to $63 000, which is 70 per cent of $90 000. If the investor had another $10 000 of shares to add to the portfolio, the shares offered as security would again be up to $100 000.

If the investor didn't have cash, she would need to sell shares. If she sold approximately $24 000 worth, her loan would reduce to $46 000. The portfolio is now worth $66 000, and with a loan of $46 000 there is a lending ratio of 69.7 per cent ($46 000 ÷ $66 000). If the lender was forced to sell, this is what it would do. A combination of putting in extra cash or shares and selling shares is also possible.

If you are forced to sell shares to meet a margin call, you are almost inevitably selling shares that have fallen, therefore taking losses (or taking reduced gains). For that reason, it is usually better to add cash to your margin facility, if you have some available.

Don't get caught with your pants down (like former PM Malcolm Fraser did in 1986 in a seedy Memphis hotel) when it comes to gearing with margin loans. The best defence against a margin call is not to be geared too highly. For those starting out, it can be best to use a leverage ratio of 50 per cent, or even less. If you had $50 000 of your money and $50 000 of a margin loan, your $100 000 portfolio would have to fall in value to about $66 500 (assuming a 75 per cent leverage ratio) before you got hit with a margin call.

Bob the (investment portfolio) Builder

Now let's have a look at the power that leverage can bring to an investment portfolio, with a portfolio that can be built with leverage into both shares and property. While the following portfolio starts with a share purchase, it could just as easily start with property. And even though it is starting with a significant first-up investment, you could start with whatever amount makes you feel comfortable with (which may not include gearing at all, although Gen Xers heeding Debt Man's advice should consider gearing with time).

One way of controlling risk on investment debt is to build leverage over time. Start with small debt amounts that you are comfortable with. If you were to make your first investment today, it might take a couple of years to get used to the impact on your cash flow, to build some equity in that investment and to become comfortable with the first load of debt.

Over time, hopefully, two things happen. The first is that there will be some capital growth in the value of your investment. The second is that the income (rents or dividends) will rise.

Assuming there is modest growth in both, you might want to purchase a second major investment in a few years. Then you'll have two investments appreciating in value and growing in income each year. A few years later still, with further growth, you may be able to purchase a third. And so on.

Let's introduce Greg Gearer. Greg is 38 and has accumulated $100 000 over the last 10 years. He wants to massively reduce his working hours at about age 56, then coast through until he turns 60, when he can access his superannuation. Considering these goals, he has decided he wants to invest aggressively. (To find out how Greg might have $100 000 to begin this investment, see step 8, which covers the different ways people can go about achieving big dream savings/investment sums.)

Greg decides to buy a geared share investment portfolio as his first investment. He'll spend a few years getting used to how that impacts on his cash flow. In year five, Greg will buy an investment property. Then every two years after that, Greg will alternate between buying a geared share portfolio and an investment property.

Where will this lead Greg? We'll work through the numbers in tables 6.4 and 6.5. But let's start with a few assumptions:

◉ total returns average 12 per cent a year—5 per cent income and 7 per cent capital growth

◉ our investor starts with $100 000 savings for the first investment

- the first investment made is a share portfolio worth $300 000 (in year one), using his savings and $200 000 of debt
- in year five, he buys an investment property worth $393 200. Then he alternates between buying shares and property every two years until year 13
- from year five, he borrows the entire investment, plus purchase costs
- purchase costs (stamp duty, conveyancing, brokerage, and so on) for properties are 5 per cent, and 1 per cent for shares (although that's being a little unfair to property)
- the loans are interest only at 8 per cent.

Table 6.4: building an investment portfolio

	Year 1 $	Year 5 $	Year 7 $	Year 9 $	Year 11 $	Year 13 $
Purchase price						
Shares	300 000	393 200	450 200	515 500	590 100	675 700
Property		393 200	450 200	515 500	590 100	675 700
Shares			450 200	515 500	590 100	675 700
Property				515 500	590 100	675 700
Shares					590 100	675 700
Property						675 700
Total asset value	300 000	786 400	1 350 600	2 062 000	2 950 500	4 054 200

Table 6.5: debt costs and cash flow for a growing portfolio

	Year 1 $	Year 5 $	Year 7 $	Year 9 $	Year 11 $	Year 13 $
New debt	200 000	412 900	454 700	541 300	596 000	709 500
Total debt	200 000	612 900	1 067 600	1 608 900	2 204 900	2 914 400
Interest costs @ 8%	16 000	49 000	85 400	128 700	176 400	233 200
Income	15 000	39 300	67 500	103 100	147 500	202 700
Cash flow	**−1000**	**−9700**	**−17 900**	**−25 600**	**−28 900**	**−30 500**

By year 13, Greg will have:

- three share parcels and three properties worth $4054200
- total debt of $2914400
- an interest bill of $233200 a year
- the income from rent and dividends of $202700
- a portfolio that is negatively geared to the tune of $30500
- a net worth from these investments of $1140000
- a net after-tax cost of the portfolio of approximately $16300 (if he was in the top tax bracket).

Around year 12, Greg became a 'millionaire' from these investments alone. But look at what happens if he stops purchasing assets right there and just allows the power of compounding to do its thing (see step 2). In another 10 years (at year 23), Greg's assets would be worth approximately $7.975 million, he would have a net worth of $5.06 million and he'd have a positive income of $165500 a year. And things only improve from there.

Obviously, it's not that simple and risk free, or we'd all be squillionaires. Property and shares can, of course, go backwards in value in some years. (And our example doesn't take into account insidious inflation (see step 2). The value of $5.45 million in year 23 is the equivalent of $2.84 million now, assuming 3 per cent inflation.) But don't get disheartened, we are talking about creating wealth. And the alternative is putting it into a bank account, which I showed in step 2 was not really an alternative at all.

But when gearing is introduced into an investment strategy, it automatically begins to introduce bigger numbers into the equation.

Maximising investment debt

If you had to have $500000 of debt, where's the best place to have it? Clearly, in the great debt category.

So, if you own two big assets—a home and an investment property, or a home and a share portfolio—the most tax-effective way to hold that debt would be to have the entire $500 000 against the investments.

If you had an interest-only loan for that $500 000 at 8 per cent on your home, it would cost you $40 000 a year to service. But if the debt was for an investment, it would cost as little as $21 400 after tax (for those on the highest tax rate in Australia in 2008).

But you can't just choose where your debt is, just like you can't choose that you'll be having dinner tonight with Val Kilmer or Kelly LeBrock. When it comes to tax, the tax deductibility of a debt is related to the purpose of the loan. You can't just declare your home loan to be an investment loan and start claiming a tax deduction for it. For the same reason, you can't buy items like cars against your investment property and claim them as a tax deduction.

It does mean that you should put thought into how your

STRUCTURED INVESTMENT PRODUCTS

The amount of control you exert over your investments is your decision. Direct property investments can be quite time consuming from a management perspective, particularly when you're purchasing the asset and if there are problems along the way. Real estate agents can make some of those decisions for you. Running your own share portfolio can be easy, if you take advice from a stockbroker, or absorbing, if you are going to do it yourself. Managed funds are generally less time consuming. You need to monitor the fund manager, but you don't have to make the individual investment decisions.

If you want to invest, want to do so with gearing, but don't have the time to monitor your investments, there are a number of buy and hold investment opportunities available. One such style of structured investment is the range of capital protected products offered by large and niche financial service providers (usually available through financial advisers), usually in the lead up to June and December. See step 7 for an explanation of how capital-protected products operate.

There are many advantages to this style of invest-ment, including the diversification of funds available within them. Another advantage is that you don't need savings to begin investing. You need cash flow, which a steady job provides. This is one style of investment I was talking about in 'The X-Flips: don't save to invest. Invest to save!' in step 2.

debt is taken out, particularly your okay debt and great debt. There are ways to minimise the debt against your home and maximise your investment debt (see example in box on next page). And sometimes opportunities arise that allow you to pay down dumb debt or okay debt and increase your investment great debt.

CLIENT CASE STUDY

Some clients of mine came to see me for some financial advice. They were doing well financially. They'd recently had a baby, opened a new business and were looking to upgrade their home. We'd sifted through and found where their debt was.

They weren't struggling for money. They just weren't properly using what they had. They had no dumb debt, a little okay debt (home mortgage) and a little bit of great debt (against an investment property). But they were a perfect example of how, by rearranging their debt structure, they could save themselves about $5000 every year.

Issue one: they had about $40 000 cash sitting in the offset account on their investment property. Issue two: when they started their business, they had used their own savings of $70 000. Meanwhile, they had a home loan of about $160 000.

What was wrong? From a tax perspective, their debt could be structured better:

⦿ The spare cash in the offset account of the investment property would be far more valuable sitting in an offset account against their home loan (because investment debt is a tax deduction).

⦿ They should have used debt to put into their business instead of their own cash (a line of credit against their home, perhaps).

In total, they could have used both sums to pay down their home loan (by $110 000), for which they can't get a tax deduction. This would have reduced the interest payments on their home mortgage by around $10 000 a year.

Their overall debt position would not have changed—they would still owe the same amount of money. But had they seen an accountant or financial adviser earlier, these problems would not have arisen. As it stands, they can now only right some of the wrongs. See step 7 for the value of having a team of financial professionals to help.

We'll take a further look at the concept of debt recycling in the X-Flips at the end of this chapter.

Know where your brakes are

With all gearing strategies, it is important to know your limits. Because your gains and losses can be magnified, geared investments need to be monitored more closely than other investments.

Same went with break dancing in the 1980s. I knew my limits. I couldn't do headstands. My version of the helicopter was appalling. Performing the worm would only cause me pain. My best break dancing move was from the couch watching the *Teenage Mutant Ninja Turtles*.

The cost of your borrowings also needs to be monitored more closely. Interest rates can always increase. You need to know how your investment plan will cope if interest rates rise considerably.

You also need to consider what you'll do if the income falls. Rents and dividends from individual investments will occasionally fall. It's rarer (although possible in some bear markets) that dividends will fall from a diversified portfolio. But with properties, it is possible that in some years you will have to go without rent for a month or two. When there are many properties on the market and vacancy rates are high, rents can fall.

If you're playing with debt, you need to know your limits and be prepared to act decisively if losses, or costs, start mounting and head beyond your control.

Further, anyone considering a gearing strategy, particularly one that includes margin lending, should keep a stash of cash to cope with unforeseen cash crunches, such as unexpected margin calls or the inevitable breakdown of appliances in an investment property.

Little things...

'From Little Things, Big Things Grow' was a song by Paul Kelly.

A gearing strategy doesn't have to start out with huge loans. Depending on the investment and where you're going to source the loan, you can start with investment debt of as little as a few thousand dollars.

Some margin loan providers insist on a minimum loan of $20 000, but if you start a geared savings plan (see the box on p. 149), also referred to as instalment gearing, you might be able to start with a smaller amount.

Because direct residential property is such a big individual investment, the only way to keep your borrowings down is to buy cheaper places, save a bigger deposit, or buy the property with others.

There are other methods to control your debt levels:

- Gear conservatively. If using margin loans with shares or managed funds, start with an initial gearing level of between 30 and 60 per cent. A gearing rate of no more than 50 per cent will minimise the chance of getting a margin call.

- Add some savings each year. If you start with a portfolio of $50 000 cash and $50 000 borrowings, perhaps you could add another $20 000 from both sources in the second year.

- If you have an existing portfolio that you would like to gear, you could start small. If you had, say, $60 000 in shares, you might consider a margin loan (or line of credit) to buy another $40 000 or $50 000 worth over a period of six months.

Geared savings plans

One popular way of building a bigger investment portfolio is by way of a geared savings plan. Most of the major lenders offer this opportunity, or look for margin loans in the investment section on <www.infochoice.com.au>.

For example, you might have $20 000 saved and want to start investing and are interested in gearing. You could borrow $20 000 from a margin lender to have an initial amount of $40 000 to invest, generally in managed funds or direct shares.

The geared savings aspect of this is if you then add, for instance, $1000 a month to your investment and get the bank to match that with another $1000. At the end of the first year, you and the bank will have put $64 000 into the investment, which will have been working for you for the whole year. The alternative—putting in your own $20 000, plus $1000 a month—would have only $32 000 growing for you for the year. This also allows the investor to take advantage of dollar-cost averaging (see step 4).

Figure 6.1 shows the difference between the performance of a geared and a non-geared portfolio, using the contribution figures from above. If we assume the investment is made for 15 years, borrowing costs are 10.5 per cent and the total returns are 10 per cent (5 per cent income and 5 per cent growth), then the investor with the geared savings plan will have a net investment at the end of more than $710000, while the non-geared investor would have a return of a little over $455000. In this case, with a relatively higher interest rate being charged, the investor is still ahead by $255000 or 56 per cent.

Figure 6.1: the extra oomph of a geared savings plan

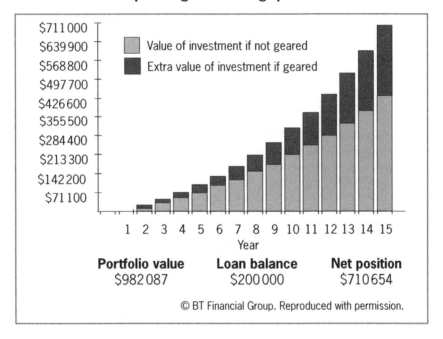

Portfolio value	Loan balance	Net position
$982087	$200000	$710654

© BT Financial Group. Reproduced with permission.

The X-Flips:
Going green—recycling your debt

In your investment life, there may occasionally be opportunities to recycle some debt—that is, effectively swap debt for which you can't claim a tax deduction for debt for which you can claim a deduction.

Consider the following example. A couple has a home worth $600000 that has a $150000 mortgage. They have a share portfolio worth $400000 with a $200 000 margin loan (that is, they have $200 000 of equity). Clearly, it would be more tax effective if the home loan debt was lower and, instead, all debt was for investment purposes. It can be done. Here's how:

◉ sell the share portfolio

◉ pay off the home loan

◉ keep some money aside to pay any capital gains tax

◉ get a line-of-credit loan against the home

◉ use money from the line-of-credit to buy back the investment portfolio (including use of the margin loan facility).

(Obviously, the devil is in the detail, so don't embark on this course without seeking advice from a financial adviser and/or qualified accountant.)

After the transactions have taken place, the couple might again have a margin loan of $200 000 and debt against the home of $170 000 (assuming a CGT liability of $20 000). Previously, only $200 000 of debt was tax deductible. Now all $370 000 of the couple's debt is deductible.

If the interest rate for the margin loan is 10 per cent and the home loan is 8.2 per cent, annual interest payments have risen from $32 300 to $33 940. However, assuming a 41.5 per cent marginal tax rate, the tax deduction would have increased from $8300 (on the $200 000 margin loan) to nearly $14 100 (on the combined $370 000 loans).

The real cost of this strategy is capital gains tax—you'll probably end up paying some. But, considering the tax deductibility of the debt, it could be something that quickly pays for itself (possibly within a year or two).

The same strategy can also work well for selling investment properties that have developed equity. However, the costs of getting into and out of property—Australia's high rates of stamp duty—can take some of the potential benefits out of this.

This won't make sense in every situation. It will depend on the couple's individual tax positions, how much capital gains tax they have to pay and how their debt is structured.

Step 6 for Gen X

The Daleks, of *Doctor Who* fame, are inherently evil. Their robotic catchcry 'EX-TER-MI-NATE!' isn't about ridding the galaxy of rats and cockroaches, but we humans and other harmless alien life forms.

Not all debt is evil like the Daleks. Some of it is. Some debt is a necessary part of life (home loans, work car loans). And some debt can actually be beneficial to your wealth creation plans.

Almost everyone employs some debt in their life. Many use borrowing to buy a lifestyle they could not afford with their regular salary, using credit cards and personal loans to buy 'stuff'. This is dumb debt.

Gearing takes investing to a different level. The rewards to patient investors can be multiplied. But if you don't have time to ride out the sometimes short-term pain and you therefore need to sell when the markets are down, the losses can also be magnified.

It's not suitable for everyone. Some of the questions investors should ask themselves before raising investment risks through gearing include:

- Does your risk profile suggest you are a suitable candidate (see step 3)?
- Do you have a long enough investment time frame (a minimum of seven years)?
- Do you have the cash flow to service the debt if the investment income falls?
- How would you feel if markets turned against you and you lost all your equity, and possibly more, because you had to sell at a bad time?

In summary, when it comes to debt, *Debt Man Walking* is about the following:

- Debt deserves respect, but it is not something to be feared.
- If there is a generation for whom investment borrowing is most suitable, it's Generation X.
- Geared investment strategies require more time and more money.
- More than other generations, Gen X has the time and money—we've got a couple of decades before we will retire and we're approaching the peak earnings of our working lives.

step 7

Q: Which American politician was responsible for the following quote: 'Government's view of the economy could be summed up in a few short phrases: if it moves, tax it; if it keeps moving, regulate it; and if it stops moving, subsidise it.'?

A: Former US President Ronald Reagan

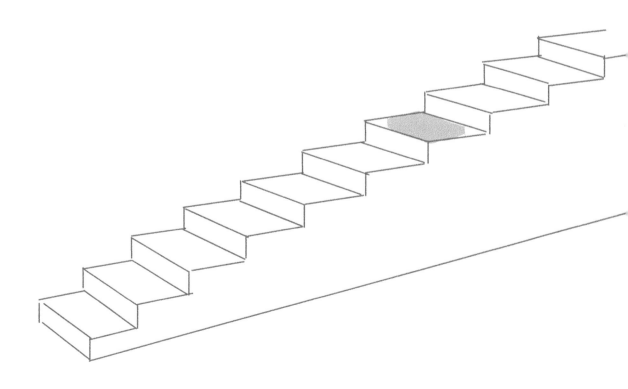

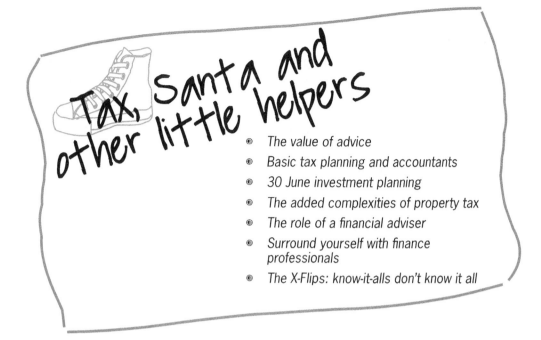

Tax, Santa and other little helpers

- The value of advice
- Basic tax planning and accountants
- 30 June investment planning
- The added complexities of property tax
- The role of a financial adviser
- Surround yourself with finance professionals
- The X-Flips: know-it-alls don't know it all

Answer the following question: 'When it comes to doing my own tax return, I would rather …

(a) visit the dentist and have two teeth pulled *without* anaesthetic.'

(b) listen to a two-hour speech from Bob Geldof on third-world debt.'

(c) watch a day's re-runs of Jon English in *All Together Now.'*

(d) sit in the front row of a Bros concert (supported by Rick Astley).'

(e) resit my final exams.'

(f) go through puberty again.'

(g) all of the above. Just promise me I won't have to do my tax!'

I don't like doing my own tax return either. So I don't. I pay someone else to do it. I don't know if my guy's a genius or not. But as far as I'm concerned, he's Santa Claus in July. If only he wasn't a Tigers supporter …

When it comes to your personal finances, your ability to plan is limited only by how much time you are prepared to put into it or how much you are prepared to pay professionals to help you. Sometimes it is as simple as just learning a few good habits. Sometimes it requires you to pay for advice—advice that could save you many times what you pay that professional. Many habits will save you a dollar or two every day. Others will save you thousands of dollars in a one-off hit.

The importance of tax to getting the most out of your investments cannot be overstated. And it's even more important where gearing strategies are involved. Proper tax planning can turn a negatively geared investment into a positively geared one. It can minimise capital gains tax. While tax should never be *the* reason to invest, it often provides a very important part of an investment's return. The after-tax outcome of any investment is the most important result, so minimising the tax you pay overall will help determine how successful your investment strategy is.

Valuing advice

When I first moved to Melbourne to work as a journalist, a good mate, Glenn Connley, put me on to his accountant. 'Dale's really good with journalists', The Con said.

So I saw Dale. I had two years' worth of tax returns to do and Dale got a tax return for me of $1000 more than I would have received had I done it myself. For a cost of $120 ($60 for each year) and two hours of my time, I'd made more than $1000. That's a phenomenal return.

Dale also told me what journalists could legitimately claim as tax deductions. He told me of the importance of keeping receipts (in a shoebox, which I've done ever since). If I wasn't sure whether I could claim something or not, he told me to put it in the shoebox and we'd go through the receipts each year.

Meeting Dale when I was 22 taught me two things. One, planning for tax can be really simple. Two, paying quality professionals for good advice can pay multiples of what their time costs you.

I can't wait to see Dale every year. I book my appointment months in advance and see him early (late July). I've referred him to two or three dozen mates over the years.

I just wish the lesson that I learnt with Dale had sunk in more deeply. While I was now getting sound tax advice, I should have widened the lesson I learned—paying quality professionals for advice—to other aspects of my life. I could have made and saved myself loads of money elsewhere also.

Yahoo Serious

There's another reason to value advice. You don't know everything. You're no *Young Einstein*. You need to accept that. It was hard, but I have.

You don't need to know everything. I have absolutely no interest in learning how to give a proper Thai massage. I'm perfectly happy to pay someone who already knows how to do it to give me one. Plus, learning how to do Thai massage wouldn't help *me* get a massage, would it?

Outsource those parts of your life about which it's not worth learning, to professionals who can do it in their sleep. They can do it in one-tenth or one-hundredth the time it will take you to do it. They'll do it better. And, ultimately, they'll do it cheaper. Why spend 10 hours to get back $500 on your tax when paying someone $200 will get you back $2000?

Do you self-diagnose your own illnesses? The internet has made that easier. But if you've got bronchitis, you're still off to go to the doctor to get a prescription filled.

You need to find professionals you're comfortable with and trust. They need to earn that trust and then they need to continue to earn it. Professional relationships can last decades. But if you don't feel you're getting value any longer, or standards are slipping, then you need to find a new professional to help you.

> You need to find professionals you're comfortable with and trust. They need to earn that trust and then they need to continue to earn it.

Most senior accountants in larger firms don't do their own taxes. True! They'll pay one of their senior staff to do it. They're better off paying one of their staff $150 an hour to do the job for two hours, while they spend two hours trying to land a client that might earn them or their firm $2000.

Tax planning 101

Book-keeping and filing doesn't have to be a chore. Basic tax planning comes down to a few good filing habits. Setting up a very basic system takes minutes. Feeding it every now and then takes seconds. Once a year, a few days before you see your accountant, you go through your files for an hour or two.

Filing for tax can be made so easy, so idiot proof, that even Frank Spencer *(Some Mothers Do 'Ave 'Em)* could do it without completely screwing it up.

Accountants—boring work, brilliant impact

They make movies and TV shows about police, firemen, journalists, lawyers, chefs, doctors, nurses, vets. But nothing about accountants. I wonder why?

DEMARCATION: ACCOUNTANTS, FINANCIAL ADVISERS AND INVESTMENT ADVICE

It is important to know that accountants are not allowed to give investment advice unless they have proper qualifications. In an attempt to protect consumers, Australian governments have separated tax and investment advice between accountants and financial advisers.

This can be a very fine line. Accountants can, for example, advise on setting up self-managed super funds (SMSFs; see step 10) and how investments are taxed within that structure. But they can't recommend that their client buy 'these shares', or 'that property trust', unless they also have qualifications to provide financial advice.

If you believe that your accountant is offering you investment advice, as opposed to tax advice, ask them if they are licensed to provide financial advice. Advisers need to be licensed with the Australian Securities & Investments Commission (unlike the property investment industry, which is unregulated). They also need to provide you with a financial services guide, which sets out the basics of how they operate, how they are remunerated and what action to take if you need to file a complaint.

Everyone who has a job *should* have an accountant. But anyone serious about investing *must* have one. Investing, particularly property investment, has some unusual tax rules that are far from obvious. Accountants can save you a fortune.

But let's take a step back. If you don't have an accountant, you might be surprised to find what items you can claim as part of your job. You may be throwing away hundreds, if not thousands, of dollars a year.

Ask around some of the older hands in your workplace or office, or older people in your industry. Do they know an accountant who deals specifically in your area? Check with your professional association or your union. Unions, in particular, tend to have lists of friendly professionals they will recommend to their members.

Tax tool one: the shoebox

An efficient, simple household tax system can be as little as two basic tools.

Get a shoebox that's wide enough to fit A4 pieces of paper. Leave it somewhere obvious—your study, on a bookshelf, wherever you keep all your bills.

Remember everything that your accountant said you could claim for your industry or for your investments. Every time you buy one of those items, put the receipt in the shoebox. Every time you get a statement about your investments (from your adviser, stockbroker, property agent, company dividend cheque, and so on), put it in the shoebox. As soon as you receive a statement about your investment loans (margin lender, line of credit, property loan), ditto.

Always read the statements as they come in. Make sure there are no obvious mistakes or charges that you shouldn't be paying. Apart from that, you shouldn't need to look in the shoebox until a few days before you see your accountant each year.

EXPENSES FOR ALL TO CLAIM

While different industries will have their own separate lists of what can and can't be claimed, there are some things that almost everyone can claim.

These include tax deductible donations, income protection insurance (see step 9), medical expenses over $1500 a year, your accounting fees, your financial adviser fees (in most cases where you pay the adviser directly), work-related clothing, work-related publications and home-office expenses.

For a list of specific items for different industry employment groups, look for 'your industry type', then 'for individuals' on the ATO's website at <www.ato.gov.au>.

Tax tool two: files and folders

The second simple tool is for longer-term investment documents—buy some lever-arch folders (and a hole-punch).

For each individual investment you make, you need to file documents that aren't necessarily related to that year's tax. For property, this will include your original purchase contract, loan documents, real estate agent agreements, tenancy agreements, insurance agreements, and so on. For shares, it will include all of your contract notes for purchase and sale, CHESS holding statements and margin loan agreements.

You might need to keep these files forever. For potential audit purposes, these files need to be kept for five years after an asset is sold.

Once you have bought and labelled the files, punching holes in the pages and filing them takes only a few seconds.

Partner up—income splitting

Having a partner has a use other than being a permanent date for Friday and Saturday nights. Turns out that 'two is better than one' has some investment and tax advantages as well.

If you're in a long-term relationship or married, there are often several opportunities to plan your tax better than single people can on their own. Sorry, but here's another few reasons that all you Bridget Joneses and Sam Malones (Ted Danson's character in *Cheers*) should think about settling down. (The upside of being single is that you don't have to share the spoils.)

There are several ways that having a partner can help the 'two-becomes-one' unit when it comes to finances:

- Those with businesses might be able to employ their husbands or wives to be involved in the business and more evenly distribute income.

- The ability to choose who holds an asset initially can help reduce tax during the holding of an investment, or reduce capital gains tax when it is sold.

- Positively geared investments can be put into the name of the lower income earner for the best tax result.

- Negatively geared income can be put in the name of the higher income earner (again, for tax).

These opportunities can include something as simple as keeping the bank account that earns a high interest rate in the name of the lower-earning partner and putting negatively geared properties in the name of the higher-earning spouse, or the spouse who will continue to work or earn the most money during the period that you are having children.

On any individual investment, or income stream, these choices can help save a couple, or a family, thousands of dollars a year.

Preparing for 30 June

What's so special about 30 June? It's really not much more than a short, dark day in the middle of winter. But it's the day that the Australian Tax Office rules off its books.

Last-minute spending to save money on tax can be smart in a number of ways. If you spend money on tax-deductible items in June, you can claim it back in July. If you buy it in July, you have to wait a full 12 months, until the following financial year, to claim it back again. This sort of tax-related spending—depending on your industry—might include a briefcase, a new set of overalls, notepads and pens, shirts, magazine subscriptions, sunglasses and sun protection. When it comes to investment, there are much broader opportunities.

In the lead up to May and June each year, a flood of investment opportunities come to market. The last day of June has become an opportunity to get people's attention when they are focused on tax. It is a marketing opportunity (like Valentine's Day, Christmas or Easter) for an industry to market to interested taxpayers.

Taxpayers might be looking to avoid paying income tax or to save a capital gain, or simply trying to get a positive start for the new financial year.

But be warned: no 30 June investment decision should be made based on getting a tax deduction alone. It's imperative that all opportunities first stack up as investments in their own right. Only then should you consider the tax consequences.

Capital-protected investments

One range of investment opportunities offered in the lead up to 30 June is capital-protected investments (also discussed in step 6), which are a type of structured financial product.

Capital-protected products are offered by the major banks and fund managers, as well as plenty of niche providers. The entire initial investment sum is usually borrowed from the provider. The money is managed to ensure that, at worst, there is enough money to pay back the initial amount of money borrowed from the provider, usually over a term of approximately seven years. If the investment rises steadily, the investor will get the benefit of most of the upside.

If you borrow $100 000, the lender wants to ensure that there is $100 000 left to repay the loan at term (most commonly seven years). There is obviously some self-interest in that on the part of the lender. But the protection mechanisms are based on formulas that ensure that if investment markets fail to perform, you won't be left having to repay the initial loan.

Capital-protected investments are suitable for different types of investors, including investors:

◉ with no savings, but with cash flow to service the loan

◉ looking for tax-deductible interest payments

◉ wanting a geared investment, but who don't have the inclination to constantly monitor their investment

◉ who would like to borrow to invest, but fear losing someone else's money.

CAPITAL PROTECTION MECHANISM There are essentially two kinds of protection used to ensure that there is enough money to repay the initial sum borrowed. These are known as 'bond and call' and 'threshold management'.

A bond and call protection mechanism sees the majority of the money (say 70 to 85 per cent) put into an interest-bearing investment. That portion grows with interest to get back to 100 per cent. The remaining money (15 to 30 per cent) is used to buy a call option, which gives leverage into the underlying investment, usually a stock market index.

Then there is 'constant portfolio protection insurance' (CPPI) or 'threshold management'. With CPPI, most of the money (70 to 85 per cent) is initially put into the underlying investment. If the underlying investment falls, money is shifted into cash, where interest rates can be accurately assessed to ensure that the funds get back to the original borrowed amount.

As you'd expect, there is a cost to this protection. Due to the way the protection mechanisms work, investors in effect give up some of the upside as part of the cost of the protection. The amount of the upside that may be lost to protection will vary depending on the performance of investment markets during the term. However, in an investment market that doubled over the course of a seven-year period, the cost of the protection might be around 20 per cent. That is, if the underlying investment (market or managed fund) rises from $100 000 to $200 000, the capital protected investor could expect to see their investment grow to about $180 000.

Managed investment schemes

The best-known 30 June investments are managed investment schemes (MIS). Managed investment schemes can, technically, be any managed investment. But for the purposes of *Debt Man Walking*, they are the agricultural-style MISs. They can be legitimate and profitable investments, but they became famous in the 1990s for dubious 'opportunities' that included emus, ostriches, films and wine. The actual investments have become a little more mainstream with time.

The concern with these products is that investors can be enticed by the tax deduction rather than the underlying investment. Invest $50000 in an MIS and receive a $50000 tax deduction (or thereabouts — Australia's GST comes into play a little and changes the numbers marginally.) This would reduce a $120000 income to $70000, saving you in the vicinity of $20000 in tax. The investor also usually borrows the initial capital. So the investor will also be claiming a tax deduction on the interest.

Investments should never be solely about tax. And 30 June opportunities are no different. No amount of tax deductions is worth an investment that is a complete dud from the beginning. If you invest $50000

DEBT MAN'S MIS WARNING: A TAX DEDUCTION ISN'T AN INVESTMENT

I have traditionally been sceptical of MIS investments. It's not that they are necessarily bad investments (although more than their fair share are dubious). But investors too often get drawn in by the tax deductions, rather than a solid underlying business case of an industry that is likely to grow over time. (And that is partly why the Australian government has moved to limit them.)

It is easy to understand the case for investing in Australian banks, retailers, insurers or miners, for example. People need these services and always will. The best MIS investments I have seen are ones where there is a clearly identifiable demand for the investment. Was there a clear and rising demand for ostrich-skin handbags?

It is easier to understand the demand for some food and timber products. The world needs more food. It needs more wood to produce paper and other products. But water resources are becoming scarce.

Speaking of liquid... MIS investments are not. Once you've invested, you're generally in it for the life of the investment. They are very hard to exit if your circumstances change. Some of the longer-term MIS projects run for 15 to 30 years.

I haven't seen enough MIS investments that properly reward investors for the risks they have taken on. Don't just chase the tax deduction.

and all you ever get out of it is a $20 000 tax refund cheque, you've lost $30 000. Anyone offered this style of investment should make sure that the person recommending the investment can explain to you why it is a solid investment opportunity and it makes sense to you.

Interest pre-payment

Another popular 30 June opportunity is pre-paying interest on investments. If you have a geared investment (such as a property loan, margin loan or structured product loan), you may be able to pre-pay your interest for the year ahead.

Why would you do this? If you have a $100 000 loan for an investment at an interest rate of 9 per cent, pre-paying your $9000 interest for the following year would allow you to claim a tax deduction sooner. For example, you could pay $9000 on 30 June 2009, which will cover your interest for the period from 1 July 2009 to 30 June 2010. You've paid your interest for the 2009–10 financial year in advance.

There are several reasons you may consider doing this:

⊛ You can quickly claim a tax deduction on the interest you have paid.

⊛ The lender might offer a cheap interest rate as an incentive.

⊛ You can lock in your interest rate for the year ahead.

⊛ Locking in might get you a lower interest rate in a rising rate environment.

Pre-paying interest can be a good idea. Your ability to do so will depend on having available cash (or the ability to fund it through a line-of-credit home loan) and how appealing the interest rate is.

Property tax — depreciation

Property needs special attention when it comes to tax. More so than most investments, real estate investors need accountants, because unlike many other investments where the reporting is aggregated for you (such as capital gains and income in managed funds), the paperwork and the tax implications for direct property have to be compiled by you.

You can claim obvious things like interest, insurance and agent's fees. You can claim trips to visit your property, postage and phone calls to the agent (or the tenant), the plumber to fix the leaky tap and the rates bill.

What isn't necessarily obvious is depreciation. This is the acceptance by the Tax Office that parts of your investment are losing value and will need to be replaced one day. Almost everything that goes into a property will eventually need to be replaced.

The curtains, blinds, carpets, dishwashers, light fittings, baths, showers, taps, decking, cupboards, stove, fans, toilets, mirrors, glass panelling, televisions, microwaves, swimming pools and sheds (to list just a few of the hundreds of items that the ATO allows investors to claim) all have a shelf life. The Tax Office will allow you to claim a portion of these on your tax each year—between a few per cent and 30 or 40 per cent.

A quantity surveyor can create a depreciation schedule for your investment property (usually for around $400 to $700), which will list the items that can be depreciated and for how long they can be depreciated.

And then there's the value of the house itself. For houses built after 15 September 1987, investors can claim 2.5 per cent of the cost of the bricks and mortar against their tax. That is, if it cost $150 000 to build the house, you can reduce your income by $3750 every year (2.5 per cent of $150 000) until 40 years after the home was built. If you buy a house

DISCLAIMER: DECLARING MY HAND

The next section of this book is about financial advisers. As I am a financial adviser (and I have said so through this book), I thought it would be prudent to remind you again before you continue, as I've written positive and negative things about the industry in the following pages.

After 15 years, I left full-time journalism to become a financial adviser at the end of 2006 so I could marry two things that I am passionate about. The first is the world of personal finance and the second is communication. I hoped I could help my clients in a simple and clear manner.

In regards to adviser specialisation, at the time of writing, I am a general financial adviser. I cover the three streams of financial advice (investment, superannuation and insurance). However, I have specific interests—Generation X finance and self-managed superannuation funds (SMSFs). Where my knowledge ends, I seek advice from other professionals or refer clients to specialists.

Fee-for-service or commission: I offer both. Some clients want to pay a set fee each quarter/year. Others would be worse off if I charged them an hourly fee. The choice is the client's and I try to educate them about this. See the Debt Man website for further details at <www.debtman.com.au>.

that was built 10 years ago, then you will be able to claim the 2.5 per cent for another 30 years, if you own it that long. Any capital improvements made to the property—extensions, renovations—can also be depreciated over 40 years at 2.5 per cent.

That's not where the complication ends. The deduction for the depreciated value of the home has an impact on your cost price, which will ultimately see you paying more in capital gains tax. If you bought a property for $300000, where the cost of building the home was estimated (by a quantity surveyor) to be $150000 and you claimed depreciation for 10 years, you would have claimed a total of $37500 ($150000 × 2.5% × 10 years). As you have claimed the depreciation, your cost base, for capital gains tax purposes, will have reduced to $262500 ($300000 − $37500).

Property investors must have accountants. Simple.

Money coach: your financial adviser

Good financial advisers are good money coaches. We can help you with life's financial basics, like budgeting, but our real talents will lie in getting you to understand how you can improve, or protect, your wealth. We also believe we can help you *not* to make some rookie investment errors. Our job is to help you to understand why doing something now—or, in some cases, not acting now—will pay medium- to long-term rewards.

Not everything we touch turns to gold (if it did, we wouldn't need clients). We can't control sharemarkets. We can't stop companies from going bust. We can't promise that we'll only ever make you money and will never lose you any. We can't promise that the only reason we are here is to help you (that's our primary goal, but not our only goal). If you stumble across a financial adviser that makes these sorts of promises, keep walking. Actually, run.

The aim of most financial advisers will be to make you wealthy (even rich), or help to protect your wealth. As a by-product of doing that job properly, we want you to happily pay us a fair fee that will, over time, make us rich also.

Advisers are constantly learning about what's happening in their industry and the investment world. We should know what's happening with investments—what's hot and what's not. Most importantly, we should be able to detail what an investment is about.

If nothing else, it can be worth having an adviser to whom you can pay a fee to have a professional, investment-related chat. You might want to talk to someone about the intricacies of property investment and paying for their time (as you would an accountant) should provide you with bias-free advice.

Advisers ain't advisers

The growth of the financial advice industry has been rapid and it is fast becoming specialised. Advisers are increasingly specialising in just one of the three tools of the industry (insurance, investment and superannuation).

There's no inherent problem with this, but you should know what sort of adviser you're seeing. Do they cover all three branches of financial advice? Do they specialise in one and outsource the rest?

For instance, stockbrokers are financial advisers who specialise in buying Australian shares. They might not even ask whether you have any personal risk insurance cover (see step 9). They're unlikely to care about your superannuation, unless you have a self-managed super fund (see step 10.) Specialist insurance agents will probably pass you on to someone else when it comes to your super or investments.

ADVISERS: A PROFESSION UNDER ATTACK

The financial planning industry has earned a poor reputation over the years. And in some respects, quite rightly. There are some bad eggs in the industry.

But show me an industry that doesn't have a few *Dirty Dozen*. There are criminal lawyers (that is, lawyers who are criminals, not criminal defenders), police, doctors and accountants. Some bank managers are so slimy that you wish you were dealing with Betelgeuse (Michael Keaton in the movie *Beetlejuice*) rather than the guy standing before you. Used-car salespeople didn't earn their reputation from being St John's Ambulance volunteers in their spare time.

Regulators are doing a far better job of weeding out the bad guys in the financial planning industry than they are in, say, real estate or the nation's police forces. Check the website of the Australian Securities & Investments Commission for how many advisers and stockbrokers get banned from practising every month.

Despite what parts of the media suggest, the world of financial advisers is not full of crooks. It inevitably has a few, because shonks are attracted to money like some of us are attracted to members of the opposite sex who are just a little bit bad—like Mickey Rourke in *9½ Weeks* or Sharon Stone in *Fatal Attraction*.

Many people will have several financial advisers. They might have a stockbroker to buy direct shares and see a general adviser for their insurance and super.

How can they help you?

In a perfect world, a financial adviser's role is to make sure that you've covered all your financial bases. However, 'You can lead a horse to water, but you can't make it drink'.

Some people, no matter how much information they receive, don't feel they need to worry about certain aspects of their finances, are simply not interested or have other priorities for their money. That's a client's prerogative—that's *your* prerogative.

In my opinion, our role is to make you aware of the areas of your finances that you should be covering. We do this by getting to know where you are financially, right now. We need personal and financial details to understand your financial knowledge, previous financial experiences and how much thought you have put into your finances.

This usually involves an initial consultation where we prod you with questions. It should be a pleasant chat. The details we take down tell us your story. It's just as important that you ask questions to find out about us, our skills and our experience. We need to know what you want to achieve (reward) and how desperate you are to do so (risk).

Some clients only want advice on one specific area. Others come in as a blank canvas—they don't really know how they got to where they are or how they've managed to survive thus far, like anyone who reached a really big score in Pac-Man or Space Invaders.

SALES VERSUS ADVICE
An ongoing concern in regards to the financial planning industry is about whether advisers are 'sales driven' or 'advice driven'. Is your adviser driven by trying to give you the best financial advice that he or she can? Or is his or her motivation what products he or she can sell you? This debate is being played out as the fee for service (advice) versus commission (sales) debate.

The financial planning industry grew out of the old life insurance sales industry where agents were paid by commission. The more an adviser sold, the more commission he made. The financial planning industry is in the process of evolving. There is a growing acceptance that commissions might cause a conflict of interest for many advisers; that is, the best product or advice might not always be given to a client. But there is still an acceptance that the clients who most need advice (those with the least money) might not get advice if commissions were banned, because they might not be able to afford the adviser's hourly rate.

Where's the issue? Let's assume the adviser's upfront commission is 2 per cent (with a 0.75 per cent trail) or he charges an hourly rate of $200. Furthermore, the investment will take the adviser 15 hours to implement and monitor over the course of the first year.

A client with $500 000 to invest would see her adviser paid a commission of $10 000 (plus another $3750 a year for the term of the investment). If charging a fee-for-service, the adviser would earn $3000.

Another client walks in. This one wants to invest $50 000 in the same product. The commission here would be $1000 (plus $375 a year for the term of the investment). But if the adviser were to charge an hourly fee, it would still be $3000. That's more than twice as much as the commission plus trail (in the first year), or 6 per cent of the total value of his investment.

Who is in the most need of advice? The woman with $500 000 to invest, or the young man with $50 000 to invest? They both end up paying for the advice. If you pay fee-for-service, you pay it directly. If you opt to have your adviser paid by commission, then the fee is built into the cost of the product or service. You pay a portion upfront, but you end up paying more over a longer period.

In my opinion, if there is a general rule, it is that those people with a lot of money to invest would be better off paying a fee, while those starting out will be better off with commission.

Ask your adviser about whether he offers an option. If you have a personal preference for fee-for-service, discuss it with the adviser.

Team building

Bringing on board an accountant and a financial adviser isn't the end of the team you're putting together. There are other finance professionals you should have. You might already use some of the following professionals. They each have a role to play in planning your financial future.

Lawyers

Some Gen Xers probably haven't spent any time thinking about lawyers—not since Harry Hamlin, Susan Dey, Corbin Bernsen and Jimmy Smits on *LA Law*. But you are getting to the age/stage where you need to. Wills are imperative for anyone who has made any of life's major 'M' commitments—marriage, mortgage or midgets. They are also important for anyone who has sufficient valuable assets.

Are you married? De facto? Divorced? Have you been around on that merry-go-round once before (or too many times to count, like Joan Collins)? Do you have substantial debt that you share with someone else? Have you already built equity in your home? Do you have children?

If you answered yes to any of those questions, you need a will to make sure your assets go where you want when you die. Say you had a long-term, live-in relationship with someone, but that ended three years ago. They might still be your common law husband/wife and entitled to everything. Your parents and the person that you've been dating for several years (but haven't been living with) might be entitled to nothing.

Having a will isn't a guarantee that the right assets go to the right people because people left out of the will are still entitled to challenge it. However, a lawyer can help make challenging the will harder by properly drafting the document in the first place.

At the same time, you should also talk to your lawyer about whether you should have an enduring power-of-attorney (a critical financial planning tool) and/or a testamentary trust. An enduring power of attorney ensures that someone you trust can make decisions for you when you no longer can (if you are in a coma or mentally incapacitated). A testamentary trust comes into effect when you die, which may be appropriate to help you look after those you leave behind.

Bankers/mortgage brokers

Shopping around banks for your first home loan is a thing of the past. Everyone should see a mortgage broker when they first intend to get a loan, or every few years to check that they're getting a good deal with their current bank.

Good brokers will have a number of lenders on their list that they are licensed with. Ask any prospective broker to tell you how many they have and which ones, to make sure they have a wide selection and that you've heard enough of the names.

Brokers can often get you a better deal with a lender than you could get on your own and they tend to know which lenders are doing the best deals, or have the best service.

Real estate agents

If you are getting involved in property, then you do have a choice about whether you use a real estate agent to look after your property or you do it yourself.

I strongly suggest using an agent. Tenancy laws are complex and your time is going to be better spent learning something other than those laws. Agents tend to charge between 5 and 8 per cent of the monthly rent (for residential properties), plus an upfront fee of one or two weeks' rent to have the house initially tenanted. So, for $70 to $120 a

OTHER PROFESSIONALS FOR YOUR TEAM

I see these professionals as the key professionals in your financial life. But they're not the only ones to consider.

You may also wish to consider developing relationships with other professionals, including quantity surveyors, stockbrokers, specialist life insurance advisers (if your regular financial adviser doesn't do insurance) and real estate valuers.

month, someone will collect the rent, deal with tenants, meet tradesmen at your property, enforce rent increases, chase up late rent and protect your interests if the tenant takes you to court or you need to take the tenant to court (sometimes for an extra fee).

Even if you have a trouble-free tenant, or you don't put a very high value on your time, you should still consider hiring an agent, because at the first sign of trouble, good agents know how to deal with the issues quickly and effectively.

General insurance brokers

If your household is running a house and two cars, then you may well be paying insurance of around $2000 to $2500 a year. You will probably benefit from finding a general insurance broker who deals with general insurance.

General insurance brokers can save you money (and time) because they know the best policies on the market.

The X-Flips:

Know-it-alls don't know it all

Learning can be a wonderful hobby or a great part-time job. But if learning about something isn't fun, or you just can't get enthused about it, then adopting an attitude that 'life's too short' could actually save you both time and money. (No matter how much friends and family warned me, I didn't really comprehend how much time children can take until they arrived. They've taught me a lot about how to value time.)

Whatever your job, your business or your industry, you are generally better off to 'stick to your knitting'. Learn all you can about the industry you work in (or the one you *want* to work in), so that you can make the most of the opportunities available.

Don't be stubborn when it comes to using professionals. By that, I mean:

1   Don't put off taking control of your finances because you don't know where to start and you want to learn how to do it yourself. It may take you years and plenty of rookie errors. It may be better to seek help first and learn as you go.

2   Don't think that you can do everything, or know everything, yourself. Pay professionals to help you fill your knowledge gaps.

I'm not saying you should get professionals to do everything for you. But you need to understand your limits and the value of your time.

Step 7 for Gen X

If you make money, you've got to pay tax. And if you lose money, you might be able to claim a portion of it back on your tax. Tax is a critical element of the success of your investments, because it's only what you get to keep *after tax* that really matters.

Too many people don't do tax well, because they don't plan for it. But planning for tax doesn't have to be difficult and it can save you thousands of dollars each year. It's also an imperative for investors. Consider this advice:

- Your two best advisers will be a good accountant and a good financial adviser. They can both pay for themselves 10 times over, every year.

- Develop a simple filing system. A shoebox and a few lever-arch folders can hold everything you need to take to the accountant each year.

- Feed your filing system regularly.

- Prepare for 30 June. It is a time of opportunity and both your accountant and financial adviser can help you here.

In fact, surround yourself with quality professionals:

- Lawyers can help you with important financial planning tools like wills and powers of attorney. (And *Ally McBeal* taught us that lawyers can also be useful for almost anything else.)

- Mortgage brokers can ensure you get the best deal out of a bank by presenting your credit information in the best possible light.

- Real estate agents can save you plenty of time, particularly when things go wrong with tenants.

- General insurance brokers can regularly save you money and a lot of fruitless running around.

step 8

Q: Who followed the instruction 'Build it and they will come' from a ghost (Dead Man Talking!)?

A: Kevin Costner in *Field of Dreams*

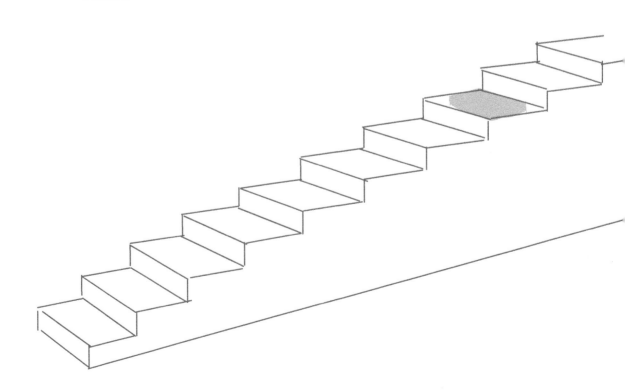

Blockbuster budgeting

- Identifying your big dream
- Money's ability to buy time
- Your $500 000 dream…
- …that's really a $713 000 dream
- Five ways to skin a cat
- Sending your savings soaring
- The X-Flips: calculate the wait, don't procrastinate

Remind me again why Kevin Costner is still famous? Is it *Message in a Bottle*? Thppppt!—only if it won a Golden Raspberry. *The Postman*? Surely not. *Rumour Has It*?

I'm running a risk of seriously boring you to death by opening one of the steps with Costner. Speaking of Costner and death—*Waterworld* and career—his first major role was supposed to be in *The Big Chill* as Alex, the guy whose death brought the crew together. But his scenes were cut and all you got to see of him was as a stiff in the morgue. It might have been better if someone had locked him in the cold storage and lost the key.

As a result, we didn't get to know Costner for another year or two. He hit the glossy magazines as a result of a string of successful films, including *The Untouchables, Bull Durham, Dances with Wolves, Robin Hood: Prince of Thieves* and *The Bodyguard*. A few of these even won some critical acclaim.

Then there was *Field of Dreams*. It got a few Academy Award *nominations*, but it didn't win a major gong. It got beaten, in its categories, by *Driving Miss Daisy* and *The Little Mermaid*. This in a year that included Gen X classics such as *When Harry Met Sally, Dead Poet's Society* and *sex, lies and videotape*.

Costner's *Field of Dreams* did give us something. It spat out the line 'Build it and they will come'.

This perfectly explains some of life's realities. Specifically, it explains why less than 10 years after a new freeway is built, peak-hour traffic is just as bad as it was before. It also gives context to the fact that when mum and dad finally put in that swimming pool, suddenly you had more friends.

In *Field of Dreams*, Costner's character had a big dream. Voices in his head told him to build a baseball diamond in his corn field in the middle of nowhere. If he did, the ghosts of great players past would come and play there.

Okaaaaaaaaay.

'I have a dream!'

If you have a spare corn field, an interest in dead baseball players and a vivid imagination, perhaps you could create your own *Field of Dreams*. And good luck with that. But if you have at least one part of your brain anchored outside of the gates of *Neverland*, you've probably got a dream that's a little more mainstream. Everyone should have a big one in there somewhere.

For some, it might be about getting some money behind them to start their own business. Others want to be in a financial position that allows them to comfortably retire. It might be to travel the world for a year or two, spending some of that time working on a humanitarian project somewhere. Others may dream of giving their children an (expensive) private school education. It could be having a weekender somewhere that will eventually become the full-time home when retirement arrives. You might want to learn how to fly a plane, go on extended sailing trips, or simply pay off your home loan sooner.

You might be aiming high. You might be aiming to achieve several of these types of dreams. Whatever your big dream is, step 8 in *Debt Man Walking* is about showing you what you'll need to do to get there.

Money's real value

If you've got enough money, you can actually buy time. It's one of money's truly great qualities.

You could buy yourself a few hours each week by paying someone to do some of the regular housework that needs doing (or should be done, but you don't get around to it as often as you should). You can pay a road toll to get to work faster so that you can stay at home a little longer in the morning, or get home a little earlier in the afternoon. You can buy a takeaway dinner, which might save you an hour preparing and cleaning up afterwards. You can afford a babysitter to spend quality time with your partner.

A takeaway pizza, or the price of using a toll road, costs exactly the same whether you're struggling through on a small wage or you're a multimillionaire. (The multimillionaire probably has a bigger house, so the cleaning bill could be a bit bigger.) But what is a $12 delivery pizza to the millionaire's weekly disposable income, compared to the struggling factory worker?

> Whatever your big dream is... Debt Man Walking is about showing you what you'll need to do to get there.

Time is ultimately what people want more money for. Money allows you to pay people to do things for you, which can free you up for the things you'd rather be doing, whether that's time with the family or in the office.

Given that, how would you prefer to spend your time? And what if I told you that the rules of compound growth for investment (see step 2) apply equally to time? That's right, investing some time now will give you more free time later.

The $500000 dream...

What's half a million dollars?

It's a little over 8.5 times the average Australian full-time wage (about $58800) in May 2008. It's more than enough to buy an average Australian home, or the average beach shack, allowing for some renovations or a boat to go with it. It would educate two or three kids in an expensive private school, with enough coin left over to fulfil some other considerable dream. With half a mill, you could certainly take a few years off to travel the world in some degree of luxury. You could start your own business, or buy a reasonably successful existing business.

This step will focus on a $500000 dream. It's pretty big, without being ridiculous. It will be a pretty big dream for some readers. For others, it will be a pretty small dream.

If you think $500000 is peanuts, then you could multiply your dream to $1 million (and multiply everything in this step by two) or $2 million (and multiply everything in this step by four). Alternatively, if you have a more modest dream that has a price tag of, say, $250000, then halve the figures. Or jump online, to <www.debtman.com.au>, and punch your own dream figure into the Debt Man 'Big Dream' calculator.

It actually doesn't matter what size the dream is. It's just a number. This section is about the different ways you can get to whatever number it is that represents a big dream for you.

Further, for the purpose of step 8, we're going to assume that the time frame for that dream is 12 years. From the publishing date of this book, that period of time will be about 2020. In that year, a Gen Xer born in 1963 will be turning 57, while a Gen Xer born in 1978 will be turning 42. (Me? I'm smack in the middle, born in 1970, so I'll be turning 50 that year.)

... that's really a $713000 dream

But what's $500000 worth in 2020? A lot less than it's worth now. If you want to keep the same purchasing power for your $500000 in 2020, you need to be aiming higher. The effect of inflation (see 'insidious inflation' in step 2), if we assume it runs at a steady 3 per cent, means that you will need to have approximately $713000 in 2020 to be able to afford what you can buy for $500000 now.

(Q: How do we figure that out? A: $500000 \times 1.03^{12} = \$712880.44$, which we've rounded up to $713000. Jump online to <www.debtman.com.au> to find out what your big dream figure will be once inflation's got a hold of it. If you decided that your dream was $1 million or $2 million, the answers, respectively, will be $1426000 and $2852000.)

That's not trying to make it tougher, but I don't want you to make a plan and then find out halfway through that you'd forgotten to factor in that it was going to cost a little more. For anyone who's looked at buying, or has bought, their first home, you might have noticed that the value of the type of house you were saving for invariably increased as you were saving.

How are we going to get there?

Using all the rules

So, how do we get from nothing to $713 000 in 12 years? There's no one simple way. What I am going to show you is that there are *different* ways of getting there—some of which are likely to be riskier, but financially less of a strain on your wallet than others. In reality, there are thousands of ways to skin this particular cat.

We're going to focus on five strategies. They run the gamut from virtually no risk to very high risk. On the risk profile scale in step 3, we'll be using risk profiles 1, 4 and 6. But that's just the first three strategies.

For the other two strategies, we head into *Debt Man* territory. Investment debt will play a role. For those who feel that *Debt Man Walking* has helped them understand and become more comfortable with the concept of investment debt, these two examples will show you some of the other possibilities out there.

As I have discussed elsewhere, there are no failsafes in investing. You can reduce risk, sure, but you can't remove it completely. The investment modelling that I use in this step has to make some assumptions. But the assumptions aren't unrealistic.

It's a large amount of money and it's a tough task to get there.

But let's start with a quick recap of the universal rules of money from step 2:

1. Delayed gratification: in order to have the money later, you can't spend it now.

2. Risk versus returns: to get a higher return, you need to take on a higher risk.

3. Compounding growth: the longer you leave an asset, the more it will grow.

4. Diversification: spread your risk by having a mixed bag of assets.

5. The power of leverage: investors with longer horizons can use debt to grow their wealth faster.

The best, safest and easiest way to get there is to use all of these rules. All of the paths lead to Bali (or Ibiza or Koh Samui) and I'll show you the calculations later in this chapter (see table 8.1 on p. 186).

1   Save away, save away, save away

Borrowing briefly from the relentless monotony of Enya, you could 'save away, save away, save away'. And that's literally what you'd be doing for 12 years if you intended to save your way to $713 000. (The title 'Sail Away' is repeated 60 times in Enya's song—no wonder our grandparents thought music from our generation was repetitive.)

Use a high-interest, online bank account and put a simple amount away each and every month for the 12-year term. Interest rates may fluctuate, but you can be reasonably confident over the period that they'll always be positive and will move up and down quite slowly. This is a virtually no risk option, but the returns will be somewhat subdued. I have assumed an interest rate of 6 per cent (see table 8.1 on p. 186).

PAYING YOURSELF FIRST There's plenty of free advice out there recommending people put away a certain amount—usually about 10 per cent—of their income each week. Some people call this 'paying yourself first'.

That's a basic starting point, aimed at getting people to save for the first time (which is not what this book is about). Imagine if you did that for your first 10 years out of school. You'd have hit your 30s in a strong financial position. It's a tough thing to do in your first decade in the workforce, when priorities are to explore your financial freedom—for example, travel, upgrade your car every few years, blow your money on being an idiot alongside your friends. But Generation X is now largely past that.

Sure, learning to save in your first few years in the workforce will help you in the long run. But life only gets more serious the older you get. You may as well have had some fun before you get saddled with life's big responsibilities.

While it would be nice to get back 10 per cent of the money blown on material possessions, alcohol, dining out, travelling, cars and petrol, turning 30 with little behind you doesn't leave you destined to die a pauper. Even turning 35 or 40 with few assets doesn't matter—it's not too late to get started.

And when they say save 10 per cent of your income, that doesn't necessarily mean stashing it away in a bank account. As we covered in step 6, it is very difficult to save your way to a fortune. I believe what it really means is committing 10 per cent of your salary to an investment program—whether that's a regular investment program, or a geared investment strategy.

2 A balanced perspective

A balanced investment approach is what investment professionals consider to be the average investor, or our prudent risk profile from step 3. This balanced investment approach would have about 60 per cent of an investment in property and shares, with the remainder in cash and fixed interest.

This is most easily obtained through a managed fund, but the DIY version would see you have the cash portion in a high-interest account and the rest used to buy non-geared shares and property assets. This is slightly riskier in that it will have about one bad year in four or five, but should perform better over the term. I have assumed growth of about 8.5 per cent over the 12-year term.

This may be stepping outside a comfort zone for Cameron Frye (played by Alan Ruck), the hapless hypochondriac who is Ferris's best mate in *Ferris Bueller's Day Off*. But for the average Gen X investor, considering the time frame and your age, this should be your absolute minimum starting point. See table 8.1 for the figure.

3 Going for growth

This is the end of the line—but not quite as far out as Douglas Adams's *The Restaurant at the End of the Universe*—as far as the *traditional* risk profiling goes. In this strategy, all investment monies are in the high-risk investment assets of shares and property. But just your own money. We're not talking gearing yet.

This is the sort of option that will keep a lot of pre-retirees—those nervously awaiting collection of their super—awake at night. This investment is 100 per cent invested in shares and property. This sort of fund will have some serious fluctuations—probably three years of negative returns in every 10 years—but should average around the 10 to 11 per cent mark over the long term. I have assumed a growth rate of 10.5 per cent. See table 8.1 for the figure.

4 One small step for Gen X…

Enter *Debt Man*. This is the first of two strategies to introduce debt directly into your investment strategy.

Our next step up the risk/reward chain is a geared savings plan. The investor will put in a certain amount of money each month and that amount is matched by a lender (which could be an amount of money coming from a line of credit on your home or a bank in the form of a margin loan). A similar outcome may be achieved with the use of geared managed funds—the fund manager takes the investors' money, adds some borrowed money, then invests in growth assets (or you could buy investment property with a very large deposit).

This is adding a bit of hired help to your investment campaign and a fairly safe entry point for those who believe they are ready to add some gearing to their investments. This is the first step into the parallel *Debt Man* universe of geared investing (like Homer Simpson discovering a *Tron*-like third dimension in *Homer*[3] behind the 'whatchamacallit-case', the bookcase).

The growth assets will still earn 10.5 per cent a year. The borrowing costs will be 8 per cent, which is closer to a longer-term average for mortgage rates. (Margin loan rates tend to be a few per cent higher.) See table 8.1 for the numbers.

5   *Extreme debt investing*

This is where *Wall Street*'s Gordon Gekko would start. While there are higher-risk strategies available, this is as aggressive as we're going to get in this step.

We're borrowing the lot. And we're not paying it back (until we sell the investment).

This option is about buying an investment property with all borrowed money, or buying a fully geared portfolio of stocks. From a tax efficiency perspective, this is the best way of buying growth assets for those who have other debt that is not tax deductible (such as a home mortgage or consumer debt), particularly when interest rates are reasonably low. Essentially, you're renting the investment capital—a fully geared investment where only the interest is paid (if you have extra money on top of this, it should be used to pay down dumb and okay debt). Another example would be the capital-protected style of investment that was discussed in step 6 (although the interest rates would generally be higher).

Again, I have assumed growth of 10.5 per cent and interest-only borrowing costs of 8 per cent.

Note: Even though you would get the tax deductions back annually (how much you get back will depend on your marginal tax rate) I have addressed the tax deductibility of the interest payments for both strategies 4 and 5 by adding back the money at the end of the 12 years.

Sooner or later, the goal will be scored

It's important to note that these examples are using mathematical averages. In reality, no investments grow at a smooth rate of return (not even cash).

As a result, in practice, if things go well, you might find that you hit your target a few years early. If the market has a slump near the start or near the end of your strategy, it might take an extra few years. It's also possible that, with this particular example, you hit your target after 10 years, but then investments go backwards for two years and at the end of year 12, you're behind your target again. Large fluctuations are, of course, more likely to happen with the riskier strategies.

Reaching that goal

Five different strategies. All five are going to get us to our goal. We're trying to determine how easily they'll get us there. This exercise is firstly based on understanding and accepting some basic investment principles, the most important of which is that shares and property will outperform income investments (cash and fixed interest) over longer periods. It also assumes that interest rates aren't outrageously high.

IMPORTANT: ASSUMPTIONS AND DISCLAIMERS

Complex modelling could be used to build in dozens of variables, but the equation could become so complex that the point might be lost.

In this step, I have ignored the effect of income and capital gains tax from the investments themselves. However, I have included the tax deductibility of the interest repayments for strategies 4 and 5, as that is a fundamental difference to strategies 1, 2 and 3. The point is to show how taking larger risks over long-term time frames can make achieving goals easier.

It is important to note that tax will have to be paid on capital gains when assets are sold or as income is earned. If you want to take into account the impact of taxation, then perhaps you could increase your target by 20 per cent. So your $500 000/$713 000 target becomes, for instance, a $600 000/$856 000 target, to allow yourself some room to pay some income tax along the way and capital gains tax at the end.

We will also assume that cash investments are returning 6 per cent and that growth assets achieve a return of 10.5 per cent from both the dividends/rent and capital growth. To reiterate, I have used 8 per cent as the interest rate for investments because this is closer to the recent long-term average.

Our example investor is on the second highest marginal tax rate, 41.5 per cent. We have also assumed that all income from the investments is reinvested.

What table 8.1 shows is that there are easier ways to reach investment targets than straight saving, or even investing regularly in a low-risk, balanced managed fund. Taking on riskier styles of investment is not only ... um, riskier ... but given long-term investment horizons it has the *potential* to make achieving goals easier.

So, here it is. Drum roll, please. Table 8.1 shows how much you would have to put away under each of the five strategies in order to reach the goal of $713000 in 12 years.

Table 8.1: five ways to hit a target

	1	2	3	4	5
	Saving	Balanced fund	Growth fund	Geared savings plan	Geared, interest only
Yearly $	$42257	$36466	$32348	$26781	$21026
Monthly $	$3521	$3039	$2696	$2232	$1752
After 12 years	$712880	$712880	$712880	$712880	$7128801

As mentioned previously, with strategies 4 and 5 the tax deduction incurred for the interest payments along the way has been added at the end of the investment and is included above. If you want to find out how the numbers would work for your own target, log on to <www.debtman.com.au> and look for the 'Big Dream' calculator. Punch in your own long-term target and how many years you've got to get there, and it will show these five calculations for you. It must be a *minimum* time frame of 10 years.

So, what do these figures show us? There are at least five very different ways to skin this cat. (There are actually thousands of ways of doing it.) And they show that from one extreme to the other, the amount of money that you would need to put away each year to hit your target can halve. Table 8.1 shows that if you wanted to save your way to the $500000 target (after inflation = $713000), you would have to put away approximately $42257 a year.

At the other end of the scale sits a strategy that involves a much higher amount of risk. Under strategy 5, if an investor was prepared to borrow approximately $263000 (to buy shares or property), then they would have to make interest repayments of only about $21026 a year. This is just less than half what you'd have to commit to achieving your target if you were going to save your way there.

This mathematical exercise shows what's possible when extra risk is added into investment portfolios. No investments grow as smoothly as mathematical models. They can grow faster, or slower. And *Debt Man* is *not* suggesting that investors move from one end of the scale to the other. However, if you know your risk profile, then you might be able to see how moving along one further step has the potential to make hitting your long-term target easier. (And you might be able to see the step *after* that and consider working towards it.)

For instance, if you consider yourself an aggressive investor (from the risk profiles in step 3) and are open to taking a slightly higher risk for a longer-term goal, then you might be prepared to move into a geared savings program. Under the aggressive option (strategy 3), you needed to put away $32 348 a year. However, under the geared savings program (strategy 4), you had to put away only $26 781, or nearly 11 per cent less. If you're already comfortable with geared savings, a strategy that saw you borrow the full amount at the start (strategy 5) would reduce your annual contributions to just $21 026 a year.

This doesn't mean that strategy 5 is the way you should go if you're in a hurry to get somewhere, or you're looking for the cheapest way to get there. Far from it. Strategy 5 is high risk — although there are higher risks that can be taken — and you are playing with other people's money. You'll have to

REPETITION: LONG TERM, LONG TERM, LONG TERM I use the phrase 'long term' repetitively in *Debt Man Walking*. I do, and I make no apologies for that.

That's because it must be understood that shares and property can go backwards in some years, sometimes backwards for many years in succession. When they start growing again, they can make up for several years of losses in one year and continue strong runs for several years in succession.

Like John Travolta. After *Grease* and *Saturday Night Fever*, there was a long, dark, cold winter of celluloid duds until his career was resurrected as Vincent Vega in *Pulp Fiction*. Things got so bleak, he had time to go off and get qualified for a real job — as a pilot.

You can't go into shares or property, particularly when it includes a gearing strategy, expecting to make a quick killing. Some people will get lucky and do that. Others will suffer from horrible timing and will get badly burnt.

Traditional theory suggests that if you are going into an all-growth strategy of shares and property, you should expect to be in the investment for a minimum of seven years. If you are including gearing in that strategy, seven years becomes an absolute minimum, but it should be more like 10 years.

pay it back, even if you lose it. It would not be an appropriate strategy for everyone. And it certainly wouldn't be appropriate for anyone to have all of their investments in strategy 5. Even the most aggressive investors would not have all of their money in this risk category (see breakout box below).

For examples of how these risks can play out and how Australian and international sharemarkets can outperform and underperform over long periods, see the tables in step 3.

In step 3, we looked at risk profiles and I suggested that given your age (if you're a Gen Xer, younger Boomer, or Generation Y) that moving up even one risk profile would deliver long-term benefits to any investment strategy you took on. Those who are naturally in an assertive or aggressive risk profile are probably good candidates to begin using gearing in their investment strategies. But there will also be others who are the prudent or judicious investors, for instance, who could be candidates for some investment gearing under the right circumstances (such as, potentially, structured products where there is a level of protection).

You might have looked at one of these strategies and said to yourself 'that is a risk I would feel comfortable with'. Have a look at the next higher strategy. How much of a difference would that make? In general, if you're Generation X, you've got the time to make these strategies work, so long as you feel comfortable with the higher risks.

A REAL LIFE AGGRESSIVE INVESTOR

To show you what I mean, let's use an actual example...me.

Even though I am what would be considered an assertive or aggressive investor, I use a combination of most of the five strategies above, depending on what the time frames for my investment needs are.

My investment properties (which I buy with the intention of owning forever) are essentially strategy 5 because they are fully geared. Most people's homes, including mine (but don't forget that we discussed in step 5 that homes aren't strictly investments), are largely strategy 5 also. I began my share-based investments, which I hoped would be the education fund for my children, as strategy 4 with some of my own equity and a margin loan (although those plans were changing in 2008 and my aim is to run them as strategy 5, using both a line of credit and a margin loan, so that all of the money being contributed is debt funded). My superannuation covers a multitude of strategies. It is running predominantly as strategy 4 (with self-funding instalments), with a bit of strategies 1 (cash) and 3 (direct shares and managed funds) thrown in. I've got investments on behalf of my children (who are clearly too young to have their risk profiles tested, but I see it as a 21st birthday investment for them, so they certainly have a long-term investment time frame) that are essentially strategy 4.

But I always make sure that I have a reasonable chunk of my personal money in cash—strategy 1. For example, I like to try to be ahead in my mortgage, so that there is rainy day money if required. No matter how aggressive your investment strategy, you need to have access to some cash, because you never know when you're going to need it.

The point is, while I'm a fairly aggressive investor, I don't have everything in the most aggressive investment strategy. As you'd expect from someone writing a book called *Debt Man Walking*, I believe that investment debt, used correctly, is worthwhile and I use it to varying degrees across my personal life.

Savings known, strategy unknown

We know how much money you need to hit a defined target, while taking on different risk strategies. Now let's have a look at the reverse—you have a defined level of savings and you want to know how those savings would go in each of the investment strategies we've used in this step.

I'll use $30000 a year—somewhere near the midpoint of the figures used in the first group—which is $2500 a month. Now, if that $30000 a year was put into each of the five investment strategies, here's how they would come out after 12 years (see table 8.2, overleaf).

Table 8.2: $30000 a year invested in our five investment strategies

| | 1 | 2 | 3 | 4 | 5 |
	Saving	Balanced fund	Growth fund	Geared savings plan	Geared, interest only
Yearly $	$30000	$30000	$30000	$30000	$30000
Monthly $	$2500	$2500	$2500	$2500	$2500
After 12 years	$506098	$586477	$661132	$798566	$1017135
Inflation adjusted	$354967	$411343	$463705	$560098	$713098

To keep the comparisons fair with the first calculator, we have added in what that 12 years of investing will be worth in today's dollars. That is, we've included an 'inflation adjusted' line at the end of the table to show you the real value of those investments after insidious inflation has taken its bite.

A reminder that there are no guarantees and that we are using figures that hopefully replicate something like the long-term return from various asset classes. But, using mathematical averages, you can see the potential of using higher-growth strategies to achieve financial goals.

Putting the same amount of money into all five strategies will produce incredibly different results. Again, don't forget that the risks in strategy 5 are alluring on the outside but are very high-risk plays, like James Bond in any Bond film, or Bo Derek in *10*. But they can behave a bit like Sharon Stone in *Basic Instinct*, or the sweet-talking parolee Brad Pitt in *Thelma & Louise*.

You will find another calculator, the 'Savings Known' calculator, on <www.debt man.com.au> that will allow you to perform this calculation for your own savings. You'll need to know how much you've got each month or year for your investment plan and how many years you're intending to take to get there. The calculator will punch out how your money will fare using each of the five strategies plus make the calculation for inflation.

The X-Flips:

Calculate the wait, don't procrastinate

'Can't do it this year.' 'Our mortgage needs attention.' 'We have to update the car.' 'We need a holiday.' 'All our bills have just come in.'

Finding excuses is easy—there are loads to choose from. If you're ever struggling, just punch 'excuses' into an internet search engine and you'll get thousands. There's always a reason for putting off getting started on a plan to change your life. But you're reading this book because you don't want to procrastinate any longer. You want to do something about it now, don't you? Let's just have a look at how much putting things off for a few years will cost you. I'll keep it simple.

The stork dropped by last night and left you a present. Actually, two presents. You've got twins. Not Cabbage Patch Kids. The real thing. And you've decided that since you didn't have to go through the whole pregnancy thing, you'll make up for it by sending them to a nice, expensive, private school. (If the kids thing doesn't do it for you, imagine you're saving for a nice big deposit for a beach house...in the south of France.)

You need $200 000 in 12 years. And we'll assume that your money is earning 10 per cent a year. Following is a list of how much you'd have to save in order to hit that $200 000 target, depending on when you start:

- The *start-now* option: if you started saving the day you picked the babies out of the vegetable garden, you'd need to save $8500 a year ($708 a month).

- The *procrastinate-for-four-years* option: start after four years and you'll need to save $15 900 a year ($1325 a month) for the remaining eight years.

- The *procrastinate-for-eight-years* option: If you leave it until they start grade 3, you'd need to save $39 200 a year ($3267 a month) for the last four years.

The point is that taking the medicine earlier (delayed gratification) will save even more serious pain later, because of *the power of compounding*—the money put in early is growing for the whole 12 years.

Step 8 for Gen X

Melbourne pub rockers The Uncanny X-Men, led by the '80s icon Brian Mannix, posed a rhetorical question about what we'd be doing in their song 'Fifty Years'.

Like me, you probably thought Brian was being utterly ridiculous by talking about such a stupidly long period of time, in what was essentially a love song. Here's the scary bit—the song was released in 1983. That 50 years is half up already—a quarter of a century. I bet you can't even remember who you were pashing back then.

So, are you going to blow another 25 years?

Everybody should have at least one big, long-term financial goal. Step 8 is about understanding that saving for your goal—by putting away a set amount of money each month—with a bank account is the most painful way of getting there. If you've got a reasonable time frame (a minimum of seven years), then understanding how slightly higher investment risks can help you achieve those goals is important.

More so than any other age group, Generation X can afford to get into bed with investment debt. That doesn't mean that it's right for everyone. Or that gearing for the sake of gearing is right—each investment opportunity has to be looked at on its own. And it certainly doesn't mean that gearing till it hurts, or stops you sleeping at night, is a good idea. It isn't. But if you're reading this wondering if you could be achieving financial goals more efficiently, then it's time you considered looking for smarter ways to get where you're going.

step 9

Q: Which American actor played a
   civilisation saviour both in the past
   as an archaeologist and in the future
   as the Millennium Falcon's pilot?

A: Harrison Ford as Dr Jones in the *Indiana Jones*
series and Han Solo in the *Star Wars* series

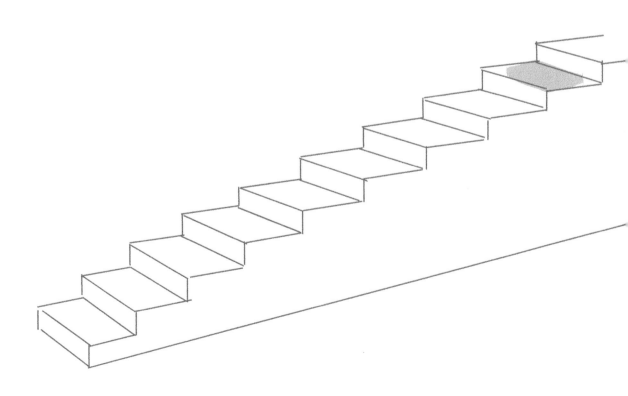

Cover your ass(ets)

- Car, house and contents—basics covered
- Covering the irreplaceables
- It won't happen to me…
- How much? How long?
- Putting it on the 'super credit card'
- Shit Creek paddle salesman
- The X-Flips: protect your greatest asset

So, here we are. Step 9. And that, when you've got 10 of them, must be the penultimate step.

In any good book, the *last* chapter is always the happily-sail-off-into-the-sunset chapter. Granted, that's the recipe normally associated with fiction titles. But maybe the same formula *can* work in a *finance* title. And I've certainly left the 'sunset step' until step 10.

Sticking with that successful formula/theory, the chapter before the happy ending must be filled with drama. Action aplenty. Disaster, even. Heroes never get to board the boat without having their cages rattled a little bit.

In earlier steps, *Debt Man Walking* encouraged you to take a step or two out of your comfort zone. But now it's time for *Debt Man* to yank you out. And this time you might not like it. Sorry, but it's time to scare the crap out of you.

You should now be feeling comfortable and resolved that the goals you wrote down in step 1 are eminently achievable. There is a path (with steps!) that'll lead you right there. Wealth creation isn't rocket science. Getting rich is far more about following a process than it is about becoming a high-finance genius. It's more about understanding and managing risks than flirting with them. *Debt Man Walking*, I hope, has demystified the process. Now, just get out there and push yourself a little.

> Life is full of potential nasty incidents. The risks that confront you from the time you wake up till the time you go to bed are endless...

But as this is the chapter before you figuratively board *The Love Boat* with Captain Stubing, Gopher and cruise director Julie McCoy, I want to know if you've got a backup plan. Are you prepared to deal with something nasty and unexpected around the corner?

Think *Raiders of the Lost Ark*. After the running battles across northern Africa and the chase scenes, hundreds of Nazis have congregated to witness the opening of The Ark. Hell is about to visit Earth. Thousands of people are about to die. Above the howling, ghostly winds, Indiana screams to Marion the secret that saves them both ...

But I'm not Harrison Ford and I don't want you to close your eyes.

'What, me worry?'

So says MAD magazine spokesman, Alfred E Neuman. Or, as the bumper sticker reads, 'shit happens'.

Some shit that happens doesn't matter. Who would have cared if a piece of Skylab landed in a back paddock of a 200 000 hectare farm? Other shit that happens does matter. You wouldn't want the comment made by Dustin Hoffman's character in *Rain Man* about Australia's national airline ('Qantas never crashed') to suddenly be disproved on your holiday.

Life is full of potential nasty incidents. The risks that confront you from the time you wake up till the time you go to bed are endless (never forgetting that, with age, the chances of waking up and getting out of bed in the morning diminish). We don't spend much time dwelling on most of them because the risk of them happening is quite small. And life would be no fun if we did. Many of the potential consequences are, let's face it, fairly minor and unlikely to have too much of a lasting impact.

For example, your house/flat could be robbed (it's happened many times to me). Your car could get broken into (it happened so often that I barely even bothered to lock it for a time). You could find yourself in a spot of international trouble in, say, Guatemala (where my wife, Genevieve, and I were fleeced of money, a passport and non-refundable airline tickets, because we relaxed for a second and didn't lock our bag on a 'chicken bus'. D'oh!). You could lend your car to someone, only for them to wrap it around a tree late one night after a 7-Eleven run. (Gen's car. Occupants, thankfully, undamaged.) Some do have a lasting impact. Your own home could burn down (which happened to my cousin and his family in the 2003 Canberra bushfires).

Things can happen to your possessions. Accidents, theft, flood and fire. They reckon global warming will mean that cyclones will hit as far south as Sydney within the next few decades. Arguably that's another Boomers' poop-on-the-footpath left behind for us to clean up.

If you've got to your age without having lost something, then you must have a special aura around you. But you can't relax yet, my friend, as yours is probably just around the next corner.

Get it? Got it? Good

But you know what? *You* know that. You understand the need to insure your stuff. Insuring your car, insuring your home and insuring your contents are things that most people understand. The stats say that.

Research compiled by CommInsure from several sources shows the following:

- 89 per cent of consumers have their motor vehicles insured
- 87 per cent have their home contents insured
- 77 per cent have their home building insured.

Most personal finance books start their section on insurance (if they have one) with the importance of making sure that your home, car and contents are properly covered. But between three-quarters and nine-tenths of Australians have this under control. So I'm not going to waste too much of your time on it.

Most of these sorts of property risks are events from which there is some financial pain, but are generally recoverable. However, it's a bit disturbing that only 77 per cent have their house insured. How would the other 23 per cent cope if their house burned down? (There are 10000 house fires in Australia each year.)

If you lost your uninsured $20000 to $30000 car, then that would be nasty. But you could get around in a cheap car for a year or two while you bounced back. Your home being robbed is also unpleasant. But, again, so long as you weren't there when it happened, you'll hopefully be able to recover reasonably quickly (financially at least).

Possessions. We love 'em. But you can always replace them. There are far bigger concerns that are far less understood.

The irreplaceables

It's the stuff that can't be replaced that people tend to say they care about. You always hear from house fire victims that they tried to save their photos. You can't insure your photos, but digital cameras now mean you can store your images safely.

But photos, really, pale into insignificance when compared to some other things that can't be replaced, such as your life. There's some stuff that you can't go out and repurchase after the event:

- If you're dead, you can't go out and buy yourself a new life.
- You can't buy a lost arm, leg, or set of eyes.
- You may not be able to buy back your health if you develop a life-threatening illness, such as cancer, heart attack or stroke.
- If accident or illness means you can't work for an extended period, you can't buy back your job. If you can't work through illness or injury, the government will give you a little bit of money. But if you're used to a $60000, $100000 or $200000 salary, surviving on $15000 a year of government benefits is going to be a struggle.

People are not replaceable. A wife or a husband is not replaceable. A dad is not replaceable. A mum is not replaceable.

If you're the household breadwinner, what would happen if you went off to work on Monday morning, but didn't come home? What would happen to your partner? Your family? What's your legacy? Is it a mountain of debt with no way of paying it off? How many plans did you make? How expensive were they? Is your partner going to be able to continue with those plans, or provide for the children, without your income there?

Death, disease, illness and accidents—there's a chance they could happen to you.

There's a solution. It's called life insurance.

It won't happen to me

Sure it won't.

No doubt the 50000 people who die each year of cardiovascular disease and the 1500 people who die in car accidents in Australia each year thought that. As do the 2500 men who die from prostate cancer each year (while 10000 were diagnosed with it).

The one in four women and one in three men who suffer from cancer before they turn 75 didn't think they'd contract it. Today's 40-year-old male has a one-in-two chance of having coronary heart disease before he dies, while a 30-year-old male has a one-in-three likelihood of suffering serious injury or illness before turning 70 (statistics compiled by Asteron).

That's a lot of bullets to dodge. But it's only the start of the potential onslaught.

You got a bit of Keanu Reeves in *The Matrix* in you? Or you're more the *Superman* type and bullets just bounce off you?

But the bullets didn't bounce off *Superman* actor Christopher Reeve when he was off screen. In 1995, Reeve fell from a horse and was paralysed for the remainder of his shortened life. In further bad luck, his wife, Dana, died soon after him, aged 44, from lung cancer. She had never smoked.

Or, perhaps you reason, 'workers' compensation will cover me'. Maybe. But less than 50 per cent of people who suffer accidents or injury at work receive workers' compensation (Australian Bureau of Statistics). And what happens if the accident doesn't happen at work?

I was born in 1970, so I'm smack in the middle of Gen X. I've had young friends and colleagues die in sad (arguably preventable) circumstances. I've also had friends killed by indiscriminate, horrible illnesses that had nothing to do with lifestyle. And thankfully, there have been some powerful, uplifting stories of survival to tell. But there hasn't been one example where the lives of those afflicted or those left behind wouldn't have been made easier by proper insurance plans being in place.

Gen X's needs are different

Gen X's needs, when it comes to life insurance, are fundamentally different to those generations on either side.

Gen Y has not had the time to accumulate much in the way of wealth, or income, to protect yet. Older Baby Boomers should have largely paid off their home, kicked the kids out of it and be preparing to 'spend the kids' inheritance' (some of that is *our* inheritance).

This is not to say that Gen Y and Boomers don't need to protect their lives—they do. But their needs are different.

When the life insurance industry talks of a severe underinsurance problem, they're talking to Gen X and younger Boomers in particular. These are the generations who are largely married, have big first or second mortgages, investment debt (which you also may have after you read *Debt Man Walking*), debt on the family business and children. They've got the triple Ms—marriage, mortgage and midgets. And that's not to mention your biggest asset—your ability to work.

Our best years are still ahead of us

I know, that sounds corny. But it's no worse than how Steven Spielberg gets that stranded alien E.T. back aboard the mother ship with bikes flying over forests.

Gen X's most productive work years are still ahead of us. Statistics show that the peak age for earning is between 45 and 50. That's when our employment skills will be most sought after and therefore when we're likely to be earning the big bucks in our chosen careers. Either side of 50 is when our generation will be the captains of industry, and leaders in politics and the community.

> Gen X's needs, when it comes to life insurance, are fundamentally different to those generations on either side.

At that time, we won't yet have hit the point where ageism sees people's wealth of knowledge sadly devalued. (Except if you're a musician. In that case you'll be under-valued during your 40s. You're currently working on other projects because the band broke up years ago, following *that* incident. It's still at least five years before the lead singer and the drummer will start talking to each other again. After *that* comes the reunion tour. Sorry. However, Led Zeppelin's reformation proves there's hope for you.)

For the rest of us, the big years are still ahead. We will soon be expected to take the reins from the Boomers, who have already peaked and started their move into retirement.

Protecting yourself and your family

Your life and your livelihood are what you *need* to protect, both for you and your loved ones.

If something happened to you or your partner, would you be able to continue to pay the rent or the mortgage on your current home? Would the kids still get the education you'd talked about?

The statistics show that this is something that not too many people have put much thought into. But think about it for a second. If you're the breadwinner, how would your partner cope without you around? What sort of a life would the kids have without mum or dad? What if you couldn't work?

Get a piece of paper and put a line down the centre. On the left-hand side, put the value of your appreciating assets—the home and any investments. On the other side put your debts—the mortgage/s, the credit cards, the car loans and anything else on which you owe money. The assets may, or may not, make an impressive list. The real question is this: how is your partner going to look after the debt side of the equation if you're not around?

If there's little debt because you've chosen to rent, the question becomes 'who's going to pay the rent for the next 40 or 50 years?'

Protecting your most valuable asset

What is your most *valuable* asset? I'll let you think about it for a little. While you do, I'll just play some of Bon Jovi's 'Livin' on a Prayer', from *Slippery When Wet*, in the background.

(The choice of song wasn't a subliminal message that if you go without insurance, you're 'livin' on a prayer'. Honestly, it was just opportunistic. I'd got to step 9 without getting Bon Jovi into this book and my 'inner bogan' would never have forgiven Debt Man if I hadn't got Jon and Richie Sambora in. Oh, and maybe a little of the subliminal bit.)

Again, what is your most valuable asset?

It's not designed to be a trick question. But people's answers are usually predictable—home, beach house, family business, share portfolio and, occasionally, super fund. Perhaps, if you were late to the starting grid because you've just returned from a stint in London, it might be your dad's old Holden Kingswood (or, if your dad was *Kingswood Country*'s Ted Bullpitt, you still wouldn't own it, much less be allowed to drive it: 'You're not taking the Kingswood! I've just chamoised the dashboard!').

In most cases—particularly that last one—these answers are wrong. The correct answer for all Gen Xers, all of Gen Y and some younger Boomers is the same thing. And it's none of the above.

Your most valuable asset is actually *your ability to earn an income.*

Think about it for a minute. If you work until you're 65 and are earning:

- $45 000 at age 30, you'll earn $1.575 million by the time you retire
- $60 000 at age 35, you'll earn $1.8 million before retirement
- $100 000 at age 40, you'll earn $2.5 million
- $150 000 at age 45, you'll earn $3 million.

These figures don't take into account the impact of inflation, or that the biggest income earning years are, on average, still ahead.

Personal risk insurance

But let's take a step back.

The life insurance industry isn't as old as prostitution, which is said to be the world's oldest profession, but it has acquired a similarly sordid reputation over the years. In the public perception stakes, insurance salespeople sit near the bottom of the table, alongside used car salesmen and journalists. (In career terms, I've moved from journalist to financial adviser, who recommends insurance as part of a comprehensive financial plan. I'm not sure whether I've moved up or down the list.)

Insurance is about grouping people who face a defined set of risks, so that if something happens to one, there is a pool of money to compensate the person to whom the event happened. For example, let's say that the statistics show that, in any given year, for every 10 000 people aged 40, six will die. An insurance company can then charge a premium based on that risk, in the understanding that they will need enough money to pay out, *on average*, for the death of six 40-year-olds each year.

There are four types of personal risk insurance (sometimes broadly referred to as the life insurances).

Life insurance (death)

Straight life insurance is often called death cover or term life insurance. It's a relatively simple concept. If you currently have a pulse, then you can take out insurance to pay a lump sum to someone (such as your family) in the event that you stop having a pulse in the future. That is, you're either dead or alive.

(And every time I hear those words, I can't stop myself singing, poorly, Bon Jovi's 'Wanted Dead or Alive', also from *Slippery When Wet*. Couldn't slot them in until step 9 and then it's twice in a few pages. That should please the inner bogan.)

This is also known as the 'fog the mirror test'. An agreed lump sum is paid if you can't perform that simple life chore anymore.

Straight life insurance is cheap as chips for most Gen Xers, although the actual cost depends on your profession and age and, obviously, how much of a lump sum you seek. As the chance of something happening to you is relatively low, so are the premiums.

Total and permanent disability insurance (nearly died)

Total and permanent disability insurance (abbreviated to TPD) is sometimes also referred to as accident or disability insurance. The accident or illness didn't kill you, but has left you totally and permanently disabled and unable to work (for six months or more).

The sorts of accidents for which TPD insurance can provide cover are loss of eyesight, loss of limbs, quadriplegia, paraplegia, tetraplegia and major head traumas. TPD insurance may also cover illnesses including multiple sclerosis, motor neurone disease, dementia, Alzheimer's disease, muscular dystrophy, Parkinson's disease and loss of hearing/speech. This is not a definitive list, but covers some of the major illnesses covered by insurers. Not all insurers cover the same illnesses and diseases and the variances between the policies offered by insurers are vast. This is one area where a good financial adviser will prove a great help.

Typically, a TPD policy will be taken out as a *rider* to a life insurance policy; that is, it is offered in conjunction with a life insurance policy. However, it can be taken out on its own.

Trauma insurance (seen the other side)

Trauma insurance is actually part of Generation X history in that it only came about in our lifetimes.

Following major medical breakthroughs in the 1970s in dealing with victims of heart attacks, strokes and cancers, doctors realised patients were surviving illnesses which had once been death sentences. However, while they survived the surgery, when they awoke and were shown the invoice, it would send them straight back into cardiac arrest.

So, a South African doctor named Dr Marius Barnard suggested that insurers create a new product to help patients deal with these bills and other major costs that can be incurred with serious illnesses.

The big three traumas are heart attack, stroke and cancer.

COVERING THE KIDS: A NOTE FOR GEN X PARENTS

Something that is often provided as an option with individual trauma insurance is child trauma cover. This is a lump sum paid for defined illnesses that occur to children.

While it can be a difficult topic for many people to consider, imagine that your child was diagnosed with a life-threatening illness that required months of hospitalisation. Would you want to be at the hospital with your child? Would you be able to concentrate at work anyway? Child trauma cover might allow you to take as much time off work as you need to allow you to be with your child. Cover is generally only available for children over two years of age.

But most policies will cover many more illnesses, including blindness, accidentally acquired AIDS, chronic organ failure, dementia, diabetes, loss of limbs or speech, muscular dystrophy, multiple sclerosis and Parkinson's disease. Again, this is not an exhaustive list.

In essence, trauma cover is a lump sum which should be useful for three main areas:

- to cover bills not covered by other health insurance
- to pay for lifestyle modifications (stamp duty if you need to buy a new home, ramps, grab rails, frameless showers, wider doorways, a new car, and so on)
- to provide financial breathing space while you recover.

Income protection insurance (seriously crook)

Income protection insurance is different to life, TPD and trauma insurance, which all provide a lump sum. Income protection (also known as salary continuance) is designed to provide an income stream, potentially for decades.

Income protection allows you to cover up to 75 per cent of your salary to continue in the event of you not being able to work. It is the most flexible of the risk insurance products, from a cost perspective, in that you can choose when the insurer's payments kick in and when they stop. The choice comes through how long a waiting period you're prepared to take until the insurance kicks in (from two weeks to two years after the accident/illness that prevents you from earning a living) and how long a policy will run for (the options run up to age 65).

A 37-year-old female manager, earning $80000 a year and living in Sydney, who chose a 30-day waiting period, could get a good quality policy in mid 2008 for approximately $1450 a year. For a 90-day wait, the premium would fall to $870 a year.

That 37-year-old woman is effectively insuring $1.68 million of income ($80000 × 28 years × 75 per cent) for less than she pays to insure her car every year. But wait…in almost all cases, income protection policies are tax deductible. So, depending on your marginal tax rate, you will get up to 46.5 per cent of the cost of the policy back on tax.

Income protection is considered by many experts to be the most important insurance for Generation Xers. But, sadly, it is one that too few people take out. People won't quibble with spending $1200 a year insuring their car, which, on average, might be worth $40000 or less (and losing value every day they own it). But they baulk at spending a similar, *tax deductible*, amount insuring millions of dollars of future income.

DUTY OF DISCLOSURE EXCLUSIONS AND LOADING

Underwriters are experts in predicting injury and death for large groups of people and have spent centuries creating mortality and morbidity tables. The likelihood of a personal risk insurance event occurring is directly proportional to a few important facts. Age, sex, occupation and whether or not you are a smoker are the primary variables when determining the cost of an insurance premium.

After that, insurers want to know about your personal health. You've got to be completely honest about your medical history — it's called a duty of disclosure. It means you have to tell them about anything that might change the risk that you pose to the insurance company. Your lifestyle is an important consideration. The type of hobbies you have (backgammon versus rock-climbing, for instance), how much you drink and genetics (how healthy your parents and siblings are) are factors that determine how much risk a life insurance company is effectively taking on.

Whatever your previous health issues, the insurance company has a right to know about them before they agree to insure you. If you aren't completely honest, they could void any future claim payouts if your non-disclosure was significant to the risks that they perceived they were taking on.

If you've had specific, serious health issues in your past, insurers might opt to put an *exclusion* on cover for certain events occurring to you, or put a *loading* on your policy (a premium multiple of perhaps, 25, 50, 100 or 200 per cent on your policy). Don't panic if your financial adviser or insurance company comes back to you with a loading or exclusion. If you're using an adviser (which is almost a necessity when it comes to insurance), talk to them about your options.

But you should still seriously consider taking the policy. The loading will generally reflect the extra risk you pose. In some instances, it might be a lifestyle wake-up call. But in many cases, a loading might add less than a few hundred dollars to your policy. And that could be a small price to pay for the cover it will bring.

Don't think that life insurers are simply looking for excuses not to pay. They paid out nearly $2.1 billion in claims to Australians during 2007.

How much insurance do I need?

Twee, maybe, clichéd, possibly, but here's a better question: 'How much do you love those around you?'

If you died tomorrow, your personal dreams are finished. But how much money would your family need to carry out the dreams that you had for them?

If you had a major accident tomorrow and you could never work again, how much money would you need to be able to still provide a good quality of life for your family? If you were diagnosed with cancer, or had another life-threatening illness that was going to keep you off work for a year, how much money would you need to ensure that you could get the treatment you wanted and keep all the other financial wolves at bay? If you couldn't work for an extended period, would you have enough of an income stream remaining to pay the mortgage?

Do you want to know why most people lose their homes? Read these statistics. House fires get shown on a regular basis on the nightly news. But for every one family that loses their home because of a fire:

- four families lose their home because of the death of a breadwinner
- more than 40 lose their home because of a short- or long-term illness (because they can no longer meet mortgage repayments).

That's terrifying.

If the breadwinner dies, the chances rise dramatically that the family will lose the home. And if you can't work for an extended period, you might not be able to afford the mortgage. If you can't do that, you will have to sell the house, or you may be kicked out of it.

For renters, could you cover your existing rental payments?

Insurance is how you transfer some of those financial risks to someone else.

Full Metal Jacket

The only relationship that I'd want to draw between Stanley Kubrick's film and this step is that the realities are both terrifying. Nothing, not even full insurance cover, can make you bullet proof.

But if you're going to cover all the possibilities that insurance will allow and protect yourself and your family as best you can, these are the general rules you'd want to follow. Following is the sort of protection that every investor, particularly everyone taking on *Debt Man*-style investment debt, should have.

As stated previously, a financial adviser is essential for a proper risk insurance plan. But the following scenarios are the sorts of things a financial adviser would run you through.

Note that everyone's situation will be different, but when it comes to straight term life insurance (death cover), the following is a very rough guide to the sorts of level of cover you should be considering:

- about eight to ten times the salary of each household earner, if you don't have children

- about 12 to 13 times the salaries if you do have young children. This should generally cover all debt and provide a further lump sum for investment to replace the income of the deceased

- in the event of the death of a stay-at-home parent, enough money to pay for full-time care of the children for as long as is required.

For total and permanent disability insurance (TPD), you should have enough to pay off all non-deductible debt and a leftover lump sum to create an income stream (for both parents, whether working or not).

You should have enough trauma cover to provide for two to three years of income for one or both income earners. For a non-earner, you should have enough to cover a year's salary of the earner.

Income protection is probably Gen X's most important cover. You should insure 75 per cent (plus superannuation guarantee payments), to cut in from one, two or three months, to last until you turn 65.

Some financial advisers (particularly specialist risk advisers) will use quite complicated formulas in order to tailor a level of risk insurance to your personal needs.

All well and good, but how much will it all cost? It shouldn't matter, but obviously it will. You will probably find that a good portion of it can be covered on the great 'super credit card'—the cost of life, total and permanent disability, and income protection insurance is available through most superannuation funds (see later in this step). In many cases, the only thing you might have to cover out of your own pocket will be your trauma cover.

Anything less than the sort of full coverage outlined above means you are effectively retaining risk yourself, rather than transferring it to an insurer. Obviously, some cover is better than none. You may wish to cover some risk now, with a view to filling out your insurance later.

It's not an 'optional extra' for investors

Let's say that after reading *Debt Man Walking* you are fired up enough to make a list of five things you intend to change about your future. It's clearly a list you'd keep in a separate place to the list of five celebrities that you're allowed to sleep with without it being considered infidelity, à la Ross and Chandler on *Friends*.

Fast forward a year and you've now got a margin loan against some shares and, after studying the property market, you bought yourself a modest investment property six months ago.

Why did you do it? To make your future life more comfortable for you and/or your family. In making this decision, you have run up some debt—about $100000 on a margin loan and $400000 on a property. Your disposable income has dropped a little because of the negatively geared property, but you're prepared to make that sacrifice in a calculated gamble that it will help put the kids through school.

What happens if you now die? Or you are diagnosed with cancer (even if treatable), or have a serious accident on your way home from work/tennis/a few drinks? Or maybe you've got a sporting rival, like ice-skater Nancy Kerrigan had in Tonya Harding…

> If you're about to start a major investment program, particularly one where you will take on considerable debt, then having adequate insurance is not an optional extra

If you're about to start a major investment program, particularly one where you will take on considerable debt, then having adequate insurance is not an optional extra. All your good work would come to nought if your partner, while trying to deal with your death, had to sell the very assets you'd bought to take care of them in the future.

Valuing domestic duties

When considering insurance, there is a tendency to fail to have the stay-at-home mum, or even *Mr Mom*, properly covered.

Unless you're earning a real fortune, there could be a serious strain on the family budget caused by the death, disablement or illness of the domestic goddess/god. If the kids are young, you might have to get longer childcare, a nanny or after-school care. Don't forget who does the housework. If the spouse who does the housework dies, the housework would now have to be done by someone else. Enough money for a housekeeper could take that pressure off.

The death of a spouse is an intensely emotional and difficult time for anyone. Don't compound it by failing to cover them. The extra cost for even $300 000 to $500 000 of life insurance for the stay-at-home partner won't be significant. You should aim to have a full package (complete with TPD and trauma insurance), to make sure that a serious illness, injury or death won't destroy the family's finances for decades to come.

How long do I need it?

Until you've made it! That is, until your net assets are worth enough that it wouldn't so much matter *financially* if something happened. That might not be until you are about to retire. It might be when you're well into your 50s.

Insurance is priced according to risk and is, therefore, generally fairly cheap for young, fit, healthy people, who are less likely to die, have accidents or illnesses. Insurance in your 30s and early 40s is generally cheap as chips. It tends to start becoming expensive in the late 40s, or the early 50s for some.

The need for insurance will increase as you take on more debt and have a more expensive lifestyle, but should eventually decrease with age as you create wealth. By the time most people are 55 or 60, the home might be paid off. Your superannuation should start to look like a substantial figure. And if you've been consistently following an investment program, you should even have a reasonable level of non-super assets.

Figure 9.1 shows the general need for insurance for people as they age.

Figure 9.1: age and the need for insurance

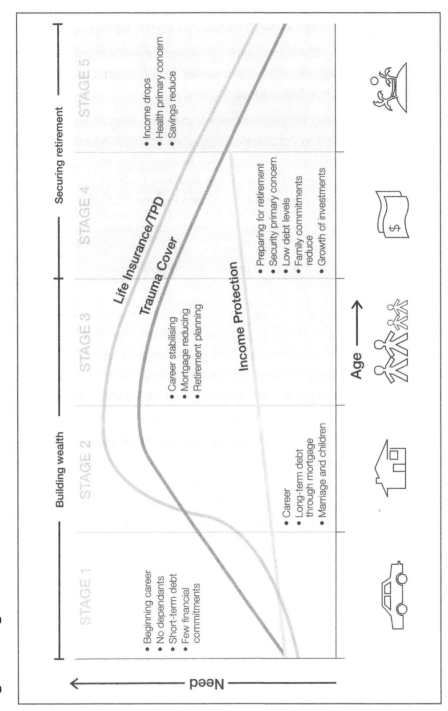

Saving bucks with the super credit card

When it comes to getting all the insurance you need, there is some good news. For most Generation Xers, big licks (mmm, remember Smurf ice-creams?) of what you need should be obtainable within your super fund.

Yep, you can use that lump of money—which may not amount to much yet and whose payoff date seems forever away—to give you something now! This means two things. The first is that you may not have to open your wallet and pay for it with after-tax dollars. The second is that, if it is available through your fund, there is almost no excuse not to have proper life, TPD and income protection insurance.

Superannuation acts like a special sort of credit card for life, TPD and income protection insurance—a kind of 'buy now, pay later' plan. You can buy insurance now (obviously in the hope that you'll never need it) and the negative comes down the track, in the form of less money for your retirement.

Another advantage is that super funds are allowed to claim a tax deduction on the premiums for life, TPD and income protection insurance (only income protection is a tax deduction in your personal name). This gives super funds a tax deduction of 15 per cent on the premiums. So, for every $100 of policy premium, your super fund will have $15 returned as a tax refund, reducing the after-tax cost to $85.

Using superannuation to pay for your insurance is a trade off; you will have less superannuation when you're ready to retire. This could be overcome by making small extra voluntary payments to your super fund (see step 10). Also, particularly in the case of TPD and income protection insurance, the super fund's trustees have to approve payment to the member. In most cases, this won't be an issue, but it could be in some unusual circumstances. Speak to your financial adviser about this.

Shit Creek paddle salesmen

A great Australian saying about being in trouble and strife is 'up Shit Creek without a paddle'.

I was at a seminar when we were asked to write mission statements: an 'elevator statement' that either got across exactly what you did in 10 seconds, or got people so intrigued they wanted to follow you out of the lift to get the full story. Most of the answers were pretty standard.

One guy, an adviser called Lucas Barsby, came up with the most brutally honest, catchy answer. When he got asked what he did by friends or people at a dinner party, his answer was 'I'm the Shit Creek paddle salesman. When you're up the creek, I'll be the one who hands you the paddle'.

That stops people in their tracks or makes them laugh. And he's right. If you've bought life insurance, then your adviser will be the one who hands you a financial paddle when you most need it.

Life insurance salesmen don't promise financial riches, except under the worst imaginable circumstances. Being properly covered is an important part of any financial plan, so find someone to sell you some paddles in case you're ever up the creek without one. Most general financial advisers can help you with your life insurance protection requirements. And those who don't should be able to refer you to an industry colleague who does.

Health insurance

And then there's health insurance. It's neither general insurance nor personal risk insurance.

It's a grey area of insurance, because governments can't decide whether medical coverage should be free for all, or whether there should be a minimum level of free coverage but people should have private cover for the rest.

It is an area of fundamental difference between the major political parties. Labor would err towards free healthcare for all, paid for through taxes. The Coalition would arguably love a much smaller Medicare system and a larger system of private health cover. But political parties are nothing if not pragmatic, meaning Australia has a nasty and often confusing mix of both public and private health insurance funding.

Carrots and sticks—government and private insurance

First, there's Medicare. We've all got it and we largely all pay for it. It covers some stuff, but not other stuff.

Medicare coverage is a lot like being pregnant the wrong way—Arnold Schwarzenegger in *Junior*. It covers some really important medical costs, but not other really important medical costs.

Private health cover is designed to cover you for most of the stuff that Medicare won't. The Australian system of private health insurance has two core values. It is designed so that if you earn enough money, you should pay to have your own private health insurance. If you don't, the government will beat you with two big sticks, which are penalty taxes and penalty insurance rates.

If you earn more than $50000 as an individual (or $100000 as a family) as at September 2008 and don't have private health insurance, the Tax Office will slug you an extra 1 per cent tax a year on your whole income. That is, if you are single and earn $120000 and you don't have private health insurance, then you'll be up for an extra $1200 in tax.

If you leave getting private health insurance until you're older than 30, insurance companies must charge you an extra 2 per cent for each year you are above 30 on top of standard premiums. If you join at 37, you'll pay 14 per cent more than a 37-year-old who joined at age 30.

The carrot is governments will refund 30 per cent of the cost of private health care.

The X-Flips:

Protect your greatest asset

Stop treating life insurance as a grudge purchase.

It's almost incomprehensible that the majority insure worldly possessions, but don't insure that which is really most precious and valuable to them—their life, their health and their ability to work. And it's a sad reflection on our priorities when the least valuable item (of cars, homes and contents) is the most likely to be insured. One year of your income is almost certainly worth more than your car. Which would you be worse off without?

Earlier in this step, we went through the percentages of how many people have insurance for particular possessions. Now, let's look at the same figures for life insurance. There's a serious contrast (these figures are again compiled by CommInsure):

- 14 per cent of consumers have life insurance

- 6 per cent of people have income protection insurance

- 5 per cent have total and permanent disability insurance

- 2.5 per cent have trauma insurance.

What's more valuable? Your $25 000 car? Or the $2 to $3 million you will earn between now and age 65? It seems particularly silly when the cost of insuring your income is probably less than the cost of your car and is a tax deduction, and when so many of your insurance needs are available through super.

Step 9 for Gen X

Sit down (with your partner) and canvass a few scenarios. Think about the household's finances if one of you were to die. What about if one of you developed a serious, but not life threatening, cancer? What happens if you had an accident or did your back and couldn't work for an extended period, or potentially ever again? Could you really survive on a government disability pension?

Once you've really considered the risks, call your superannuation fund and find out if you can get your life, total and permanent disability and income protection insurance needs through super if you do not wish to pay for them personally. For whatever you can't get, including trauma, see a financial adviser. These policies vary widely in quality and cost and you should seek professional help.

step 10

Q: What was the name of that bizarre-
looking magical animal that seemed
to be part dog, part rabbit and part
mouse in *The Neverending Story?*

A: Falkor, the Luckdragon

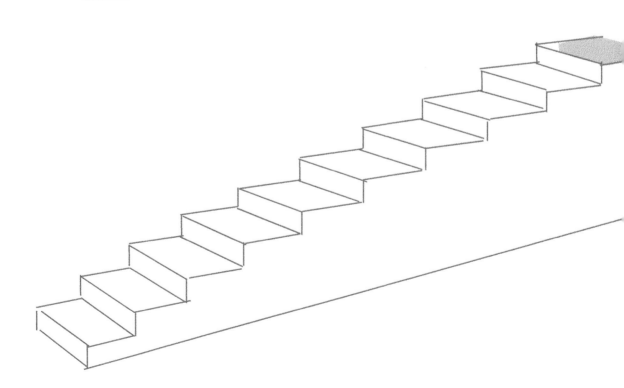

Choose your own...neverending story

- Super—soon, sexy and stripped down
- Your super. Where? What?
- Double your super with 15 minutes' work
- Super's warring factions
- Managing your own super (SMSFs)
- Super's gearing options ('Super Debt Man?')
- The X-Flips: time to Care Bear about super

In 2006, when I was still a fulltime finance journalist, I went to France with wealth manager AXA on an 'educational' trip. Okay, so it was a junket. Over a period of about three or four days as AXA's guest in Paris and at their Suduiraut winery in Bordeaux, eating six-star French food 17 times a day and drinking French wine by the bucket of an evening, I put on about three or four kilos. A kilo a day! The food was *that* rich and the wine was *that* good. It wasn't just an eating-contest-cum-drink-a-thon, even if that's how it might be perceived that I treated it. The days were spent being lectured at. And I did file a few stories for the paper.

When you're being entertained by a wealth manager, you inevitably spend a lot of time on the issue of retirement. That's what they're managing most of their customers' money for. And if you're being forced to talk about other people's retirement—particularly when your own seems to be an insignificant speck in the distance—what better place to be discussing the topic than a winery in the south-west of France?

One of the lectures was on the topic of how people around the world view retirement—quite differently as it turns out. At one stage, the subject turned specifically to Australia's compulsory superannuation system. Being one of only two Aussies in the room, it fell to me to explain how super worked. I said something along the lines of: 'The government forces business to pay a portion of people's wages into super, where it is taxed at a special low rate. They can also put their own money in. That money is invested and any earnings are also taxed at lower rates. People can get that money when they retire, yet again taxed at lower rates. Really, it's just one big legal tax dodge'.

The foreign business journalists were gobsmacked that a little backwater like Australia could have invented such a simple, almost universal way of forcing people to save for their retirement. I was answering questions from them for about 40 minutes, until they cut the session for…another six-star meal with copious bouteilles du vin.

> *…it is possible that you can have a big impact on your super now and therefore improve your retirement.*

That sums up superannuation in Australia. As a concept, it is simple enough. But anyone who has taken the time to have more than a cursory look at it knows that it is anything but simple in practice. It's a hotch-potch of inconsistent rules that are constantly tweaked by politicians trying to make their mark over nearly three decades.

But it is possible that you can have a big impact on your super now and therefore improve your retirement. It's *Choose Your Own Adventure* meets *The Neverending Story*.

'So Far Away'…

Just like Dire Straits, we're ageing. But unlike Mark Knopfler, who has hit retirement age, we've still got some way to go.

When the rules are constantly changing, it's understandable that Generation X struggles to get excited about superannuation. As a generation, we are, on average, still more than 20 years away from being able to access it. Extrapolating past legislative experience means politicians will make approximately 4 637 864 largely unnecessary changes to the superannuation rules before the average Gen Xer hits retirement.

You don't have to get excited about super. But failing to take some care now could severely impact on the quality of your retirement.

What if I said that with about 15 minutes of work now, most readers could double, or nearly double, their superannuation in retirement? Instead of, say, $300 000, you could have $600 000. Instead of $1 million when you retire, you collect $2 million. Seriously.

Want to know how? 'Patience, young grasshopper.'

Actually, it's not so far away

How could anyone get excited about retirement when starting work in their late teens or early 20s? And anyway, your first super statement probably was something like $383.67. Even less to get excited about.

That first work gig was some time ago. We've largely been working for a decade (or two or three) now. Gen Xers, in general, will have something between $25 000 and $150 000 in super. Some might have considerably more.

And it's no longer 40 years away. For the oldest Gen Xers, turning 60 is only about 12 to 15 years away. That's sort of on the horizon. And if you've always ignored your bi-annual super statement (and my experience as a financial adviser is that about two-thirds of people have never done anything with their super) you might have already cost yourself tens of thousands of dollars.

Access to super

How early you can access superannuation depends on when you were born. Everyone born after June 1964 can't get access to super until they turn 60. If you were born before July 1960, you can access it from age 55. Those born in between have a sliding scale from 55 up to 60.

Why? Just because some politicians decided that 55 was too early. Not too early like River Pheonix's checkout, but too early nonetheless.

You've got to start thinking 'super is sexy'

Because it's a pot of savings that you can look at, but can't touch, super does get sexier with age because it grows (well, most years it does).

Take Jane Seymour and Sean Connery. Jane was one of the early James Bond girls. She played Solitaire in the 1973 version of the Bond classic *Live and Let Die*. More recently, she played *Dr Quinn, Medicine Woman* in the 1990s. And then there's Connery, Mr James Bond himself. They both just seem to be getting sexier with age. If Catherine Zeta Jones and George Clooney age half as well, we've got some good cinema to look forward to.

You might think your superannuation currently looks about as attractive as the little fat kid from *Hey Dad...!* But at some stage over the next decade, it will, miraculously, start to look like Catherine or George.

Whether your super ages as well as Sean and Jane will depend on what you do with it *now*.

Your retirement—caviar or cat food?

Governments say they're committed to handing out the old age pension indefinitely. That might well be the case. But that doesn't mean that they have to be very generous with how much they give. And they could further restrict who can have it.

But that's not really important. Who wants to live on the government age pension? Let's face it. It would suck. It would be a meagre, hand-to-mouth existence at best. Paying bills would be a constant struggle, updating the car a pipe dream and enjoying your retirement with the odd stay in a chateaux to sample wine in Bordeaux nothing more than a fantasy.

Super was invented to force people to save for their own retirement and to take the strain off the government age pension. But the government can't make people care about it.

Super: me love you long time

Current average retirement age: about 59 for men and 56 for women. Average age of death: about 79 for men and 84 for women. That's in 2008. By the time I turn 60, medicine might well mean that Sean Connery is still making movies at age 100. By that time, the average age of a man falling off the perch will probably be close to, or even exceeding, 90.

Your super needs to last you a long time. The best way of having your super last as long as you do? Have an obscene amount of it in the first place.

Gen X has got to start seeing super as sexy. And the sooner the better. It's a lump sum that will come back to you at some stage, and the more you make of it the bigger it could be.

REGULATORY RISK: DONALD RUMSFELD'S APPLICATION TO SUPER POLITICS

Like children in a lolly shop, our elected leaders can't help themselves when it comes to tinkering with laws. Making laws is obviously what we send them to Canberra for. But sometimes it feels like they just change things for the sake of it.

Superannuation is a perfect example. It has been tinkered with a thousand times. It's rare that a federal budget passes without super getting a prod. In recent years, thankfully, most of those changes have been positive, making super more attractive. But that hasn't always been the case.

Therein lies one of the great risks of superannuation, and it is particularly important when it comes to Generation X.

When Generation Xers hit retirement age, superannuation will not look like it does right now, that's a certainty. Superannuation today doesn't look much like super of 10 years ago. And it's unrecogniseable to superannuation of 20 to 25 years ago.

The rules will change regularly. They might change the age at which super can be accessed (if anything, delayed) or they might change super taxes (up or down). Governments are usually painfully aware of annoying voters close to retirement and accessing their super, but they are less likely to care about the votes of people who don't care so much about super (like, say, us now).

To quote Donald Rumsfeld, when it comes to super the concerns lie in the 'known unknowns' and the 'unknown unknowns'. For this reason, committing too much too early to superannuation is a potential hazard to keep in mind when considering putting extra into your super in your 30s or early 40s. While super is almost the ultimate use of the law of compounding growth, there are better options for younger Australians, particularly those under 45, than locking money away until you're at least 60.

Comes as standard

Our great grandparents won the minimum wage. Our grandparents earned the right to paid holidays (one week became the standard in 1941!). Our parents were in the first generation where women had to be paid the same as men for the same work.

Us? We are the first to have super installed as a standard working condition. Prior to us, super was an optional extra—business really only offered it to senior employees as a reward/retention strategy. Outside of that, only the wealthy had super funds.

The standard super payment started off in 1992 as 3 per cent—that's how much of an employee's wages an employer had to contribute to super. That has since grown to 9 per cent.

Those who crunch numbers on these sorts of things believe 9 per cent is still not enough. (There is occasional talk of the superannuation guarantee amount being lifted to as high as 15 per cent, or that the government could force employees to start putting in up to 3 per cent of their own money as their contribution.)

> So, why do we have super? Essentially, it's designed to be savings and investments to look after us later in life.

Given a lifetime of working and normal investment market returns, it is certainly capable of becoming a reasonable sum, even if it's not enough to sustain the same standard of living until death. The 9 per cent standard contribution didn't occur until after 2000, so it won't be until about 2040 to 2045 that we'll see the first employees to have had a full working life (say, 40 years) with a full 9 per cent of their incomes put away for their retirement.

Super made simple

So, why do we have super? Essentially, it's designed to be savings and investments to look after us later in life. To that end, the government taxes superannuation at reduced rates (15 per cent as a maximum within super, versus up to 46.5 per cent for income earned in our personal names).

Contributions

How does the money get into super? There are a few ways, and it also depends on whether you're an employee or self-employed.

Superannuation guarantee

If you're an employee (above certain minimum incomes), your employer has to pay 9 per cent of the salary paid to you into superannuation, which is known as the superannuation guarantee. It was designed to get employers to shoulder some of the burden of making sure their employees have something in retirement.

It's worth checking once or twice a year that super is actually being paid into your account, as some companies try to shirk their superannuation responsibilities. If you are concerned about this, call your super fund. They should be able to tell you quickly whether payments, and the right payments, are being paid into your account.

If you're earning $80000 as your full-time salary, then your employer will have to put in $7200 a year (either through monthly or quarterly contributions). Australia has a contributions tax of 15 per cent that is charged to money that has not been previously taxed on the way into the fund. That means that of your $7200, there will be a net $6120 ($7200 minus 15 per cent) in your super fund to invest for your future.

Salary sacrifice

Salary sacrifice is one way that regular employees are encouraged to put money into super. It is based on the understanding that the government will tax you less if you agree to sacrifice a portion of your future salary to put away for your future retirement. As a result, you can only agree to sacrifice salary that you have not yet earned. (That is, to stop tax evasion, you can't sacrifice income you have previously earned in a financial year, only income that you have yet to earn.)

The money you salary sacrifice into super is also taxed at 15 per cent on its way into the fund. (If you took it as salary, you would lose up to 46.5 per cent in income tax and the Medicare levy.)

For example, if someone is earning $100000 in Australia in the 2008–09 financial year, their marginal tax rate is 41.5 per cent. For every dollar they earn above $80000, they will pay 41.5 cents in the dollar in tax. If they were to take their last $10000 in the normal way (that is, as salary) they would lose $4150 in income tax, leaving them with $5850 to be paid into their bank account. However, if they salary sacrificed that $10000 into super, it would be taxed at 15 per cent—of the $10000 of salary paid into super, $8500 would make it into the fund. In this instance, salary sacrificing would result in $2650 less tax being paid overall.

GEN X AND SALARY SACRIFICING: DECADES OF LOST ACCESS

I'm not a great fan of too many Generation Xers doing too much in the way of salary sacrificing — yet. Superannuation is a great savings vehicle for retirement, but it has one big drawback. You can't touch it until you hit your access age. A 35-year-old salary sacrificing now is going to have a wait of a minimum of 25 years before they'll be able to spend that money. (Those Gen Xers on very high incomes, say above $200 000, might have something to gain from salary sacrificing some portion of their income.)

I believe that by following the *Debt Man* investment principles, Gen Xers can do far more with the money in their hands now, and over the next decade or two, by using some gearing with their investment strategies. Plus, if something happens, or they decide they want the money for some other plan (such as upgrading the home, paying for the kids' school fees or starting a business), it's available. It's only under the worst of circumstances, such as severe financial stress or disability, that you can get early access to your super, and even then it is severely restricted.

There's nothing wrong with salary sacrificing at any particular age. It is a great way of saving for retirement. But salary sacrificing works best as a strategy when there is less than 10 years to go until retirement. Most Generation Xers (those born after June 1964) will be able to get access to their super from age 60, so salary sacrificing as a strategy is probably worth looking at from about age 50.

Prior to that, stick to other investment strategies where you can continue to get access to your investments. You can do some tax-advantaged investing through the other principles in *Debt Man Walking* in your personal name now and begin a salary sacrificing strategy a little later. You can reduce your tax overall with negatively geared investments (if you decide that is your thing) without losing access forever.

Self-employed

There is nothing stopping people who are self-employed from contributing to their super, but there is no requirement for them to do so. As a result, the self-employed often don't contribute anything to super in the years when they are building up their own business. They will often leave contributions to later on, losing the benefit of compounding over extended periods.

They can contribute along the way, of course, and there are tax advantages to doing so. The government will allow the self-employed to claim a full tax deduction for any money they contribute to their own super (up to certain limits).

If they earn $120000, but make a $15000 tax-deductible contribution into their super fund, they will be taxed only on earnings for the year of $105000. (That $15000 contributed to super will also lose 15 per cent in contributions tax on the way into the fund.)

GEN X AND NON-CONCESSIONAL CONTRIBUTIONS The same general principle applies to Generation X making non-concessional contributions as it does for salary sacrificing (see box on p. 226).

The loss of access for an extended period means making significant non-concessional contributions before you turn 50 is probably not advisable. It's a strategy best left until you're in your last five to ten years before retirement.

Hopefully, *Debt Man Walking* has shown you that there are better investment strategies that can be used, outside of super, to help you achieve other shorter- and longer-term goals.

That doesn't mean that you should be doing nothing with your super. We'll get on to what you can do to improve your super a little later in this step.

Non-concessional contributions

All super fund members can put some of their own money into their fund. This is called a non-concessional contribution.

As full tax has already been paid on the money and no-one is claiming a tax deduction on the contributions, no contributions tax is charged as it enters the fund.

There are limits to how much you can put into super through non-concessional limits. This limit is $150000 a year (or $450000 can be put in at once, which will cover three financial years for those below age 65).

How super is invested

Superannuation fund managers invest in the basic investment assets that we have talked about already in *Debt Man Walking*—cash, fixed interest, property and shares. At the end of 2007, nearly $1.3 trillion was invested through superannuation in Australia. The meltdown in share and property markets in 2008 meant there was considerably less than that by the middle of the year.

At the moment, most superannuation is managed fund superannuation. That is, the trustees of large super funds pool the money from members and place it with fund managers.

Because most people don't take an active interest in their superannuation and how that money is invested, super fund trustees have to choose a default option. This is usually into a balanced fund, which is the equivalent of the prudent investment style that we discussed in step 3. About 60 to 70 per cent of the money is invested in shares and property and the remaining 30 or 40 per cent is invested in cash and fixed-interest investments.

Is balanced super right for Gen Xers?

Is a default balanced option appropriate? There would certainly be a lot of people who should be invested in a balanced fund. But it is a style that neither takes into account the age of the investor nor their risk profile. It's the safe option for trustees or employers to take, like putting Billy Joel or Phil Collins on as background music at a dinner party. It's not great, but it's unlikely to make anyone angry.

A balanced fund doesn't recognise, for instance, that a 25-year-old joining the workforce can afford to take on bigger risks because they have longer to retirement. The fact that Gen Xers have such a long time to retirement and can afford to take on more significant investment risk is central to the investment ideas of *Debt Man Walking*.

Younger people can afford to take longer-term risks (as discussed in step 3). Gen X still has at least 15 to 20 years until they turn 65 and about 35 to 40 years until the average age at which they are likely to die (assuming current life expectancies). The youngest Xers have more than 35 years until they turn 65 and more than 55 years until they will turn 85. Lumping all new employees into the same balanced fund is ridiculous. Should the rampant Republican Alex P Keaton (Michael J Fox in *Family Ties*) be in the same fund as any of the *Golden Girls*?

That's a long time frame for investing. And being in a balanced fund isn't likely to have them exposed to the sort of growth that will best help them fund a satisfactory retirement.

And tax free from 60

The most positive changes to superannuation in recent years came into effect on 1 July 2007. And with the standard warning about how super laws can change over time (see 'Regulatory risk: Donald Rumsfeld's application to super politics' on p. 223), interest in super has soared since the government decided to make it tax free for the over 60s and removed reasonable benefit limits (which effectively limited how much money could be held tax effectively in superannuation).

Turning 60 in itself is nothing to get excited about, particularly if you're still in your 30s or 40s. But it's promising that governments have allowed super to grow up. And making it tax free when you turn 60 is about as positive as anything that could have been done to encourage people to save for their own retirement.

FINDING LOST SUPER In 2007, there was something like six million lost super accounts, worth a total of \$12 billion. This often happens because of short-term or casual employment.

The good news is that it's not hard to track it down. There are dozens of internet sites where it can be done online.

The best place to start is the Tax Office's Superseeker site. Go to <www.ato.gov.au/individuals/content.asp?doc=/content/16442.htm>.

Where's your super hanging out now?

It's surprising how many Gen Xers don't even know the basics of their own super. Given that it is now a reasonable sum (or is fast approaching being so), it's pretty scary how many people don't know the basics about where a large wad of their future prosperity will come from.

Off the top of your head, can you answer these two basic questions?

1   Who has your super?

2   How is it invested?

Now…go and grab your last super statement. If you've answered both correctly, then congratulations, you've reached a bare pass mark—you may well yet graduate from Summer Bay High (and hopefully get to leave behind *Home and Away* for good!). (To achieve a 'B' or even an 'A' you would have to know the answers to: How much is in there? How has the fund performed? How high are the fees? Does the fund offer me the insurance I need?)

If you have previously filed everything without reading it, you may have just discovered that your super is invested in something that is about as exciting as a Barry Manilow concert (with a set that included 'Copacabana (At The Copa)' and 'I Write The Songs'). Your fund name might have the word 'balanced' in it, or something equally unappealing, like 'moderate', 'balanced growth', 'defensive growth', 'moderate growth' or 'conservative'.

The titles mean nothing. Any of these terms can mean anything. A 'defensive' fund can actually be quite aggressive and a 'growth' fund can be quite conservative.

> By definition, your superannuation is a long, long-term investment.

You need to dig a little deeper. Call your super fund and ask them, 'Of the fund that I'm invested in, what percentage is invested in Australian shares, international shares, property, fixed interest and cash?'

Add the percentages for shares and property together. Separately, add up the fixed interest and cash percentages. Then put the two separate figures together as a ratio (such as 70:30, or 60:40) and find out what sort of investment it is the equivalent to from the risk profiles in step 3. The first part is the amount of your fund in growth assets (shares and property) and the second part is the portion in income assets (cash and fixed interest).

Is that where it should be?

Estimates put about 80 to 90 per cent of Australians' super sitting in a balanced fund. Is that where they chose to put it? Often it is not. Generally, it's there purely because it is the default fund. Is that where *your* superannuation should be? Think back to the risk profile questionnaire in step 3. Probably not.

Where your superannuation should be is critical to your long-term investment strategy. Largely, you can't touch it until you are 60. The average Gen Xer now is about 38 years old. That's an average of 22 years to accessing super. By definition, your superannuation is a long, long-term investment. Considering what *Debt Man Walking* covered in steps 3 and 4 in regards to risk, reward and growth assets, if you could just take one step further—move yourself one step further up the risk ladder—there would be significant advantages.

Part of the *Debt Man* philosophy is to take the time to understand risk, particularly that time reduces the risks of short-term volatility in share and property markets.

How you can double your super in retirement with 15 minutes' work now

You: 'Gimmick for your book, right?'

No, it's not. It simply takes into account the principles of *Debt Man Walking* and allows time to work some magic for us. Not *everyone* will be able to double their money. Older Gen Xers probably don't have enough time to double their money, but they could certainly improve their super by a minimum of 30, 40 or 50 per cent.

How can this be done? Let me show by example.

Sally is a 30-year-old earning a salary of $70 000 a year, with $50 000 already in super. She is getting $5355 ($70 000 × 9% − 15% contributions tax) paid into her super fund each year by her employer.

Sally is currently in a balanced fund, which is 60 per cent invested in shares and 40 per cent invested in cash and fixed interest. She's too young to know when she might retire, but admits that she's a bit of a spender, so she might have to work a little longer, perhaps to age 65. So she has 35 years until retirement. Sally did the risk profile test and found out that she was an assertive investor. After reading *Debt Man Walking*, Sally feels comfortable with how time can iron out the fluctuations for property and share assets, and is comfortable that her super can be invested with even more risk. Sally decides to switch her super from the balanced option to a high-growth (all shares and property) investment option.

If her money had stayed with the balanced investment option, she could have expected to receive a compound annual return of approximately 6.6 per cent a year after fees and taxes (because a portion of her money is invested in lower return cash and fixed-interest options). If that assumption turns out to be correct, Sally could look forward to having approximately $1.24 million in her super fund when she retires. We have ignored salary inflation in this section, so that the dollar numbers are effectively in today's money.

SURELY THERE ARE RISKS? Of course there are. The main risk is that you switch from a balanced fund to an all-growth fund and the share and property markets poop themselves the following day, the following month, or potentially even the following year.

You could reduce this risk by deciding to make the switch over certain defined periods. You could switch one-quarter of your balanced fund into all-growth now, one quarter in three to four months' time, another in seven to eight months' time and the last quarter about one year after you made your first switch. Your super fund should be able to help you with doing that.

That won't remove all of your risk, but it would substantially reduce it. But don't forget that even if the market does melt down soon after you switch to an all-growth strategy, your balanced fund strategy would have had about 60 to 70 per cent of your super in the falling growth assets anyway.

An all-growth fund is likely to have a higher return over the same period. If Sally's fund were to return 9 per cent a year (after tax and fees), then her super would be worth approximately $2.495 million when she retires. That's slightly more than double the balanced option.

Even though the performance wasn't double (6.6 per cent for balanced, versus 9 per cent for growth), the difference eventually becomes double because of the compounding nature of that few per cent a year over time.

You, again: 'But that's 35 years! How does she do it in 15 minutes?' Sally grabs her last super statement and finds out that she's invested in the balanced fund (one minute), calls her super fund (gets stuck on hold for two minutes) and asks her super fund to send her the forms for an investment switch (another two minutes). So far, five minutes.

A week later, Sally gets a letter from her super fund in the mail. She opens the letter, reads the investment documentation (four minutes) and fills in the form (four minutes). Sally finds an envelope and a stamp (two minutes). She'll post it on the way to work tomorrow. Total: 15 minutes, spread over two days.

And that's the long, old-fashioned way of doing it. With most super funds, you can download the documents and forms you need from the website, print them and post them in.

Even if your risk profile says that you are a prudent investor and you only want to take a small step up the risk ladder to assertive, the difference it could make to your super could be financially significant.

Let's say Sally moved her funds from balanced to assertive. If we assume that the growth in the assertive-style fund (after fees and taxes) is 8 per cent, then her fund would likely end up at about $1.856 million—almost 50 per cent higher than the balanced option.

Assuming most of the same figures from above ($50 000 in super now, salary of $70 000), let's have a look at some other examples:

- If someone with 15 years to retirement moved their super from balanced to assertive, their super should increase from $271 800 to $321 300.

- If someone with 15 years to retirement switched from balanced to aggressive, their fund should grow to $362 800.

- If someone with 23 years to retirement moved their super from balanced to assertive, their super should increase from $517 200 to $669 200.

- If someone with 23 years to retirement switched from balanced to aggressive, their fund should grow to $808 000.

Super's warring factions

The superannuation industry employs tens of thousands of people, as could be expected of an industry in which almost everyone in the country has a personal interest.

But it is far from being one happy little family. There's more factionalised fighting and strained alliances in the super household than in any single episode of *The Brady Bunch*. And since the introduction of Super Choice in 2005—which allowed about half of Australia's workforce to be able to choose any fund they wanted to invest their super—there hasn't been a day of peace.

They are fighting over more than $1 trillion in funds, billions of dollars in profits, tens of thousands of jobs, just as many shareholders, and a public concerned about how they are going to fund their retirement. Big stakes. Big bucks. Big egos. And a flammable mix when thrown into the same pot, like the Carringtons and the Colbys in *Dynasty*.

Industry funds

Industry funds were traditionally run by trade unions. They are low-cost, non-profit organisations that plough profits and costs savings back to their members to improve retirement benefits. They normally offer some insurance (life, TPD and income protection), as far as it can be purchased or paid for through superannuation. But they are unlikely to offer members much in the way of financial advice outside super. While they do offer financial planning services, those services seem to be limited in nature, outside of super, insurance and retirement planning.

> **THE VALUE OF ADVICE**
>
> I believe in the value that financial advisers can provide. I know that when I sit down with a client, I can help them improve the financial path down which they're headed.
>
> The bickering that goes on between industry funds and retail funds is as ridiculous as it is bitter. If the industry funds are right and the average cost of their super services is 1 per cent lower than a retail fund, then that could, indeed, make the difference of 30 per cent over a 20-year period.
>
> But what if the adviser attached to your retail fund helps you get started in some non-super investments? What happens if that $50 000 investment in shares turned into $150 000 by the time you were 40 or 50? That investment could be the one that helps educate the kids, helps you pay off your home loan sooner or allows you to start up that business you've been dreaming of running for years.
>
> If there is a problem with industry and corporate funds, it's that they have no interest in your finances outside of your superannuation. And there is so much more to investing than superannuation.

Corporate funds

Corporate funds are usually sponsored by major employers for their staff. Like industry funds, they tend to be a low-cost, low-advice model that is unlikely to offer financial advice outside of superannuation and insurance advice. Employers themselves used to run corporate funds, but nowadays businesses tend to hire outside fund managers to run their super for them.

Retail funds

Small employers and individuals often use retail funds to administer their super. They are also often used by those who have changed jobs on a regular basis. Retail funds tend to charge higher fees for their services, because they are dealing with individuals, rather than a large employer base. They are also private businesses and need to turn a profit. They are likely to have financial advisers aligned to them, who can service clients more broadly and potentially offer them investment opportunities outside of superannuation.

Self-managed super funds

Think you know a bit about investing? Think you could do a better job yourself than the industry/corporate/retail super fund that's been looking after your money? Well, a self-managed super fund (SMSF) could be for you!

Hold on a second there, Kermit. Not so fast now, my little green friend. There are now more than 370 000 SMSFs in Australia. Their membership numbers are growing faster than the turnstile spins at a *Star Trek* convention. And they are controlling an ever-increasing slice of the superannuation pie.

The real draw of SMSFs is that they offer their members (who must also be trustees of the fund) the ability to control their investments. If the fund is big enough, an SMSF also has the potential to be able to reduce the overall fees that you pay for the management of your superannuation. That is, it

CONTROL: A DOUBLE EDGE SWORD

An SMSF can be a great vehicle for many people. But it can be a disaster for others, who may believe they are suited to be their own trustee and investment manager. But some people are simply not suited.

Be careful. This not an idea that should be acted upon on a whim. If you don't know what you're doing, don't have enough to make it worthwhile to start with, or you aren't prepared to pay professionals to help you, then finding another way to exercise more control over your super might be a better idea. You could use a retail fund that gives you access to funds or opportunities (such as geared funds or individual ownership over shares) that aren't available through industry funds or employer-sponsored funds that might be lower cost, but with a restrictive choice.

doesn't take a lot more work to do the accounting for $2 million of assets in super than it does for $200 000 of assets in super. It also allows the members to have greater control over the fund's taxation, because they can decide what assets to buy and the timing of the sale of those assets.

You also have more direct control over the personal risk insurance held through an SMSF. You can buy directly your life, total and permanent disability and income protection insurance. (Potentially, you may also have your trauma cover inside super. However, the trustees might find it difficult to make a payment to a fund member under the relevant super law. In my opinion, unless the member is approaching, or over, 55 years of age, trauma insurance is generally best taken outside of super.)

While you have considerable control over the risk you take with a managed fund super, an SMSF allows the super fund trustees to take on levels of risk that aren't available to ordinary super fund members (particularly thanks to the new super fund gearing rules, covered later in this step).

An SMSF operates under a trust structure. The trustees of the fund are responsible for making sure that the super fund complies with all super laws. And there are many rules to know. You need to know the rules yourself, but you may also end up paying professionals (accountants and financial advisers) to help you with this. If you are considering going down the SMSF path, I would recommend that you read further (perhaps Trish Power's *Superannuation For Dummies* second edition).

While an SMSF gives the trustees some choice about how things are invested, it's not open slather. There are still things that an SMSF can't invest in.

And there are inescapable costs involved in running a super fund. Predominantly, these are accounting, audit and government fees and some transaction costs. Because of those fees, it is generally accepted that a member, or members, should have a minimum of $200000 before setting up an SMSF (some experts argue that it should be more like $250000 or $300000).

Geared super (*Super* Debt Man?)

Plenty of Australia's smartest minds work in the field of superannuation. So what do they discuss when big groups of them get together? What's the dinner party conversation among a group of super professionals?

In 2008 I can tell you that it was gearing into super. A seismic change in the SMSF landscape occurred in late 2007 and the aftershocks were still occurring well into 2008.

In September 2007, a decision was made by the Australian Tax Office that has been every bit as contentious as the winged keel on *Australia II* that helped us win the America's Cup in 1983 (and nearly as memorable as then–Prime Minister Bob Hawke's comment that 'Any boss who sacks anyone for not turning up today is a bum!').

The announcement opened the door for super funds to take on debt to acquire assets. Suddenly SMSFs could borrow to gear into property or shares, on a much broader basis than ever before. They could even negatively gear themselves into assets.

Super fund gearing options

Super funds have had limited access to gearing since the early 1990s. The September 2007 changes expanded the previously limited options.

Be warned: the new super rules don't allow an SMSF to just go out and get a loan to buy assets. There are strict rules in place. The debt-funded assets will largely need to be purchased under regulated contracts and lenders have developed special loans to cater for this new market. The loan must meet certain

SUPER GEARING AND THE NEW WORLD OF DE-LEVERAGING

The timing of the super gearing changes has been (as the Hoodoo Gurus would say) bittersweet. As we mentioned in step 6, the world is going through a process of de-leveraging.

This was also occurring in Australia in 2008, but for slightly different reasons. While Australia could not escape being affected by what was going on globally, our own de-leveraging was being exacerbated by high interest rates.

When the Reserve Bank raised rates in March 2008, it was the twelfth time that rates had been raised since May 2002 and the fourth time they'd risen in seven months (August and November 2007, plus February and March 2008). On top of that, banks, which were suffering from the global credit crisis, had also lifted rates separately to the RBA's increases, meaning Australian borrowers had endured the equivalent of more than six interest rate rises in seven months — enough to give even the most optimistic great debt users cause for pause.

And, as it turns out, the timing of the new laws coincided with the top of the stock market boom. The new laws allowing super funds to gear came into effect on 24 September 2007. Just five weeks later, on 1 November, Australia's stock market peaked, before going into nearly a year of falls.

conditions — including that the loan must be limited recourse (which introduces further risk to the lender and will mean higher interest rates).

In 2008, lending products that meet the new super lending rules criteria are still thin on the ground. New loans and products are entering the market every month. So, how can super funds gear? Under the new rules, there are approximately four broad options for gearing.

Geared share funds

Most managed funds in Australia collect money from investors and then invest that money in the markets. However, there are some funds that gear internally. That is, they use their investors' money, then borrow some more money, and invest the entire sum. This tends to give investors about twice the investment fire power.

The advantage of this sort of fund is that you have a professional fund manager managing your investment and a cheap source of funding, because the fund manager can generally get the debt cheaper than an individual investor.

This is one of the few options that is potentially available to members of some retail managed fund super companies. It is also available to SMSFs. It is not generally available through industry or corporate funds, because managers of those funds are trying to keep costs down and, quite likely, because it would provide a potential risk headache for the trustees.

Self-funding instalment warrants

Self-funding instalment (SFI) warrants are, in essence, partly paid shares. They are usually offered only over the biggest companies listed on the Australian Securities Exchange.

With SFI warrants, the investor pays about half of the value of the shares now, with the other half to be paid off later (usually in five or ten years). That other half of the share is wrapped into the warrant as a loan (and the provider makes their money through the interest on that loan).

The process allows investors to get, on average, greater leverage to the underlying share's value (but with an important difference in some inbuilt protection in the warrant (see the box on p. 239).

For example, one share in company DEF is worth $20. An SFI warrant provider (the largest are Macquarie Bank and Westpac) creates a warrant with an internal loan of $10. The investor might pay about $12 for a warrant in company DEF. Dividends paid by the company, usually every six months, go directly to paying down the $10 loan. And once a year, interest on the loan is added back on to the debt.

At the end of the five- or ten-year period, the $10 loan might have been paid down to, say, $2 through a combination of rising dividends and steady interest rates. If the underlying shares have grown to $40, then the warrant itself may now be worth around $38.

For a $12 initial investment, the investor now has equity in a warrant of approximately $38 ($40 minus the remaining $2 loan), through a combination of share price growth and dividends paying down a loan.

Listed instalment receipts

Listed instalment receipts are shares offered with a part payment (first instalment) up front, with what is usually a second instalment in the future. They are essentially partly paid shares, but unlike SFI warrants, there is no inbuilt protection mechanism.

One example of this is the third tranche of Telstra shares that were offered to investors in late 2006. Telstra offered the partly paid shares for approximately $2 each, when the full Telstra shares were trading at about $3.60. Investors paid $2 in November 2006, with the remaining $1.60 to be paid in May 2008. But, in the meantime, the $2 instalment receipt tracked the underlying fully paid (and more expensive) Telstra shares.

In regards to holding an asset in super, listed instalment receipts will usually be directly available only to SMSFs.

WARRANTED PROTECTION

One of the important elements of SFIs is the element of protection they provide the investor. In the above example, the investor paid $12 for a warrant over a $20 share. Essentially, that is $10 for half a share and $10 for a loan. The other $2 that the investor paid is used to buy a put option over the share. This is a sophisticated protection mechanism that allows an investor to walk away from the debt if the value of the underlying share, on which the warrant is based, collapses.

Let's say that $20 share is only worth $2 at the end of a 10-year term. However, the inbuilt loan is still at $5. The investor technically owes the provider $5. But, because the shares are worth only $2, the warrant is likely to be worthless. Because they paid for a put option as part of the warrant, they get to walk away from the $5 loan without having to repay it.

And now ... Almost Anything Goes!

Like the title of that 1970s game show (which later returned as *It's a Knockout*), the rules of the super game have been dramatically broadened. It's not, however, *anything* goes and the new rules are quite strict. But a super fund can now use debt to buy any type of investment that it is allowed by the relevant law (which is the *Superannuation Industry (Supervision) Act 1993*, which lists things that an SMSF may not invest in).

These new rules are going to be of greatest advantage to property investors. The problem that has previously confronted most SMSFs is that they have not had access to enough money to be able to buy an investment property within their fund, because properties are big, expensive assets. The advantage of the new super rules is that super funds will be able to fund a property through debt. The first lenders in the space were offering to lend between 55 and 70 per cent of the purchase price.

AND THE ALLOWABLE ASSETS DON'T STOP THERE Loans under the new super gearing rules won't be limited to shares and property. Technically, an SMSF will be able to borrow to buy other assets as well, including works of art, vintage cars and wine. But seek advice before purchasing these sorts of assets within your super fund. The sole purpose test for SMSFs means that the purchase of any assets within a fund must be for the sole purpose of providing retirement benefits for members.

You obviously can't drink the wine. Driving the vintage car for pleasure would be an issue. And hanging the works of art in your home would mean that you are deriving benefits other than retirement benefits from owning the art.

The rules that govern SMSFs are serious. It's not a plaything for your personal use and it's something that the Tax Office will continue to crack down on, harder and harder.

SMSFs will also be able to borrow to buy shares, although it won't be open slather access such as margin loans. Commercial lenders will tightly control these products, particularly because of the fact that they are limited recourse loans (the bank can't get other assets from the super fund if the fund fails on its loan repayments).

Speak to an adviser

Anyone interested in running their own SMSF should, at a minimum, speak to an accountant who has experience with SMSFs, but should also consider taking on a financial adviser.

SMSFs are complex beasts. The obligations of trustees can be quite onerous. And as much as you pay others to make some decisions, the ultimate responsibility lies with you as the trustee. You're the one the Tax Office will come after.

Under the law (in 2008), accountants are allowed to advise on setting up SMSFs and how SMSF taxation works, but they are not allowed to advise on investments. Unless you feel confident with your own ability to run your own investments, you should have a financial adviser on your team.

The X-Flips:

Time to Care Bear about super

I know superannuation is something the vast majority of Gen Xers don't care too much about at present. The care factor probably fits into the same category as:

- Whatever happened to Andrew Ridgeley? (The ugly half of Wham!)
- Who killed Laura Palmer? (*Twin Peaks*)
- What possessed them to name the band Spandau Ballet?
- Why would New Zealanders even think about spending 'Six Months in a Leaky Boat'? (Split Enz)
- What the hell was 'Whip It' referring to? (Devo)
- When did video stores officially turf all those betamax movies?

Yawning questions all. They're hardly going to keep you lying awake at night.

At our age, super shouldn't keep us awake either. But superannuation was designed for us, for our generation. They—those people who called us Generation X—thrust compulsory superannuation upon us so that the state's responsibility for our future retirement finances would diminish and we could largely look after ourselves.

Show a little care for your super. Now. No, right now. Go grab your last super statement. Check it out. Give it the time of day. It could have a huge impact on your future. Accept that superannuation is an ultra-long-term investment and take a longer term view on your investments in it.

With 15 minutes of care now, to raise your investment risk profile, you could double your super. That's not a promise. And it's not a guarantee. But it is a mathematical *likelihood*.

Step 10 for Gen X

I hate to point it out, but retirement is no longer 40 years away. For some, 10 years have passed. For others, 25 years have slipped by. Some Gen Xers will be able to access their super in less than 10 years.

And if you've had a look at your super balance lately, you'll notice that it's probably no longer an insignificant amount of money.

Here are some hard truths about retirement and superannuation:

- You don't want to end up relying solely on the government age pension—there's no fat in that budget.

- You've got superannuation anyway; you might as well make the most of it.

- While you might retire at 60, the likelihood is that you'll live until your early 80s (if modern medicine doesn't improve things), but possibly into your 90s. That's 20 to 30 years of supporting yourself without working.

- If modern medicine does improve, we might be surviving for 30 or 40 years in retirement.

- Accept that super is a long-term investment and consider the benefits from investing your own funds a little more aggressively.

- The ability to gear into super could be appropriate to start considering for those who understand the risks and have an interest in taking an even more aggressive Debt Man–style long-term approach to their super.

And there's nothing wrong with managed fund super (whether it's an industry, corporate or retail fund). The problem is that most Australians tend not to put any thought into it until they are approaching retirement, when they are some time in their 50s. That's usually too late. By that stage, they have generally been sitting in a balanced fund for 10 or 20 years and they have missed the chance to have grown their super by considerable amounts through a couple of stock market booms.

Think about it.

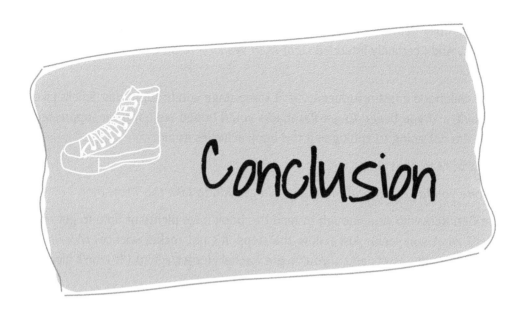

Conclusion

The 11th step...

Phew. That's a bit full. Like the bag you used to get when you asked for 20 cents worth of mixed lollies. Nowadays, you'd be lucky to get a couple of chocolate freckles.

So there you have it. *Debt Man Walking* is now complete. Nearly. There's a little bit more. And, like the credits in a Monty Python film, there's still a gem or two to come.

You'll find a punchy, cut-down version of the 10 X-Flips, a 100-term glossary (where I've found some new Gen X targets) and a list of 50 *DMW* rules. That's 20 investment rules, 20 gearing rules, plus 10 rules that should serve as advance warning to civilisation about how Gen Xers see things and how we intend to run the planet when we take over (which is fairly soon). I'm hoping you might help me expand on that list at <www.debtman.com.au>. Look for the 'Gen X Rules' tab (sign up for your regular newsletter at the same time and try the investment calculators).

I set out with the intention of making *Debt Man Walking* different to the other books on the bookshop business shelf. I think I've covered debt uniquely. I believe

I've successfully delivered Australia's first finance book aimed specifically at Gen X's needs. And I certainly intended *Debt Man Walking* to be a bit of fun. I enjoyed writing it.

If some childhood angst resurfaced … if at some stage you thought this 'Smells Like Teen Spirit' … if you began to get flashbacks you'd hoped were forever suppressed … well, I'm not going to apologise if this book achieves its aim.

'And, Debt Man, that aim is …?'

To inspire you to get your butt into gear! To get you to take the 11th step!

Those Gen Xers who care enough to read this book have plenty of time to get rich (if that's what you seek). Just follow the steps. It's not rocket science. Mix time, debt and the right assets and … you've got Rachel Hunter again! ('It won't hippen overnight … ')

The 11th step is something you need to make. You need to at least make a *decision to act*—perhaps to find professionals to work with. If you need some help, want further advice or want to sit down with an adviser to find out how they work (or more accurately, how I work), I'm pretty easy to contact. (Hint: <www.debtman.com.au>.)

It would be way too corny to cue 'Time of Your Life' by Greenday as you work your way through the credits. So, I won't. I'll keep it simple.

Walk this way to wealth.

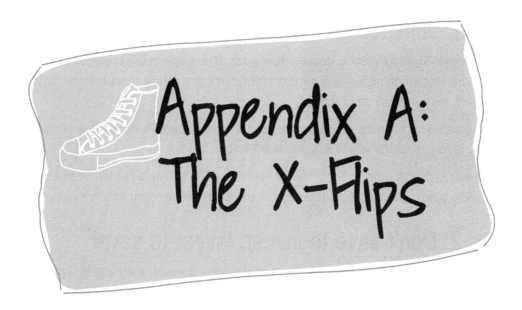

Appendix A: The X-Flips

Debt Man Walking aims to send Generation X readers down a different financial path. It's a path that is littered with scenic memories, good and bad, about the world we grew up in. It was a fun world. Well, most of it was. I hope the flashbacks don't cause you distress. 'It's okay, it's okay! You'll never have to listen to Charlene's 'I've Never Been to Me' again!'

That different route involves deconstructing some old, ingrained bad habits and biases that we've picked up. Society is an odd beast. The 'rules' society spits out are designed to be failsafe, idiot-proof, lowest-common-denominator rules. We learn some odd stuff from our parents, our friends and from the society that we live in. Many of them are, to be honest, not good for your wealth at all.

Debt Man Walking's X-Flips are designed to get you thinking differently about 10 financial matters. Flip your thinking or get you motivated. Make you see things from the opposite viewpoint. Just to make sure you got them, here is a cut-down version.

Step 1: Just…say…yes!

Say yes more. Start by writing down a few goals. The single most important thing about achieving anything in life is getting started. It's that whole 'a journey of 1000 miles starts with a single step' thing.

Stop saying no to building yourself a better financial future. Putting off an action isn't going to get you to where it is you want to be.

Remember Rachel Hunter in those awful Pantene ads? 'It won't hippen overnight. But it will hippen.' Saying yes to the steps in this book will see you achieving goals.

Step 2: Don't save to invest. Invest to save!

We've always been taught that we should save some money, then invest. There's nothing wrong with this. Saving is a slow and steady way of reaching a target. But is it always the best way?

For life's really big financial goals, Gen Xers should consider taking the opposite approach: *don't save to invest, invest to save.*

Instead of putting a little away each week or month, you could use that money as the interest payments on an investment. It will allow you to buy a much bigger investment initially. For example, saving $300 a week for two years would give you about $32 000, including interest, in a savings account. But with the same amount of money, you could have:

● invested in a geared savings program (with a margin loan) and had an investment of $60 000 to $125 000

● invested in $200 000 to $300 000 of structured investment products (such as capital-protected investments)

● bought a $300 000 investment property.

Reversing the idea and investing to save could give you a much bigger asset to start with. A sum of $32 000 that increases in value at 10 per cent a year for the next 10 years will be worth nearly $90 000. However, a $300 000 investment property appreciating at 10 per cent a year for 10 years will be worth more than $778 000.

The risks are obviously higher, so this sort of strategy should be used only for long-term investments. But changing your thinking on this could make a phenomenal difference to your wealth.

Step 3: Stop worrying about today

You won't be able to stop worrying about *today's* money problems until you've done something about *tomorrow's* finances.

By tomorrow, I don't mean the day after today. The day you should be worried about is five or ten years from now. Or when your kids are due to begin school, or when you want to buy the holiday home. It's about the big financial targets you've set yourself.

That's what you should be aiming at. Following the steps in this book will get you there. Start working towards a bigger target.

Step 4: Diversification is portfolio protection

Making just one or two investments is akin to gambling. It might make you rich. But let's face it, it probably won't.

You need to diversify your investments, both in type and in timing. Diversification helps remove the risk that you'll choose an investment just before everything plunges. If it's only one of ten investments that you've made over five or ten years, then it won't matter so much if one of them doesn't do well.

Some investments simply don't work out. Some perform spectacularly. It's far more dangerous to pin all your hopes on the one investment than it is to have a dozen.

Step 5: Manage your mortgage, then manage your wealth

Within five years of getting a mortgage, most people should start to have things under control. The mortgage should no longer be a stress.

You could reward yourself with a more expensive lifestyle, trade up to a bigger home, accelerate your repayments or use the extra funds to start an investment program that could help you pay off your home loan faster, or do a combination of all of these.

You'll never earn an income from your home, so it's time to move from managing your mortgage to managing your wealth. Start using some of your excess cash in broader investments.

Step 6: Going green—recycling your debt

In your investment life, there may occasionally be opportunities to recycle some debt; that is, swapping over debt for which you can't claim a tax deduction into debt for which you can claim a deduction.

How is this done? If you have equity in some investments, then you might be able to sell the investment, pay down your home loan and take on investment debt to buy back the original investments (or a similar investment in the case of property).

This strategy may incur capital gains tax, but may pay for itself inside a year or two in many cases.

Step 7: Know-it-alls don't know it all

Life's too short to waste time learning stuff you don't want to, or doing chores you don't enjoy. So don't be stubborn about the cost when it comes to hiring finance professionals. They will often save you both time and money.

Don't put off taking control of your finances because you don't know where to start. Find some professionals to help you. And don't think you know everything. You don't. The right professionals are often going to be worth their weight in gold.

Understand your limits and the value of your time.

Step 8: Calculate the wait, don't procrastinate

Finding excuses is easy—there are loads to choose from. If you're ever struggling, just punch 'excuses' into an internet search engine and you'll get thousands.

Let's say you have a goal that requires $200 000 in 12 years. Delaying your attempts to hit that $200 000 target can be costly:

- The *start-now* option: you'd need to save $8500 a year ($708 a month).

- The *procrastinate-for-four-years* option: you'll need to save $15900 a year ($1325 a month) for the remaining eight years.

- The *procrastinate-for-eight-years* option: you'll need to save $39200 a year ($3267 a month) for the last four years.

Taking the medicine earlier (delayed gratification) will save even more serious pain later, because of *the power of compounding*.

Step 9: Protect your greatest asset

Stop treating life insurance as a grudge purchase.

It's almost incomprehensible that the majority insure worldly possessions, but don't insure that which is really most precious and valuable to them—their life, their health and their ability to work. What's more valuable? Your $25000 car? Or the $2 to $3 million you will earn between now and age 65?

Step 10: Time to Care Bear about super

For Gen Xers, super is an ultra-long-term investment. Given that, it doesn't make sense that so many of us have so much of our money sitting in balanced funds.

With 15 minutes of care now—to raise your investment risk profile—you could double your super. That's not a promise. And it's not a guarantee. It's a mathematical *probability*.

If *Debt Man Walking* has taught you enough that you feel comfortable with a bit of extra risk, then call your super fund and ask what you need to do to get your funds invested more aggressively. You don't have to go for the most aggressive investment options. Even one shift up the risk scale should, given the time frame, deliver substantial rewards.

Appendix B: 50 investment, gearing and 'Gen X Rules' rules

We've had the 10 Steps, the 10 X-Flips, five global money rules and five Australian money rules. So why not end the book with another worthy list? Here are the 50 investment, gearing and 'respecting our generation' rules.

'Whaaa?'

I've broken it down to 20 investment rules and 20 rules about debt. But that's only made 40, which is not a particularly memorable number. So, I've included a further 10 rules as the *start* of a list that I hope we can use to define how Generation X intends to run the planet, when we are in charge. If you have any other great ideas, you can add to the list by visiting <www.debtman.com.au> and searching for the 'Gen X Rules' tab.

Twenty rules about investment

1   Set yourself financial goals and write them down. There is no point investing without them. Goals keep you focused. They might stop you from chucking in the towel too early, or remind you that small sacrifices can lead to great rewards. And make sure you have a long-term, big-dream, goal. Whatever it

is, there are a multitude of ways of getting there, depending on how much risk you're prepared to take.

2   Learn the rules. How can you consistently win at any game without understanding them?

3   Time helps reduce risk. Time irons out fluctuations. The longer the time frame, the more likely an investment will perform close to its long-term average.

4   Time brings greater rewards. There are many risks involved when measured over short time periods. The risks lessen considerably if you've got a decade or two as your time frame.

5   Get professional help where you need it. Start with accountants, financial advisers, lawyers, mortgage brokers, real estate agents and general insurance brokers to help you in specialist areas, but you may find others useful also. They'll save you time and, inevitably, money.

6   A tax deduction is not an investment. Tax is one consideration when it comes to investing and it's an important one. But it should never by the only one. Investments should first stack up as an investment, then come any tax benefits and finance rates.

7   Does the investment make common sense? If someone explains to you the reasons behind an investment, but they still don't make sense, then find out more or don't invest.

8   A home is not an investment property—the tax rules are too different. But it is a great platform from which to build your investing future.

9   Everyone has a comfort zone when it comes to everything. *Debt Man Walking* encourages you to push that envelope *a little* at a time, not a lot.

10 Most major personal risks can be managed and should be managed. Death, accidents and diseases can have devastating impacts on survivors. Personal risk insurance can help you protect your future lifestyle.

11 Diversification is more than just having two properties, or two investments. It means that you have many investments in property, shares, fixed interest and cash.

12 Renting is forever. If you never buy a home, you'll be paying rent until the day you die. Mortgages have an end date.

13 If you decide to rent, you have an even greater need for an investment plan to use the money you're saving in the short term.

14 Hundreds of years of history show that shares and property will perform better than income assets (cash and fixed interest) over longer periods. And Generation X has the time to make long-term investment strategies work.

15 Generation X also has the income to fund an investment plan. The peak income-earning period is approximately 45 to 50 years of age. Younger Gen Xers have plenty of time to build their investments, while older Gen Xers need to make the most of it now.

16 Always expect the unexpected when it comes to investing and maintain a ready access to cash. Things can turn against you when you least expect it. Make sure you've got enough money on hand to cover problems with your investment property or to fund a margin call, or you will end up having to sell at the worst possible time.

17 No investment program (geared or not) should cause you to fail the sleep test—if your investments or debt levels are making you nervous, start selling down. No riches are worth buggering your health.

18 True, superannuation is for old farts. But take a few minutes to understand what it is now and you can have a dramatic impact on what it looks like in your future.

19 Delayed gratification—if you spend money now, you don't have it to spend later. If you invest the money instead, you'll create even more money to spend later.

20 The power of compounding means that investments work best if they're given years to work, so that you can generate interest on last year's interest, or growth on last year's growth.

Twenty rules about debt

1 Debt deserves respect. But it is not something to be feared.

2 Debt-funded investment strategies create the potential for bigger gains (and bigger losses).

3   Investment debt and one-night stands don't go together. Cliché or not, it's like a marriage—a relationship that needs time, patience and plenty of monitoring. If you haven't got time to make it work, then you don't have the time to gear your future.

4   Some debt is daft, dumb or dopey. Or all three. Typically, if you incur debt for something that *could* be saved for within a month or a year, it fits in the dumb category. The dumbest debt is also usually the laziest and easiest debt to come by—the credit that banks, retailers and car dealerships throw at customers. They'll generally have the highest interest rates and the worst fees.

5   There is such a thing as okay debt. This is debt that is either (a) a tax deduction such as a car used for work, or (b) used to buy an asset that appreciates in value, such as a home.

6   Then there is great debt. Great debt is both a tax deduction and used to buy investments that will increase in value, such as shares and property. Funding them at least partially with debt can form the basis of creating real wealth for your future.

7   The only time a negatively geared investment makes sense is when the value of the asset is growing at a faster rate. If the negative cash flow is $10000 a year to hold the investment, but the investment's value rises by $30000, you're ahead.

8   If there is a generation that can handle investment debt, it's Generation X (and younger Baby Boomers and older Ys). Generation Y is still grappling with basic finances and older Boomers are too close to retirement to risk losing what they've achieved to a geared investment strategy if they haven't done it before.

9   Interest rates are a fairly accurate indicator of risk. The higher the rate being charged (in comparison to home loan rates), the higher the risk for the lender. A home loan is cheaper than a car loan is cheaper than a credit card is cheaper than store credit for exactly this reason.

10 The higher the interest rate, the less likely you should have the debt in the first place.

11 If you want to know which of your debts to pay off first, look at both the interest rates and the deductibility of the loan. The decision should be made

based on which loan is more expensive once interest rates and the deductibility (or not) of the loan have been taken into account.

12 If a lender gives credit too easily, or doesn't ask you enough questions, they might have motivations other than your financial health at heart. Some lenders are wolves in sheep's clothing. A general rule is that the ones with the biggest reputations have the most to lose. The ones with no reputation have nothing to lose.

13 There should be no debt for debt's sake.

14 No matter what your risk profile, some people just can't handle debt—not for personal use, not for investment purposes, not for any reason. If you can't balance your own home budget, then you've got little chance of being able to control a debt-funded investment strategy. Start by getting your own house in order, as it were, then return to the *Debt Man Walking* principles.

15 Don't get sucked in by the dark side, or the Darth Vader, of credit. Don't get reeled in to buy cars that are more expensive than you know you should buy, or furniture you don't really need, or electrical equipment that's too expensive. And certainly don't get suckered in to having all three.

16 If you're starting out with investment debt for the first time, start out small. Take a small margin loan. Buy a small investment property. Use only a small amount of home equity from your line of credit to buy your first investment. Get comfortable with the cost and power of debt first before you grow your portfolio.

17 Manage your mortgage, then manage your wealth. After a few years (perhaps five or so) of having a mortgage, that loan should be under control, as opposed to being paid off. It's at this point that you should consider beginning your investment program.

18 Build it slow. Any investment empire should be bought and collated over time. The risks of taking on investment debt can be eased by making sure the assets are bought at different times in investment cycles.

19 Not all gearing needs to be negative. There are many opportunities to reduce your risk but increase your wealth through neutral and positive gearing strategies.

20 Open your mind to new thinking when it comes to debt and money. What society has always told us isn't always right (see the condensed version of The X-Flips).

Ten 'Gen X Rules' rules

Gen X is coming of age. We are about to take over the world. To do so, we need to learn the mistakes of our history. We need to set some new boundaries. And we need to warn other generations what sort of a world they're in for. Here's a start:

1   Paisley and tartan should never be worn together. They were bad enough on their own.

2   High-tech special effects are over-rated. *Jaws* was scary. So was Freddy Krueger. The kids of today are pathetic if they don't have the imagination to see past antique props.

3   Stirrup pants must not be allowed to make a city comeback. If you want to wear them, marry a farmer and buy a horse. And guys, unless you live on the Gold Coast, we should never see white suits and white shoes, à la Don Johnson, again.

4   They should have stopped with *Grease* (although a young Michelle Pfeiffer looked hot in the lame follow-up). Tony Barber was *Sale of the Century*. No point doing *Wheel of Fortune* without 'Baby' John Burgess.

5   Politicians don't have to be assholes. Let's vote in more Natasha Stott Despojas, just with a wider range of political views.

6   For God's sake! They're not shrimps! They're prawns!

7   'I've never been to me'. Why would you want to? Don't you get enough alone time? Did Charlene ever apologise for this?

8   To our mums and dads: apricot chicken casseroles should have been a criminal offence (with all due respect to Margaret Fulton, Peter Russell Clarke and Bernard King). To us: we've got to learn to cook from real Gen X chefs, like Gordon Ramsay and Jamie Oliver.

9   Stock, Aitken and Waterman must never be allowed to work together again … this side of heaven.

10 When Gen X is in charge of declaring global wars on evil (Reagan's 'war on drugs' or George W's 'war on terror'), let's try to make it something that can be defeated.

If you have any other rules that you believe we should warn the world will be in place when Generation X takes the reins, then jump on to <www.debtman.com.au>.

Appendix C: Glossary

A

Abba: a '70s Swedish pop band with silly lyrics who we still, bizarrely, love today. They sang 'Money, Money, Money', the anthem about wanting-to-be-rich and living in a rich man's world. It still doesn't make much sense.

Adam: everything started with Adam. Not the boyfriend of Eve, but the guy who led the Ants. Catchy tunes included 'Ant Music', 'Goody Two Shoes' and 'Prince Charming'.

B

bonds: loans to governments. Considered the safest form of investment after a bank account. Returns tend to be low. Bonds are about as common as a 'Go-Go' t-shirt these days as governments reduce their debt. Should not be a major investment class for Gen Xers at this point.

C

capital gains tax (CGT): the tax you pay for making profits. And making profits is not a bad thing, so pay it gladly. If you hold an asset for at least a year before selling it, you pay CGT on only half of your gain.

capital-protected investments: one form of structured investments where if things go bad, your initial investment amount is protected (that is, you can't lose). The cost of this protection is that you will miss out on some of the upside (that is, you won't win as much).

cash investments: considered the safest form of investment; essentially money in the bank, whether it's a bank account or a term deposit. The long-term returns from cash are the lowest of the four general asset classes.

Cecille: wrong. It was not 'I love Cecille'. It was not 'Alex the seal'. The title to The Go-Go's song was 'Our Lips are Sealed'.

commission: payments to service providers (real estate agents, financial advisers, any sort of salespeople) for their work in aiding purchase of an asset. There are two general types of commission: upfront and trail/ongoing.

compounding growth: the beautiful natural act of interest being earned on interest or earnings growing on earnings in an investment over many years.

compulsory superannuation system: Australia's government forces employers to put 9 per cent of workers' salaries into superannuation to help take care of their future.

conveyancing: the legal work that allows for the transfer of property from one owner to another.

corporate super funds: a super fund managed by an employer for their employees.

D

delayed gratification: not spending money today so that you can invest it and turn it into a larger sum to spend later.

de-leveraging: a reduction in loans. The 'sub-prime' mess in the US has caused investors worldwide to lower the debt they hold.

dinks: double income, no kids. What we were before we got midgets. The good old days that some who now have midgets long for.

distributions: the income payments paid by managed funds and property trusts.

diversification: making sure that your investment eggs are spread around a bit. See Village People and *Melrose Place*.

dividends: profit sharing by a company with its shareholders. Dividends are payments made as an income return to investors.

dollar-cost averaging: buying more shares/units in an investment because the price fell after you bought, thereby lowering the average price you have paid.

dumb debt: something that depreciates and for which you can't claim a tax deduction, such as credit card and store credit debt. This is the stuff you should have saved for.

E

enduring power of attorney: a living will declaration where you nominate someone you trust to make decisions for you if you lose your decision-making capabilities.

exclusion (regarding insurance): when an insurer excludes certain events from an insurance contract, where undue risks are evident, so that they can still offer insurance. For example, a history of back problems might see a back exclusion placed on a policy, but the person insured would still be covered for other events.

F

Fawlty Towers: a comedy that should have put people off running their own hotel forever. A criminal offence of international proportions that they only ever made 13 episodes.

fee-for-service: an agreement where a set fee is charged for a service (as opposed to a commission). A fee-for-service is usually an hourly rate, or an agreed dollar figure.

fixed-interest investments: loans to businesses who then pay interest to the investor. In terms of risk, this investment sits above cash and below property and shares.

franking credits: the tax already paid by a company and attached to a dividend. A fully franked dividend means that 30 per cent tax has already been paid, so investors don't have to pay full tax again.

G

geared savings plan: an investment strategy whereby the investor puts in a regular amount of their own capital and has another sum (usually an equal sum) of money added by a lender, on which interest is paid.

geared superannuation: superannuation that involves an element of lending, which will become far more common as a result of changes to the law in 2007.

gearing: borrowing. When associated with investment, usually means using borrowed money to increase your exposure to an investment.

Generation X: Douglas Coupland said it was people born between 1964 and 1977, but he's Canadian, so what would he know? *Debt Man Walking* defines it, loosely, as anyone born in the 1960s or 1970s (with a little bit of leeway in the late 1950s and early 1980s).

Gordon Gekko: central character in *Wall Street*, the movie about the excesses of the 1980s, who said 'Greed…is good' (see 'greed' below).

great debt: a loan used to buy an item that should both appreciate in value and qualify as a tax deduction. Investment properties and margin loans are two examples.

greed: 'Greed…is good', the famous line spoken by Gordon Gekko in *Wall Street*. Certain types of greed—for life, for love—are apparently okay. It's only the greed and money bit that people get a little antsy about.

growth assets: investments that create returns for the investor through growth in the value of the asset rather than from income. Predominantly shares and property. These are the assets Gen X should be concentrating on.

H

home: where you live (derr!). Importantly, a home is different from an investment property. Firstly, tax makes them different. Secondly, a home is about a place to live. An investment property is about making money.

home affordability crisis: what? Apparently, when the price of homes is rising there is a home affordability crisis. But if property prices are rising, then people are, by definition, able to pay more for them. An affordability crisis should, actually, be when prices are falling because people can't afford to buy them. Strange media and political phrase that one.

home equity: the portion of the value of a home that is not made up of a loan. If a home is worth $600000 and the loan on the house is $250000, then the home equity is $350000.

I

income assets: assets where the majority of the returns are expected to come through income, such as interest. Cash, fixed-interest and bond investments.

income protection insurance: insurance that will replace approximately 75 per cent of your income if you can't work. Can be taken inside or outside of superannuation. Generally qualifies as a tax deduction.

income splitting: taking advantage of tax rates by spreading income over two people, rather than one.

index funds: plain vanilla managed funds, except that they don't manage funds. They just buy shares according to an index (like the All Ordinaries or the Dow Jones Industrial Average), to mimic the return.

industry funds: low cost, union-run super funds. Cheap as chips, but unlikely to offer much advice outside of super and insurance.

inflation: insidious termite-like effect of the rising cost of goods. If inflation is 3 per cent, then what would have cost you $100 a year ago will now cost you $103.

interest pre-payment: advance payment of interest on an investment so that you can claim the tax deduction sooner.

investment property: a property you buy with the sole aim of making money, through rent and/or capital gains. Your home is not an investment property because the tax rules are too different.

L

leverage: another name for gearing. Using borrowed money to increase the amount of assets under investment control.

life insurance: (a) a lump sum of insurance that covers you for death; (b) a general term to describe the suite of personal risk insurance that includes life, total and permanent disability, trauma and income protection.

line of credit: a finance facility, generally against your home or investment property, available for those who have equity in a property asset. This is a good source of funds for investment for most mum and dad, or retail, investors and generally the cheapest.

listed instalment receipts: a partly paid share that allows investors to gear into an underlying asset (such as Telstra's T3), with a second instalment due later.

listed investment companies (LICs): companies listed on a stock exchange that invest in other companies. Examples include Australian Foundation Investment Company and Argo Investments.

listed property trusts: listed companies that invest in property. Now known as real estate investment trusts, or REITs.

liquidity: a measure of how quickly an asset can be turned into cash. Some assets, such as directly held investment properties, are considered illiquid. Most of Australia's 200 largest listed companies are fairly liquid in that their shares can be sold, usually the same day, and turned quickly into cash. Cash is the ultimate in liquidity.

loading: (regarding insurance) a higher rate charged for an insurance premium, for people identified as posing an increased risk, so that standard conditions can still apply.

Locklear, Heather: hot as hell as Sammy Jo in *Dynasty*. Still had it 10 years later as Amanda Woodward in *Melrose Place*. Ages gracefully, like a good investment portfolio.

LVR: loan to valuation ratio. The percentage of your asset, or asset base, that is a loan. For example, a $500 000 property with a $300 000 loan has an LVR of 60 per cent.

M

managed funds: a broad name for almost any investment where investors can buy units in a fund run by professional investment managers.

managed investment schemes: usually offered in the lead-up to 30 June each year and are typically agricultural or timber investments. Investors will usually get a big tax deduction upfront and hope to make a return after that. Tend to be primarily tax driven, rather than being driven by investment fundamentals.

Mannix, Brian: so short he'd almost have made more money being a jockey. But, as frontman for The Uncanny X-Men, created a bunch of Australian Gen X 1980s rock classics such as 'Everybody Wants to Work', 'Party' and '50 Years'.

marginal tax rate: the highest individual tax bracket on which an individual worker or investor pays tax. The rates in Australia (in 2008) are 0 per cent, 15 per cent, 30 per cent, 40 per cent and 45 per cent (not including the 1.5 per cent Medicare levy).

margin call: a time not to answer your phone! Kidding. A margin call occurs when you have a margin loan that breaches its thresholds and you need to act quickly.

margin loan: a type of loan that allows investors to leverage into share or managed fund investments.

Meldrum, Molly: the rock guru who got us all home by dinner time on Sunday nights to bring us the latest hits on *Countdown*. As Gen X an icon as there is.

Melrose Place: a lesson in diversification. If you're into property, don't sink it all in one apartment block leased to the best looking people on the planet. It was inevitable that things would eventually get so hot, some script writer would have to blow the place up.

Milli Vanilli: fakes. Stone cold talentless frauds. 'Blame It On The Rain'? No, blame it on greed. One thing's for certain: Debt Man, as vocally hopeless as he is, can sing better than you two.

mortgage: when the title to a property is held by someone else (possibly a bank), usually because there is a debt owed on the property.

muppets: twits who don't *get* the need to invest. Will be stuffed like the Swedish chef, as bitter and twisted as the two old hecklers, or have the propensity to conduct wealth creation experiments with failure rates like Beaker.

N

negative gearing: when the costs of an investment, including the interest, outweigh the income of the investment.

neutral gearing: when the costs of an investment, including the interest, are roughly equal to the income the investment generates.

non-concessional contributions: the name for personal contributions made to superannuation where tax has been previously paid. It is therefore not taxed on the way into the fund.

O

okay debt: debt that's not too bad. It is used to buy either an asset that will appreciate in value or an asset that will qualify as a tax deduction, but not both. Examples are a house or a work car.

P

passive income stream: an income earned where the receiver does not have to undertake paid work. Rent from an investment property, dividends from shares and distributions from managed fund investments are three examples.

period: what no-one wanted to mention when *Women's Weekly* became a monthly, but they didn't want to change the title.

pool room: as in *The Castle*: 'That's going straight to the pool room'. A present or idea so stupendously brilliant that it has to go on a mantelpiece straightaway, where it will probably only ever be marvelled at, but never used. What you'd do if someone gave you a boxed set of *Knight Rider* videos.

positive gearing: where the income from the investment (rent or dividends) is higher than the costs of the investment, including the interest.

property depreciation: investors in properties built after 20 September 1985 can claim a cost for the depreciation of the value of the bricks and mortar.

property managed funds: these are not REITS or LPTs, but managed funds that invest in property.

R

Ralph: (a) to vomit, usually after drinking a litre or two of West Coast Cooler or Fruity Lexia; (b) the name that author Judy Blume made her character Michael give his penis.

real estate investment trusts: the new name for listed property trusts (LPTs). These are companies listed on an exchange whose primary business is investing in and managing properties.

risk profile: a ratings system designed to give investors an indication of how they would probably be most comfortable investing. (*Debt Man Walking* has used a six-tiered system, but every investment business will have its own ratings system.)

S

salary sacrifice (super): an agreement with your employer (and the Tax Office) to put some of your salary directly into your super fund, where it is taxed at 15 per cent instead of your marginal tax rate.

self-funding instalment warrants: in essence, a partly paid share, where you have contributed some equity and the remainder of the share is wrapped into the warrant via a loan. The dividends earned are used to pay down the loan, while interest is added back on to the loan.

self-managed super funds (SMSFs): a small fund for four members or fewer where the members (you) are also the trustees of the fund, the managers of the fund and the people ultimately responsible for the investments in the fund. There's no-one else to blame.

shares: a legal part-ownership of a company. When we talk shares in *Debt Man Walking*, I generally mean the top 300 companies on the Australian Securities Exchange.

sleep at night test: if your investments are causing you to lose sleep at night, then your investments are too aggressive or your investment debt is too big. You shouldn't be worried about your investments to the point of being stressed.

stamp duty: a state government levy on the purchase of some goods and services. This is most annoyingly, and outrageously expensively, charged on property, which can be as much as 6 per cent of the property purchase price in Australia.

structured investment products: a name for the types of investment products that have been manufactured to be more appealing for investors. The alterations might include wrapping in a loan, capital protection or foreign exchange into the investment.

superannuation: a special low-tax investment environment designed to allow and encourage individuals to save for their retirements. Access is restricted to age 60, for those born after 1 July 1964. Those born earlier might be able to get access as early as 55.

T

tax deduction: an item or expense that the taxman will allow to be claimed against your income to reduce the tax you owe.

testamentary trust: a trust structure that comes into place at the time of your death. An important part of estate planning for those with complicated asset structures or difficulties with asset transferral, who may want to provide options for benefactors after their death.

Tossers: (a) complete wankers; (b) an embarrassingly inept group of lowly graded indoor cricketers based in Melbourne whose *Biggest Loser* weight loss competitions are inevitably doomed to failure because they don't commit any dough to the cause.

total and permanent disability insurance: also known as accident insurance. This is designed to pay out a lump sum in the event of a major accident (that typically includes the loss of limbs or eyesight).

trauma insurance: provides a lump sum in the event of a traumatic illness. Up to 40 or 50 illnesses can be covered in some policies, but the most common illnesses covered are heart attack, stroke and cancer.

trauma insurance (children): lump sum cover for major children's illnesses (such as leukaemia, cancer, strokes, burns, meningitis and blindness). Allows a parent to take time to be with their child, potentially for long stays in hospital.

U

unlisted/direct property funds: pooled property investment opportunities that are not listed on the stock exchange.

V

Village People: a catchy, but camp (as in gay icon) 1980s band made up of characters dressed as a police officer, an American Indian chief, a cowboy, a construction worker, a leather man and a military officer. Say, what?! A good example of diversification.

virgin: something that Madonna was never like, despite the song. The pointy boobs, the *Sex* 'coffee table' book, and the early (hairy) *Playboy* issue put paid to us believing that.

W

wealth accumulation: like football cards, or Barbie Dolls, the act of collecting money. The generation known as wealth accumulators are generally those aged 30 to 50, roughly Generation X now.

will: the document you write while you're alive that is supposed to deal with your life's accumulated goods and money when you're dead. One of those documents that should be made with a lawyer.

Y

yuppies: young urban professional people. A sometimes derogatory tag used to label those who live the high life with big incomes in the inner city. Or at least appear to be living the high life. May well be funding lifestyle with dumb debt that will catch up with them some day.

Z

Zimmer frame: used by older generations as a walking aid. Slow and difficult to manoeuvre. Hopeless getaway vehicle.

Recommend to a friend

...and take the credit forever

A personal finance book that I once read changed my life. It got me thinking about investments (and investment debt as it turns out) in a completely different way. Over time, I ended up buying that book for many friends and recommending it to loads more, and almost all of them acted on the contents and turned their head to investing, often for the first time. Most of them have never forgotten that book referral and I still get thanked for doing that.

It was just the first of dozens of books that I read that have shaped my opinions on investing, but it certainly put me on the path to becoming a successful investor. It tapped the keg—a thirst for wider knowledge about how I could improve the financial situation for me and, later on, my family.

One thing led to another. I ended up becoming a business journalist, a personal finance writer, an author (now of three books), a columnist and a financial adviser.

If you've just read *Debt Man Walking*, and it made sense to you and gave you a laugh, do a friend, a sibling, a cousin or a colleague a favour and recommend it to them (or buy them a copy). They might forever thank *you*.

I'm passionate about what's in this book. I really believe that those members of Generation X who care enough to educate themselves just a little can have a huge impact on their financial future. If you believe it also, feel free to jump on to the website <www.debtman.com.au> and let me know what you thought.

Index

DEBT&MAN

BRUCE BRAMMALL

A book ... a website ... and a lone financial adviser with a big dream—like Sylvestor Stallone when he wrote the original *Rocky*—to inspire Gen Xers to attain their birthright as the wealthiest generation on the planet ...

That's all Debt Man is. At the moment this book went off to the printers.

Now that you've read the book, check out the website, <www.debtman.com.au>, where you'll be able to:

1 Sign up for regular Debt Man newsletters, columns, radio and TV podcasts.

2 Access *Debt Man Walking*'s purpose-built investment calculators (from step 8).

3 Contact Debt Man's alter ego (Bruce Brammall).

4 Find more investment information that will add to the lessons in *Debt Man Walking*.

5 Read up-to-date news about debt.

6 Inquire about making a financial planning appointment with Debt Man.

7 Buy extra copies of *Debt Man Walking*.

8 Find more Generation X trivia.

9 Add to Debt Man's Gen X lists.

10 Book Debt Man to speak at your next function.

Debt Man Walking was fun to research and write. And I hope it was an enjoyable read. But there's an obvious serious side to this book and that is: what's next for *you*? What steps are you going to take in regards to improving your finances from here? Your options are endless, but here's four:

1 You can do nothing (in which case I hope that you at least enjoyed the book).

2 You can attempt to do everything—the research and the investing—yourself. (And best of luck with that. It can be a very enjoyable and personally rewarding, though time-consuming, process.)

3   You can do parts of it yourself and outsource those parts that don't interest you (as I recommend in step 7).

4   You can surround yourself with a team of professionals to help ease the time strain and allow you to concentrate on what you're good at (also what's recommended in step 7).

If the idea of professional help appeals, then perhaps you'd care to see if you and Debt Man might work as a financial team!

As a financial adviser, I take my role and responsibilities very seriously. If you would like to contact me about your financial planning needs, then please do so by emailing <bruce@debtman.com.au>. The first appointment (about 1 to 1.5 hours), which is about making sure you and I are on the same page and believe we can work together, is free. The options can be discussed after that.

A copy of my Financial Services Guide is available on the website.

Printed and bound by CPI Group (UK) Ltd, Croydon, CR0 4YY

13/04/2025

14656609-0001